Democratizing Development

Democratizing Development

The Role of Voluntary Organizations

John Clark

KUMARIAN PRESS

Democratizing Development: The Role of Voluntary Organizations

Published 1991 in the United States of America by Kumarian Press, Inc., 14 Oakwood Avenue, West Hartford, Connecticut 06119-2127 USA.

Cover design by Laura Augustine
Cover photo by Ian Mayo-Smith
Typeset by Rosanne Pignone   Proofread by Beth Penney
Index prepared by Alan M. Greenberg

Printed in the United States of America on recycled acid-free paper by McNaughton & Gunn, Inc. Text printed with soy-based ink.

Library of Congress Cataloging-in-Publication Data
Clark, John, 1950–
    Democratizing development : the role of voluntary organizations / John Clark.
        p.   cm. — (Kumarian Press library of management for development)
    Includes bibliographical references and index.
    ISBN 0-931816-91-2 (acid-free paper)
    1. Non-governmental organizations—Developing countries. 2. Non-governmental organizations. 3. Poor—Developing countries. 4. Developing countries—Economic policy. 5. Democracy. I. Title. II. Series.
HC60.C514   1991
338.9′009172′4—dc20   91-7371

01 00 99 98 97   10 9 8 7 6   1st Printed 1991

Contents

Tables   vi
Acknowledgments   vii
Preface   ix

Part One   Voluntary Organizations:
**   Their Contribution to Development**   **1**

  1   Setting the Scene   3

  2   Democracy and Development   12

  3   What are Voluntary Organizations, and Where
       Have They Come From?   29

  4   Magic or Muddle?   45

  5   Relationships between NGOs and Governments   64

Part Two   NGOs: Impact in the South   **71**

  6   Scaling Up   73

  7   Project Replication   82

  8   Building Grassroots Movements   89

9   "The Unreasonable NGO": Influencing Policy Reform   104

Part Three   Redefining Development   **123**

10   International Lobbying   125

11   New Pragmatism   150

12   NGOs and Structural Adjustment   165

13   Structural Transformation   186

Part Four   Conclusions   **201**

14   Think Locally, Act Globally   203

References   213

Index   219

Tables

3.1   Voluntary (private) and Official Contributions to NGOs   40
3.2   Total Official and NGO Aid   41
3.3   U.S. Support to its NGOs   43

11.1   Trends in Social and Productions Indicators   160

12.1   Policy Conditions of Adjustment Lending   178

Acknowledgments

MOST OF THE FIRST draft of this book was written during a six-month sabbatical for which I was based at the Center for African Studies, Cambridge University. I would like to thank Oxfam UK, my employer, for making it possible for me to have this sabbatical and for the support and encouragement it gave me during it. I also thank John Sender, Paula Munroe and others at the Center for African Studies for their constructive help, and Wolfson College for generously accommodating me during my spell in Cambridge.

Few authors look back at early drafts of their works with anything other than embarassment. I am no exception. In my case the transformation from early to later drafts owes much to the constructive criticisms I received from a number of good friends who are also talented workers in the development field. For this I thank, in particular, Jim Monan, David Beckmann, Tim Brodhead and David Korten as well as Oxfam UK colleagues, especially Frank Judd and David Bryer.

Many other people furnished me with useful information, inspired me with ideas, gave me valuable advice on particular sections or contributed to the book in other ways. I would like to mention in particular Elena Borghese, Guy Stringer, Doug Porter, Judy Henderson, John Toye, Simon Maxwell, Robert Chambers and others at the Institute of Development Studies, Anne Gordon Drabek, Jean-Marie Hatton, Henri Rouillé d'Orfeuil, John Schlanger, Max Van den Berg and others at Novib, Saidur Rahman, David Lehman, John Mitchell, Robert Molteno, Donatus de Silva and others at the Panos Institute, Edgardo Valenzuela, Mark Robinson and others at the Overseas Development Institute, Paul Spray, John Mitchell, M.D. Mistry and Czeck Conroy.

I know how busy all of these people are and am doubly grateful to them.

I thank them for their specific contributions and I thank them for the immense encouragement their involvement has given me. Their views have done much to sharpen my understanding and mold my thinking on the issues dealt with in this book. None of them, however, share responsibility for either the opinions or for any possible errors contained within. Full responsibility for these reside with the author.

Finally I would like to acknowledge that without the peace and tranquility of "Upper Island" this book may never have been completed.

John Clark

Preface

WEST BENGAL, SEPTEMBER 1971. The rich green fields indicated a good growing season. All looked well. Overhead the dark clouds of late monsoon rolled threateningly.

These were not the only dark clouds on the horizon. Flooding over the borders came the refugees. By this time more than ten million refugees from East Pakistan, as it was then known, had escaped the torture they feared from the West Pakistan army. The East Pakistan people had been guilty of winning a democratic election for their candidate, and were facing reprisal. This was only weeks before the India–Pakistan war, and three months before the new nation of Bangladesh was to be born.

Some two million people were killed in this war or simply never returned to their homes. Never in all time has there been such a dislocation of people. Ten million refugees. That is more than the population of Greater London. More than the entire population of Belgium.

The conditions for the refugees can hardly be imagined. The authorities—try as they could—were not able to keep up with the pressure to set up new camps, erect shelters, build clinics and dig latrines. And the monsoon rains didn't help. People were living up to their waists in mud, latrines overflowed into the drinking water, disease spread like wildfire and shipping food in was a neck-and-neck race against starvation.

Just a few miles away from the border sprawled Calcutta. Everything possible had to be done to stop the refugees breaking their way into the city. There were far too many beggars on the streets as it was.

One community of beggars lived on the streets around Chowringee, the hotel area of Calcutta. With the monsoon, and the troubles, there were few tourists around and so the beggars were having a very tough time. They scavenged for scraps of food to eat among the vast rubbish bins at the backs of the hotels—scarcely a human existence. Every morning the local Salvation Army ran a soup kitchen. The beggars would line up in their hundreds to get a bowlful of hot, nourishing food. In their lives absolutely nothing was certain, nothing could be depended upon, except this daily hand-out.

But the beggars were from the same land as the refugees. They had come from what was then East Bengal at the time of Partition, when—shortly before giving independence—Britain divided her colony into two countries in an effort to avoid communal warfare between Hindus and Muslims. They remembered the journey, and they knew the transit camps. They could guess how the refugees would be suffering today. And they wanted to help. They, who had nothing, wanted to help their brothers and sisters who were even worse off.

One day the leader of the community knocked at the door of the Salvation Army hostel. He had come to talk to the person in charge. He explained what the beggars had been discussing, that they were determined to do something to help, and called on the hostel for their assistance. His plan was this: the soup kitchen should cut their rations in half from now on, so that the other half could be sent to the refugee camps. It is barely credible that a group of people who were so poor, for whom life was a day-by-day battle for survival, who, by any standards, were themselves malnourished, was prepared to sacrifice half of the little they had, for people they didn't even know.

This puts into sharp relief our fine sense of charity in the rich world; the voluntary contributions we draw from our surpluses. But in Calcutta this contribution was drawn from no surplus, neither was the action one of charity. It was a simple act of solidarity. No doubt countless similar acts of solidarity take place every day throughout the Third World. But this one was different for me: I was there.

I was a student traveler, staying in the Salvation Army hostel. And it was over cornflakes at breakfast that one of the staff told me of the beggars' action. It moved me more than I can describe. That we with our comfortable homes and our secure lifestyles in the West do so little, while those battling constantly against adversity, living on the streets of Calcutta, would sacrifice so much. Over the years my thoughts have frequently returned to that day. And that one event—augmented a few days later by a grim tourist visit to one of the camps—did more than a little to bring about my career shift from science to development.

The lesson I have learned from this experience is not the one I first thought of, that of Western guilt, but of the power of solidarity. This has been reinforced for me countless times in the slums, shanty towns and villages I have stayed in subsequently throughout the Third World. The poor are not passive victims of circumstance, but active players in the battles against suffering and injustice. In contrast to the cynical self-interest behind much official aid, the actions of the poor themselves seem so genuine in their motives. If development organizations—official or voluntary, Northern or Southern—are to make meaningful contributions toward alleviating poverty, then they must learn to follow the people, not expect the people to follow them. The poor themselves know the capabilities of their communities, and know what needs to be done. Development is done *by* people, not *to* people.

Throughout the 1970s and 1980s I have worked in one way or another in the development field. In some senses it has not been very encouraging. The wealth gap between nations and within nations has grown and there are more malnourished people now than there were at the start of the period. What has been immensely encouraging, however, is the evolution of powerful grassroots organizations within the Third World. I have been fortunate that my work enables me to witness this and to see the difference it is making. I am quite sure that the fisher-folks' associations in the Philippines are doing more to stem the environmental destruction of the coastal waters than any large-scale project or government ministry. I am quite sure that the peasant movements in Bangladesh are doing more to fight for the rights of the landless than any political party. I am quite sure that voluntary action in the cities of Zambia is doing more than any official aid agency to protect the poor from malnutrition. And I am quite sure that it is the women's movement the world over that is slowly liberating one-half of humanity from centuries of oppression.

If there is one single message it is this. Voluntary organizations will only achieve their full potential if they develop a more strategic, coordinated way of working. Their projects are important and will remain so, but in themselves do no more than create islands of relative prosperity within an increasingly hostile sea. These projects should be seen not as ends in themselves, but as starting points. They are demonstrations, catalysts and vantage points. Using them as their base of experience and knowledge, voluntary organizations should help to challenge governments, official aid agencies, international companies and others to change their ways. They should strive for the changes in local government policy and practice that the poor require. They should do what they can to promote the evolution of people's organizations and grassroots democracy. And they should lobby Northern governments to make the changes necessary for international justice.

Official aid all too often strengthens governments whose policies and practices oppress the poor. It may support projects that provide the wrong service or that serve the wrong people, and may strengthen a development model to which equity and social justice are alien.

Many organizations are changing in this way or are being set up specifically for the influencing tasks required. They are having to come up with not just a new way of working, but also a new analysis and a new confidence in order to seize the high ground of international debate. Their challenge is to redefine the principles of development, democracy and sovereignty in the light of mounting poverty, growing inequalities, looming environmental threats and the ever-clearer interdependence of nations.

This demands of voluntary organizations a new pragmatism. A world view that is restricted to flagging ideas of neo-imperialism and conspiracy theory is no longer adequate if it is to catalyze change in the thinking of governments. Voluntary agencies are well placed to challenge official development thinking and to advocate a new order to take its place, based on human values and environmental sustainability. But they will make little headway unless their ideas are well grounded in economic reality and unless they search for positive as well as negative lessons within the programs of the World Bank and other practitioners of development orthodoxy.

Such a new order is, I believe, possible. Global threats posed by the greenhouse effect, environmental degradation and pollution, AIDS, narcotics and other phenomena are heralding a new global political consciousness. The struggle for democracy not only in Eastern Europe but in Latin America and other parts of the world is not just because people want to vote, but because of a spreading realization that countries are more efficient and prosperous where governments are guided by strong civil societies. And the rapid advance of South Korea and other "tigers" in Southeast Asia has demonstrated the importance of economic equity as a firm foundation for sustained growth.

The eradication of poverty demands more than aid to meet basic needs. It demands equity, social justice, human rights, development that is sustainable and democracy. It is not charity that the poor require, but a transformation of development.

Part One

*Voluntary Organizations:
Their Contribution to
Development*

1

Setting the Scene

VOLUNTARY ORGANIZATIONS HAVE BEEN actors on the development stage longer than the World Bank, the United Nations or any other official aid agency. Until recently they have played minor parts—doing good works but largely irrelevant to the overall plot. Throughout the 1980s this has changed. They have moved closer to center stage.

Voluntary organizations—or non-governmental organizations (NGOs) as they are more formally known—have greater diversity, credibility and creativity than ever before. In the developing countries (the South) they have often managed to engage with local populations and to command their trust in ways which governments find impossible. Mounting public support in the rich countries of the North has given their NGOs a much stronger financial base. Northern NGOs collectively now transfer to the South more than the World Bank group does. NGOs have frequently demonstrated their ability to help those most in need who have been missed by official aid programs. And most importantly they have pioneered new approaches and challenged development orthodoxy. In particular many Southern NGOs have successfully challenged socially or environmentally damaging programs pursued by their own governments. And their Northern counterparts have used the media, mass lobbies and other devices to bring international environmental and social issues out of virtual obscurity on to the political agenda.

The enhanced role of NGOs comes at a time when the thinking of the more established actors—the official development agencies—is in considerable disarray. Development, as they define it, isn't working.

While the second half of this century has seen some important advances in the Third World, the underlying problems remain firmly entrenched. Child mortality rates have improved in the wake of medical advances and improvements in social services. But these changes have simply enabled people to *survive* their poverty, not to be freed from it. Advances in agricultural technology have helped turn countries such as India from being food-deficient to food-exporters, but there are more hungry people than ever before. Billions of dollars spent on infrastructure in Africa have improved the roads, railway lines, airports and electricity supply, but usually not in the regions where people are dying of hunger.

The orthodox approach is oriented to the technical fix for technical problems. Advanced agricultural know-how, equipment and training is the response to food problems. Immunization and health services are offered to tackle problems of sickness. And "structural adjustment" is the response to economic problems. None of these address the reasons why people cannot afford to eat, why the poor are exposed to disease, or why international forces are causing Third World economies to collapse. An NGO is more likely to see these as political, rather than technical, problems and so seek political remedies. Organizing the poor to stand up for their rights, demanding access to the clean water supply from the landlord's well and campaigning internationally for debt cancellations might be its approach.

The failures of mainstream development have been brought into sharp relief in recent years by the waves of famine in Africa, unfolding environmental disasters and the debt crisis stemming from the impossibly high interest bills developing countries are expected to pay for their debts to Northern governments and banks.

The principal development actors since the Second World War have been the international bodies—notably the World Bank and the United Nations organizations—and the Northern governments' own aid agencies such as the US Agency for International Development (USAID). They have promoted a style of development that has often been insensitive to the needs of ordinary people and to the environment. Indeed, the focus on wealth production rather than wealth distribution, production for export rather than for the needs of local populations, extraction of natural resources rather than environmental protection and Western-style technologies, for example in agriculture, have often compounded the problems we now regard as critical.

Similarly, Southern governments have typically pursued policies that serve the elite at the expense of the poor, neglect the politically disconnected or those living in remote areas and reflect short-term expediency rather than long-term survival.

There is now near-universal recognition that poverty alleviation, eradication of hunger, protecting the environment, grassroots development and safeguarding the poor from the debt crisis are priorities. But these are areas in which the official agencies have limited experience or discover tremendous operational difficulties and as a result they are actively seeking the collaboration of both Northern and Southern NGOs. The voluntary organizations often work in the areas of greatest poverty, have direct relationships with the communities of poor people and have considerable experience of tackling environmental problems.

For NGOs this makes for an exciting and challenging time. They are no longer regarded as irrelevant, but find themselves drawn into mainstream development debates. They have vast resources at their disposal. And they have the capacity to influence those who wield even greater resources. They are on the cusp of great opportunity.

Indian NGOs are now of such significance to the country's development efforts that the government's latest Five-Year Plan has a one and a half billion rupee provision for funding NGOs.[1] In Mozambique some 120 national and international NGOs dominate welfare services, and in Kampuchea the NGOs, rather than official aid agencies, are the main development partners of the government. Once content to be apolitical providers in a welfare role, NGOs are increasingly claiming an identity as challengers of oppression and injustice whether by local elite, by Southern governments or by Northern institutions.

In some countries such as Bangladesh and India, NGOs are beginning to force through the implementation of legislation concerning minimum wages, feudalism and modern-day slavery (bonded labor), legislation which, though progressive, had largely remained ignored. In Gujarat, India, for example, one NGO called DISHA has worked with the poorest and most vulnerable landless laborers and has come to understand how the landlords who employ them deny them the right to work for others. DISHA has challenged the landlords but has also taken action in the High Court, in the state Parliament and through the media on the behalf of the laborers. The situation is now improving and DISHA's leader has been invited to join an all-India government commission on bonded labor.

The popular movements of Latin America have acted as a channel for public concern even where political parties are absent or silent. In Brazil, grassroots organizations working with the rubber tappers and the tribal indians who live in the forests of Amazonia—supported both by strong national NGOs and by Northern pressure groups—have over the years shifted their government away from its indifference to environmentalism. This work started well before rainforests became a popular concern in the North.

In the Philippines, similarly, environmental organizations have succeeded in arresting the breakneck logging by huge timber concerns in the island of Palawan and have gone on to press through legislation severely restricting logging operations throughout the nation.

In the same country a wide coalition of national and grassroots NGOs as well as academics—the Freedom from Debt Coalition (FDC)—has challenged the government's meekness in continuing to service in full its external debt. FDC has pointed out the damage done to the country's economy, to the environment and to the poor by the draining of some 46 percent of the government's budget in debt service. They have pointed out that virtually all of the national debt was inherited from the era of President Marcos and his spendthrift wife, Imelda, and that much of it relates to schemes that are fraudulent or at least highly suspicious. As as result of their efforts, which have been supported by many prominent politicians, the government has established a Foreign Debt Council to examine, loan by loan, the authenticity of the nation's debts, and NGOs are being asked to to serve on this. A bill is being debated in both houses of Congress about setting a cap on debt service payments. Even five years ago it would have seemed fanciful to think that NGOs could have such political influence anywhere in the Third World.

In their search for political influence, NGOs are increasingly looking beyond their national boundaries. They are realizing the strength that comes from joining forces or networking with like-minded NGOs in other countries. Hence both Northern and Southern NGOs concerned with health have established the International Baby Foods Action Network (IBFAN) and Health Action International (HAI) to expose and combat immoral practices by manufacturers in their marketing of baby foods and pharmaceuticals, respectively. International codes of conduct and controls have been introduced by UN agencies as a result.

Similarly, the combined efforts of NGOs in Brazil, the United States, Europe and elsewhere, including other Third World countries, succeeded in persuading the World Bank to stop funding a road-building and resettlement scheme that was destroying a large tract of the Amazon.

While the early groupings tended to be rather dominated by the Northern NGOs, this is now changing. Strong Southern NGOs are coming to the fore. In some cases networks are being set up that are restricted to Southern participants. For example, the Penang-based Third World Network is a forum for sharing information and strategy on a wide range of environmental, social, economic and consumer issues. And the Forum for African Voluntary Development Organizations (FAVDO) emerged to provide NGOs from across the continent with a common platform in the build-up to the UN Special Session on Africa in 1986.

As the NGO sector becomes higher profile and engaged at a wider variety of levels, it has attracted a wider variety of supporters. This is evidenced not just by the pop music industry's backing for Live Aid, USA for Africa and other media extravaganzas, but also by the commitment being made to NGOs by prominent people from all spheres. Gro Harlem Brundtland, a former Prime Minister of Norway, made great efforts to consult NGOs while chairing the World Commission on Environment and Development. Many prominent academics are now giving their services to NGOs. And former US President Jimmy Carter is now working alongside

NGOs in his efforts to help resolve the intractable problems of conflict and hunger in Africa.

An NGO that is outspoken on political issues can expect harsh reprisals both from the government and from the local elite. For Northern NGOs this can mean slur stories in the reactionary press or the withholding of government subsidies, but for Southern NGOs it can mean imprisonment and, all too frequently, the murder of their leaders.

Size and resources may bring unwelcome responsibilities. A small NGO can work in safe obscurity, but as it grows it has to learn to coordinate with others, even, sometimes, with a government it dislikes. This can lead to more regulations and intervention than it would like. Similarly, an NGO that accepts invitations to collaborate with official aid agencies can find that its own agenda is lost, swamped by that of the larger partner. Conversely, if it resists such invitations it may find itself squeezed out by the arrival of others that don't share the same reservations or that have been formed specifically because of the opportunities for such collaboration.

Because NGOs do not have to be answerable to parliaments, electorates or any constituency other than their funders, it is easy to start such an organization in most countries (this is not so true in centrally planned countries and many African and Middle Eastern states). Providing they remain within the law of the land and can continue raising the money they need, they can chart their own course. This is a blessing as far as flexibility is concerned. It allows NGOs the space to innovate, to alter course, to grow or to die as they think best. But it is a curse as far as coherence of the sector is concerned. Anyone can form an NGO. There are rules about financial accounting, and there are rules about what you *cannot* do but, thereafter, there is tremendous freedom.

A recent phenomenon is the establishment of NGOs by government ministers and even heads of state, though this brings into question what is non-governmental about such organizations. Ministers in Sahelian countries see this course as a way of supplementing the meager resources of their own departments. And heads of state perhaps believe that results will come faster, and international support be greater than by using bureaucratic government departments—as, for example, with the King Mahendra Trust for environment protection in Nepal.

Often the new NGO arrivals refuse to recognize established conventions. In Bangladesh, for example, most of the longer serving NGOs take trouble to avoid introducing a "beggar mentality." In setting up a village credit scheme they may be prepared to prime the pump with a start-up loan, but only when the community has demonstrated its determination to recover loans made by the scheme, to administer it efficiently and to encourage its members to save. The program may also be a vehicle for adult literacy or other social development initiatives. Such schemes have, by and large, proved highly successful—to the extent that it is fashionable for Northern funders to want to support them. It is consequently easy for articulate, educated Bangladeshis to set up such credit programs and secure international funding. The more villages they reach, the more funds they can attract. Consequently, they will not require the villages to save for themselves, nor will they wait until administrative effectiveness has been demonstrated. And they certainly will not bother with the social development frills. In some cases established local credit schemes have been approached by new national NGOs and urged to accept *their* money —in much larger quantities—and to leave their original funder.

In such situations it is difficult to preserve the integrity of the NGO sector. Moreover, official aid agencies may well exacerbate the trends. For laudable reason they may seek partnership with local NGOs. (The World Bank now produces a regular list of several hundred projects in which there is NGO collaboration, or where it seeks collaboration.) Such partnership usually entails the official aid agency contracting NGOs to implement a component of *its* project, rather than supporting NGOs to expand their own programs. The NGO becomes just one of the many subcontractors engaged in the project.

The official aid agencies look for such partnerships because they appreciate that NGOs frequently have close contact with, and enjoy the trust of, poor communities. Paradoxically, those who are content to accept the proffered partnership may previously not have been ones with such grassroots credentials. However, their new status allows them to grow and prosper so that they become prominent members of the NGO community. There may be no ingredient of voluntarism within their work, and they may have no activities other than within the official programs, but they come to be, in the eyes of the official funders, the new standards by which to judge other NGOs.

It is tempting to condemn this trend as a highjacking of "the people's sector" by agencies of Northern governments. But do Northern voluntary funding agencies have any greater right to be the arbiters of what should be supported in the name of development in the Third World? They only do so if, alongside their Southern partners, they genuinely are in tune with the aspirations of ordinary people, and if they are using all possible opportunities to deliver what the poor need in both the short and the long term.

Smallness is often seen as a virtue in NGO circles, in comparison with the giant schemes of governments that are so frequently criticized. But small can also mean insignificant. The challenge for NGOs is to seek ways of maximizing their impact and of maximizing the value of the lessons drawn from their experience without sacrificing the quality of their programs.

Such "scaling-up" can be achieved by expanding their projects and their outreach and by helping others to set up similar programs and to coordinate efforts. But it can also be achieved by using their experience to persuade others to change. They can urge governments to improve services so as to be more relevant to the poor or to reform policies. They can persuade official aid agencies to modify their programs. And they can lobby internationally for Northern governments and institutions to make reforms in the global economic regime so as to allow the Third World and its people a fair chance.

These tasks are daunting, perhaps frighteningly new for most NGOs. However, there is a rich base of experience to draw on from those pioneering NGOs in both North and South who have already made remarkable achievements in multiplying their impact. This experience allows lessons to be drawn about the new skills that must be learned, the new tasks to be undertaken, the new priorities for planning and management and the new partnerships to be forged.

Whether NGOs make a lasting impression on development thinking, or whether their moment passes and they fade into the background alongside previous aid fashions depends on their resoluteness in grasping the opportunities that the present climate presents, while remaining true to their purpose. More is at stake than the health and growth of the voluntary sector. The new vision and challenges that NGOs can bring have much to offer to the survival of the planet itself.

The world is racked with crises. Yet—as if blind to these—there is still a business-as-usual complacency of our governments. Absolute poverty continues to increase. The natural resource base on which we all depend is being stripped bare or polluted to death. Per capita food production is declining. Conflict and injustice has led to a record number of refugees and dispossessed people. Tension between ethnic or religious groups is leading to more frequent violence and to violations of human rights. The global population is still skyrocketing, with over thirty developing countries having population growth rates exceeding 3 percent per annum (in other words doubling every twenty-four years). The consumption of resources in the North continues to soar and though it houses only about one-quarter of the world's population, it consumes over three quarters of the world's output of energy, paper, steel and other resources.

The world simply cannot stay locked on its present path for very long, or it will find that the business-as-usual quickly becomes a going-out-of-business sale. The world's capacity to yield the resources we consume makes this abundantly clear. Sometime next century the global population is projected to stabilize at between two and three times the present level. The South will hope by then to have gained at least today's rich-world lifestyles, which implies a ten-fold increase in their per capita consumption. This scenario would mean overall multiplying today's ecological impact some twenty or thirty times over—which is manifestly impossible.[2]

It is also fanciful to believe that the other global problems of mal-distribution, injustice and conflict will disappear by themselves. Though important progress has been made in some areas (such as reduced infant mortality, improved standards of education, improved family planning services in some countries), and both official and voluntary aid have contributed to these, this progress is dwarfed by the escalating problems.

Democratic governments are usually elected for periods of four or five years. That time scale dominates their thinking. And authoritarian, non-democratic governments are usually preoccupied about maintaining their hold on power. Problems that will take twenty or thirty years to mature can be ignored because these will be someone else's headache. Governments are concerned with today's issues, with today's popularity and with today's voters. Even now that the problems of acid rain, global warming and holes in the ozone layer are actually upon us, even now as it dawns on us that long-run ecological problems have crept up to become medium-term crises of today, governments still appear incapable of taking significant action.

The world's headlong path to catastrophe is like the airplane in the thriller movie that is flying straight at the looming mountain. The pilot wrestles with the joystick but it refuses to budge as the mountain wall gets closer and closer. But in the real world the controls *can* move. It is the pilots who are stuck. They see the rock face coming, and they say they are doing everything possible to avoid it. Everything, that is, except deflect from the very course of maximum economic growth and maximum competition that is taking us to disaster.

We cannot wait until the long-run environmental problems become issues of short-term survival. We need to chart a new course, and we need it today. Hence citizens' pressure is essential. Only this can turn the events unfolding in tropical forests several thousand miles away into a domestic political issue in the North. Only this can make the future a contemporary political issue. Only this can lead to international cooperation becoming a national priority. Such action can, and must, show politicians that they have a new mandate, a mandate to turn away from the immediate self-interest of the country and toward the long-term survival of the planet.

NGOs have a critical role to play. Because of their international structures and linkages they have the potential to construct global networks of citizens pressure. Because they command a unique vantage point they are ideally placed to study and describe how contemporary crises affect the poor. Because of their size and flexibility they are able to experiment with new approaches to the crises and so, through demonstration, serve as pioneers or catalysts for government action. Because of their access to the media they are well placed to reach out with their message. And because they do not stand to make personal profit they are trusted by the public at large.

To achieve this critical role demands, first, clear statements about the direction NGOs wish development to head and what lessons they draw from contemporary world events. Because of the diversity of the sector it is unrealistic to expect a single, coherent position; however, a wide range of influential and like-minded NGOs would be able to reach broad consensus on the most salient issues. This would enable them to exploit the unique window of opportunity that the recent tide of world affairs brings. The struggle for political liberty in Eastern Europe, and the demand for development that is for the people and by the people, are opposite sides of the same "democracy" coin.

The opportunities for NGOs have never been greater, and neither have the resources at their disposal. They have the chance today not just to influence the shape of projects being executed by official agencies, but also to influence critical aspects of development policy itself.

This new role calls for a conscious decision to move beyond a *doing* to an influencing role. It does not call for an abandoning of the NGO's projects, but instead an evolution from this starting point. Such progress will not come about systematically unless it is clear throughout the NGO that such is its agreed mission.

Whether NGOs significantly seize the opportunities or not depends largely on whether they create the space to step back from their conventional project work to be able to put effort into discovering the skills of analysis and persuasion needed to shape an alternative vision of development out of their experience of working with the poor. The challenge is to move from a tactical to a strategic approach. By doing this they have the chance to transform development.

2

Democracy and Development

THROUGHOUT THE WORLD WE are witnessing a spontaneous hunger for popular power; people are demanding the right to have a say in the shaping of their societies. The governments of the two leading centrally planned countries—the People's Republic of China and the Soviet Union—have recognized that their difficulties and inefficiencies can only be overcome through reforms. They have chosen different paths but both seek to give more economic freedom to the individual and to make their state institutions more publicly accountable.

The Eastern bloc reforms have not satisfied their populations, however, and have set off a chain reaction. There is a clamor for greater and greater reforms, for a full handing over of power from the state apparatus to the people through democratic processes. The Russian people, through the elections of 1989 and the subsequent events in the Baltic States, bit off the hand that preferred reforms and, in rejecting the candidates favored by the Party, demanded full democracy.

The students and intellectuals in China, likewise, led the Tiananmen Square revolt because they believed that the government reforms were inadequate. Whereas the Soviet reforms concentrated on political issues and skated over economic restructuring, in China it was the reverse. Sweeping economic reforms were brought in, trade barriers were dismantled, a new banking system was constructed with World Bank assistance and private enterprise was permitted. However, ordinary people remained almost as divorced from political power as they had been previously.

Crushed as the revolt was, it revealed the thirst for democracy. The leadership of China, inescapably aware of the specter of democracy that is haunting Eastern Europe, must know that this thirst remains quiescent

12

but not quenched—ready to flare up again when the moment is right. Democratic values are unstoppable, whether in China, Albania, Latin America or Africa.

A similar groundswell for democracy is evident in countries whose right wing, authoritarian governments have invested freedoms in their private sectors but not in their peoples. Dictatorships have been flushed away in the Philippines, South Korea, Chile, Brazil, Haiti, Nicaragua, Argentina and elsewhere.

In the Middle East and much of the African continent such progress has been most disappointing. While the Republic of South Africa remains the most offensive example, few states in these regions have democratic or human rights records to be proud of. Political parties are, typically, strictly curtailed or banned, and ordinary people are scared to voice the merest hint of criticism of the government for fear of reprisals.

In economic terms, state intervention remains very strong throughout Africa. The stated objective of controlling markets, prices and production is usually the need to ensure that the poor have access to the food they need at prices they can afford and the need for careful management of scarce and vital resources. Though political leadership is dressed in the rhetoric of socialism, wealth distribution remains perversely polarized. In four of the forty-six countries reporting wealth distribution statistics,[3] the richest 10 percent enjoyed over 45 percent of the total household income. Three of these (Zambia, Kenya and Mauritius) were in Africa. The fourth was Brazil.

Though state intervention can lead to improved food security and wealth distribution, the reverse can also be the case. Periodic efforts to hold down inflation in Zambia by controlling consumer prices merely leads to the hawkers deserting the marketplaces and selling their wares, illegally, from their back doors. This uncertainty pushes prices up, not down.

In Ethiopia during the famine year of 1985, relief workers tackling a localized pocket of famine in the south of the country were outraged to discover that the local state farm had, rotting on the stalks, a quantity of maize roughly equal to the relief food they were desperately trying to bring in. When the order to harvest was received most of the cobs were not yet ripe on this farm (the climate varies greatly from valley to valley) and so the laborers left them. No one in the relevant ministry in Addis Ababa thought to give the instructions to go out and pick the remaining maize, and the farm workers felt unable to do so without instruction from the center.

Such examples illustrate that the lessons of Eastern Europe have yet to be learned in many African countries. In the wake of tough adjustment programs many Africa countries, however, have now introduced *economic* reforms which divest power from the state to the individual, to the private sector, and indeed to the International Monetary Fund. But few countries have introduced the *political* reforms that would allow democracy to blossom and state instruments to become publicly accountable. Africa, as some observers comment, has had *perestroika* without *glasnost.*

Perestroika, in the form of the widespread privatization advocated by Northern governments, is not necessarily the solution for Africa. To remove basic food marketing from a parastatal and invest this vital function in a small band of wealthy merchants can worsen the situation, as it did in parts of Malawi in 1987. But introducing economic freedom is important. The exact approach must vary from country to country depending on the strengths of local institutions and traditional practices. It may involve dismantling parastatals in one country but investing in them to make them more efficient or more publicly accountable in others. It may mean state intervention to attack monopolies in some cases and removing barriers to private enterprise in others. It may mean price de-control in some countries and increasing producer prices in others. It may mean scrapping subsidies in some countries and ensuring that they reach the poor in others.

Economic decision making, in essence, should be one weapon in the pursuit of democracy.

Democracy

Democracy is not just about the right to vote in a government—important as that is. It is about a whole set of rights which citizens must be afforded if a government is to be open, accountable and participatory. These rights include freedom of speech; an independent press; freedom to associate, for example, in trade unions or pressure groups; access to state information, particularly about specific state plans for those directly affected by them and the right to be consulted in such decisions; and freedom from discrimination, whether on grounds of sex, race or creed.

Defined broadly, democracy has been advanced not just by the leaders of revolutions in Eastern Europe and elsewhere but also by the popular movements throughout the world. The women's movement has eroded many of the barriers that hold one-half of humanity in an inferior status. The environmental movement has forced the world's political and business leaders to view the natural resource base in a new light. And campaigns in many countries by tribal communities who are threatened by "progress" have brought the rights of indigenous peoples into the limelight.

The driving force for these movements is the voluntary coming together of men and women in a common purpose to improve the society in which they live by demanding change from their rulers. Their only bargaining power is the force of their numbers, the persuasiveness of their arguments and their popular appeal. They too are voluntary organizations. Alongside charities, church societies and more established NGOs, they involve their participants in the sharing of an ideal or a vision for changing society, in the common commitment to the eradication of poverty or injustice and in the voluntary making of sacrifices or taking of risks to attain these goals.

Popular Movements

In many countries throughout the world, particularly in Northern countries, the political topography can no longer be described by the familiar contours of left and right. The scenery has been made more complex by issue politics. The well-worn debates about public *versus* private ownership, collective bargaining and free markets are still important, but there are other contestants for the political limelight. In Europe the most significant campaigning causes have been the women's movement, the environmental movement, nuclear disarmament, anti-racism, the pro- and anti-abortion lobbies, freedom of information, animal rights, consumers' power, support for a national health service, protests against the siting of nuclear power stations, toxic waste dumps, new roads and many other issues.

Taken together these signal a sharp transition in popular politics. The traditional emphasis on "production politics"—capitalist *versus* socialist ownership of the means of production—is giving way to a new age of "consumption politics"—demanding a popular right to determine what is produced and how, and the quality of the society we live in.

In Britain this trend reflects a political evolution which is running ahead of mainstream politicians. The Labour Party is seen by many issue campaigners as their natural ally. But it is just that, an ally, not a leader of these campaigns. Were it seen to be putting intellectual and political leadership into the women's movement or environmentalism or some of the other causes then the party would perhaps enjoy more active and popular support than it does today.

In 1971, when Greenpeace was born, the Labour Party had 699,522 members. It would have seemed unthinkable at the time that by the start of 1990 it would have been overtaken in membership by an organization concerned about the marine environment. By the end of 1988, Labour Party membership had fallen to 265,927. The figure picked up slightly in 1989 but this recovery was not sufficient to avoid Greenpeace storming ahead as its membership rose by 70 percent, from 187,000 at the start of 1989 to 323,000 a year later. (Worldwide, Greenpeace has some 3.5 million members.)

Single-issue politics has escalated in importance in the North because, to the voters, the "old" issues of means of production have become less relevant. Through welfare programs and progressive taxation there has been a gradual redistribution of wealth and opportunity. And through pension funds and insurance schemes the *ownership* of the means of production has become more evenly spread throughout this century. However, *control* over the production process is more polarized now than it has ever been. Fewer and fewer company directors make the decisions that affect the society we live in, determine what products we are offered, what we read in our newspapers, the design of our buildings and the threats to our environment; these issues of consumption—of the shape and quality of the society we live in—increasingly motivate people to active politics. Ordinary people theoretically own more now but they probably don't even know what they own, and they certainly don't control it.

Parallel trends are found in the South. In Bangladesh—one of the world's poorest countries—the rural poor are becoming disenchanted with mainstream political parties. They have seen successive governments neglect their wonderful election promises about poverty eradication and land redistribution. They are shifting their commitment from political parties to newly emerging grassroots mass-membership organizations of the landless. These are taking action locally to oppose ruthless landlords and nationally to press for implementation of some of the hitherto ignored liberal legislation on the statute books.

In Brazil, NGOs and popular organizations are engaged in a wide range of political struggles. The ones that have received international attention have been those of the rubber tappers—who have tried to prevent the Amazon forests from being destroyed by logging companies; of the native indians—who have tried to protect the reserves on which they live from developers; and of the environmentalists—who have tried to protect Brazil's natural heritage from ill-conceived hydroelectric schemes.

Elsewhere in Latin America, grassroots movements are growing in strength and are demanding radical social changes. This sector, what David Lehman calls *basismo*, distrusts equally the bureaucracies and institutions of capitalism and the state. It seeks to reform their operations, to force them into public accountability, rather than to overthrow and replace them. In this sense, their objective is not to provide a blueprint for an alternative political model but to "transmit modernization from below," so as to ensure that their societies answer the needs of the people.[4]

Throughout the world, from Western to Eastern democracies, from developing to Communist countries, there is a groundswell of popular movements. These movements are often led by, or supported by, voluntary organizations. For NGOs in development this phenomenon will become increasingly important, though controversial, throughout the 1990s. It is not enough to be carers of the poor. If their work is to be effective, NGOs must address the root causes of suffering, not just the symptoms, and this involves taking sides and supporting the poor in their grassroots struggles. They should not shy away from political action, pressure tactics and controversy. An analysis of what poverty really is and where it comes from makes this clear.

What is Poverty?

The principal objective of development must be the eradication of poverty and its underlying causes. This necessitates an understanding of what these causes are.

Poverty concerns income and assets but it is about much else besides. It concerns health, life expectancy, diet, shelter, education, security, access to vital resources and other aspects of living standards. It is also a relative concept. The poverty of the single mother in London is the splendor of her peer in Calcutta. Both, however, are denied options routinely open to those more fortunate. There is no single measurement because of the diversity of the variables. A number of attempts have been made to calculate physical quality of life indexes or wealth indexes (the most scholarly of which is that of McGranahan et al., United Nations Research Institute for Social Development[5]), but these are usually flawed because the data that are available from most developing countries are unreliable or out of date. If the purpose of quantifying living standards is to improve policies, then figures that are more than two or three years out of date are almost useless.

The most useful rough-and-ready indicator of poverty (advocated by the United Nations Children's Fund, UNICEF) is the under-5 mortality rate (U5MR) because the statistics are relatively reliable and regularly available and because of its close relationship to all the other poverty variables.[6]

Even these figures are usually only available on a national basis, and assessments of poverty in particular regions of a country or among specific classes usually have to be determined by one-time surveys of child mortality or malnutrition.

It is sobering that, in spite of the abundance of statistics about all aspects of development, so little is known about the human condition. It is difficult to say with certainty who is poor, and are they getting poorer; who is hungry, and are they getting hungrier. For example, the World Bank's flagship, the annual *World Development Report,* contained statistical annexes with a total of some 334 columns of data in 1988. None of these indicated malnutrition rates for any age group. None indicated prevalence of tuberculosis, diarrhea or other diseases of poverty. None indicated the proportions of the populations who have access to safe drinking water. The report did, however, contain a table showing household expenditure on motor cars. Throughout the 185 pages of text the issue of poverty is not raised (except for half a page revealing it to be on the increase) until the very last page when the reader is reminded that "reducing poverty remains the ultimate challenge of development policy." (Similarly, the 1989 report all but ignored the issue of poverty, but the 1990 report is an exception. For the first time in ten years the report's chief concentration is on poverty issues.)

A compelling analysis of the causes of poverty is offered by Robert Chambers.[7] He describes an interlocking web of five factors, each of which feeds off and exacerbates the others. The factors are poverty itself, physical weakness, isolation, vulnerability and powerlessness. To Chambers's list two other factors should be added: environmental damage and gender discrimination.

Isolation means lack of contact, not just in a physical sense, through living in a remote area, but also in a social sense, through ostracism or illiteracy.

Vulnerability can be due to natural disasters, to exploitation, to physical incapacity or to social conventions (for example, the dowry system which bankrupts many families with large numbers of daughters in countries such as Bangladesh).

Powerlessness also relates to exploitation and comprises three categories:

1. Powerlessness to prevent the elite trapping all or most of the benefits of a development advance; for example, agricultural extension services favoring the larger farmers, credit schemes benefiting the already wealthy, food aid being siphoned off by government officials and so on. This phenomenon has been powerfully described by BRAC, a Bangladesh voluntary organization.[8]
2. Powerlessness to prevent robbery, deception, blackmail or violence.
3. Powerlessness to negotiate—an absence of bargaining power.

This description of poverty accords closely to surveys of poor people's own attitude toward their situation. (Sadly, few such studies have been made.) For example, a survey of poor people in two villages in India[9] produced the following criteria of poverty:

- more than one family member working as attached laborer;
- residing on patron's land;
- marketing produce through patron only;
- members seasonally out-migrating for jobs;
- selling more than 80 percent of their marketed produce immediately after harvest;
- cash purchases during the slack festival season;
- adults skipping one meal a day during the summer months;
- women and children not wearing shoes regularly;

- housing made only of mud;
- animals and people living in same dwelling.

Similarly a survey in Sierra Leone of poor farmers' perception of their biggest problems[10] yields the following issues:

- how to buy food at reasonable prices in the dry season;
- how to get credit to build up herds;
- animal and human health;
- injustice from the forest department;
- dealing with the "modern world."

It is clear that a lack of opportunity for self-determination and a vulnerability to risk are perceived by the poor as most important, but these factors are often ignored by outside agencies. Sometimes, in fact, these problems can be compounded. Diversity is the strategy adopted by the poor in the face of adversity, yet so many officially funded development schemes seek to lock poor farmers into monoculture. Other schemes increase the authority of officials or merchants over the poor.

If aid is to attack deprivation then it needs to act on all of the interlocking and underlying causes. Attending to the easier factors while ignoring others builds unsustainability into the design of the programs at the outset. Hence we see nutrition and health projects to combat physical weakness, roads and education to combat isolation, disaster preparedness and crop insurance to combat vulnerability and income generation to combat poverty. These must be combined with the redistribution of assets, freedom of political and trade union association, legislation to assure human rights, programs to elevate the status as well as income of women and environmental protection.

In most developing countries the majority of the population would be poor by Northern standards, but perhaps only a small proportion are so poor as to be physically at risk. The World Bank has commissioned a major study of the problem of extreme poverty. The conclusions of this study were that the extreme poor should be seen as a distinct social group —one that suffers from or is prone to, malnutrition—and that the World Bank should launch a major initiative to safeguard the food security of this group.[11,12] Although the World Bank has subsequently launched a number of programs designed to target the extreme poor, its efforts fall well short of the full-scale initiative the report called for.

The extreme poor have by and large not benefited from economic growth and indeed have frequently suffered from policies and projects that are otherwise "good for the economy." To help this group requires different policies geared to their health, food and production needs, to employment guarantee schemes and to land redistribution.

Michael Lipton argues that the best measurement of extreme poverty is food consumption. The group comprises those who consume less than 80 percent of the calorie intake recommended by the Food and Agricultural Organization and the World Health Organization as a minimum, or those who have to spend over 80 percent of their income on food. It comprises only some 10 to 20 percent of the population in the countries covered by the study. These are the most vulnerable people in the Third World. Globally (excluding the People's Republic of China) they comprise a total population of some 430 million and their annual income is of the order of US $100 per person. If they were able to increase their real income by 30 percent they would no longer be vulnerable to malnutrition.

The total income supplement this would require is about US $13 billion, which amounts to about one-quarter of total aid to the Third World, or one-twelfth of debt service. Unfortunately, though this comparison may illustrate that the problem is of a manageable scale, it says nothing about the practical feasibility of eradicating it. The practical problems and vested interests to overcome in order to target assistance to the very poorest means that the resources needed would be considerably greater. What is essential, however, is that, in future, very much more attention must be given towards ensuring not only that official aid is increased, but that it is directed effectively to the requirements of the extreme poor. This calls for a redefinition of development priorities.

What is Development?

The orthodox economist might define development as the achievement of economic growth and hence improved living standards. It is achieved by improving the use made of a country's human, natural and institutional resources. The gross national product (GNP) provides the obvious measurement of progress according to this definition. But this narrow definition offers little to the poor. Decades of experience have shown that economic growth does not by itself lead to improved living standards for the majority. Improving the application of human resources can be brought about through trampling on human rights. The natural resource base can be depleted for short-term profit—"environmental borrowing." Improving the effectiveness of institutions can be achieved through turning them away from the services that the local populations want of them.

The signal failure of development has been its inability to remedy the problem of hunger. In 1974 political leaders from across the world came together for the first ever World Food Conference. Shaken by the starvation that had plagued Ethiopia and other African countries the previous year, the politicians spent several days analyzing the causes of hunger and what could be done to prevent future suffering. Announcing the Conference's conclusions at the close, Henry Kissinger, then US Secretary of State, asserted the common commitment to a new approach which would mean that, within a decade, hunger would be abolished and that no child need go to bed hungry at night.

With cruel irony the tenth anniversary of that conference was marked by the worst famine that Africa had ever seen. The world's public was generous, but it was not content to donate cash. It was a time to demand change. The pop stars of Band Aid and those who "ran for the world" in Sport Aid demanded action to "change the world," to dismantle the political barriers that had obstructed international action, to cut through the red tape of European Commission bureaucracy that was hampering governmental relief efforts and so make the surplus food mountains of Europe available to the starving of Africa. And some of the major charities called on their supporters not just to give more, but also to lobby their governments in the North for action to end the debt crisis, to make official aid more relevant to the poor and to improve terms of trade for the developing countries.

Official statistics revealed that, in spite of all the fine rhetoric, the number of people who faced the daily threat of starvation actually rose over the decade which was to see the end of hunger. World Bank estimates of food insecurity put the number at 700 million.[13] It also became apparent that the prospects for reversing the trend were reducing as the wealth gap between nations widened. The threat of recession at the start of the 1980s had to a large extent been avoided, but this had been achieved by pursuing policies which created a more hostile economic environment for the Third World. The governments of developing countries in turn had pursued policies which protected their elites from the ravages of recession, but which loaded the burden of austerity on to the poorer groups. The wealth of Marcos, Mobutu and others grew to dizzy heights while the poor became poorer.

Some blame must be apportioned to the official aid agencies. Billions of dollars poured into development assistance (much in the form of loans rather than grants) have failed to solve the mounting problems of poverty. This aid has often helped the elite increase their personal fortunes or power bases. And, together with the loans that were readily available from Northern banks throughout the 1970s, it often funded expensive "white elephants"—projects that have done little for economic growth but which have contributed greatly to the Third World's mounting debt burden.

With rising interest rates and high oil prices in the 1980s, much of the Third World descended into deep economic crisis. For countries dependent on the export of primary commodities, attempts to increase their foreign exchange earnings have proved largely futile. Their rush to increase exports has led to world gluts and plummeting prices. It also became clear that the natural resource of much of the Third World was being used unsustainably to pay for debts which few had benefited from.

Though the once popular theory of the "trickle down of wealth" had largely been discredited (it being apparent that the poor rarely benefit from economic growth unless there are government policies to ensure that they do), it had become evident that the "trickle down of poverty" is a surprisingly efficient mechanism. When the screw is turned those with power can readily ensure that it is not they, but someone weaker, who feels the squeeze. Hence rich governments were able to push the burden of recession on to poor countries; the elite in poor countries were able to pass on the burden to their poorer neighbors, and through shortsighted mining of the environment the burden is being passed on to those whose voice is the weakest of all, because they are not yet even born.

Northern governments and the international institutions they dominate have given much advice to their southern counterparts on how to withstand the economic crisis. The rewards promised are new loans and a gradual route out of debt. Though many countries have accepted this advice, by the World Bank's own admission there is little light at the end of the tunnel. In spite of several years of "structural adjustment" and painful rescheduling of loans, "no country has significantly improved its debt ratios."[14] As a result the social pains and tensions continue to rise, as the growing number of food riots, mass protests against "IMF austerity" and coup attempts make clear.

Development is in crisis, and the clamor for a new approach is growing, a new approach based on a broader definition of development.

At its broadest, "development" means quite simply "improving society." Since the society comprises no more than the people it is made up of, development therefore can mean "enabling people to achieve their aspirations." This may appear a rather tautological argument, but it has three virtues. Firstly, it indicates the fundamental necessity to build any development model on a foundation of democratic processes. How else can we judge what people's aspirations are? Secondly, it reveals the need to make political choices—it goes without saying that it is impossible to satisfy *all* the ambitions of *all* the people all of the time. Choices must be made by those who wield the power about which groups' aspirations are to be prioritized. And thirdly, it speaks of "enabling" rather than "providing"— hinting that true development is done *by* people not *to* people, that development might be coordinated by the governments and official aid agencies in their provision of institutions, infrastructure, services and support, but that it is *achieved* by the people themselves.

Development is not a commodity to be weighed or measured by GNP statistics. It is a process of change that enables people to take charge of their own destinies and realize their full potential. It requires building up in the people the confidence, skills, assets and freedoms necessary to achieve this goal.

Just Development

Just development is about attacking the web of forces that cause poverty. This demands that equity, democracy and social justice be paramount objectives, alongside the need for economic growth. It must enable the weaker members of society to improve their situation by providing the social services they need and by enabling them to acquire the assets and to improve the productivity of those assets. It must combat vulnerability and isolation. It must ensure the sustainable use of natural resources and combat exploitation, particularly the oppression of women. And it must make the institutions of society accountable to the people.

A developing country has three principal assets. It has its economic resources—such as its investments, infrastructure and foreign exchange reserves, its natural resources and its human resources. Unless the country nurtures and uses each one of those assets to full potential then it will fall behind. Any country, for example, which is obliged to drain its economic resources in order to service its debts will inevitably turn to plundering its natural resources and its human resources.

Just development, therefore, comprises the following ingredients, some of which are more familiar to orthodox development thinking than the others:

Development of Infrastructure

Early offical aid strategies concentrated on infrastructure in the belief that roads, railways, ports, telecommunications, power stations and similar schemes would open up the country to future trade and prosperity. Such hopes have rarely born fruit. Infrastructure may make development *possible,* but it doesn't make development. Conversely, development, poverty alleviation and famine relief are severely hampered where infrastructure is weak or unreliable. In rural areas there is usually a marked correlation between vulnerability to hunger and lack of proximity to roads or other communications channels. Just development, therefore, must concentrate infrastructural development on the needs of the most vulnerable areas.

Economic Growth

Though sometimes overlooked by voluntary organizations, economic growth is vital for financing the improvements in the quality of life desired by the people. But it is only one component of development, as walls are only one component of a building. A house without windows or doors becomes a prison, so too a society based solely on growth becomes an economic machine.

Poverty Alleviation

People are the most precious resource of any country. There is little prospect for any country which allows its people to remain hungry, sick or ill-educated. The provision of health care, schooling, good nutrition and safe water may initially be expensive welfare measures, but in the long run, by improving the strength of the workforce, they are a wise use of resources. As Winston Churchill once said, "There is no finer investment for any community than putting milk into babies."

Equity

While some governments and official aid agencies have recognized the importance of poverty alleviation, few pay more than lip service to the concept of equity. The former, though important in terms of human capital, is generally seen as the compassionate action of a civilized regime with funds to spare. The latter implies a shift in the development model so as to invest in the poorer members of society through the redistribution of wealth and incomes. The former is a strategy of investing the surplus resources a nation generates into human capital. The latter is a strategy of generating surplus in a different way.

Equity is not charity. It should be pursued because the nation as a whole runs more efficiently and becomes better off when its productive assets are broadly distributed. Countries as politically diverse as China, Japan, Cuba, South Korea and Finland have demonstrated this. In particular, the land reform programs of the Southeast Asian examples have proved to be remarkably strong foundations for rapid social and economic improvements. The success of these countries and the other so-called tigers of the region (though their human rights records may leave much to be desired) is usually ascribed to their pursuit of export-led growth, though it would be more accurate to describe their strategy as equity-led growth.

Gender equity is also of critical importance. In most countries women comprise at least half the workforce. Any development strategy that fails to recognize this is guilty of denying this sector the chance to achieve its full potential. This is not only bad for women, it is bad for the country. Similar arguments can be made about the need for equity between nations. It is desirable from a moral standpoint, but it is necessary if we are to achieve an economically healthy and a politically stable world.

Natural Resource Base Protection

Just development must attend to future generations and to the health of the planet, not just to immediate needs. Hence it is essential that the natural resource base is used wisely and sustainably. To achieve growth by the depletion of non-renewable resources is as artificial as the achievement of short-term government spending plans by the printing of money. Both are forms of borrowing from the future. The latter, as is well known, leads to economic inflation. The former leads to "environmental inflation." It creates a legacy of environmental debt, which is a debt that cannot be written off.

Environmentalism and economic growth are not natural enemies. To replace environmentally unfriendly products and lifestyles will be costly and so growth—if it is the right kind—is important. In a production process there are two sources of "value added"—labor and nature. The right kind of growth is that which maximizes the former contribution and ensures that the latter is derived at a sustainable rate.

Democracy

In any geographic region, those countries where people are freer to speak out, to associate in political parties or trade unions, where there is a free press, where governments are open and freely elected and where institutions of the state are publicly accountable tend to fare better and to have more contented populations. The rapid transformations in Eastern Europe, Latin America and elsewhere illustrate this. Governance is improved by strong civil society.

The Soviet Union has distinguished between political democracy (*glasnost*) and economic democracy (*perestroika*). It has been more energetic in pursuing the former, but by 1990 it realized the unsustainability of political changes without parallel economic reforms. In many African countries, conversely, there have been major economic reforms, often urged by IMF/World Bank structural adjustment programs, but without political liberalization. The World Bank has observed that African countries such as Botswana and Mauritius which *are* democratic are also more economically successful.

Just development calls for an effective partnership of the government and the people, and this is only possible through the achievement of democracy in its broadest sense.

Social Justice

For a sustainable and trusting partnership between governments and the people to be possible, full human rights must be guaranteed. Social justice also demands the eradication of all forms of discrimination, whether on grounds of race, creed, tribe or gender. A country where social justice is impaired is a country divided. Its human assets will not be used to their full potential. Factionalism will lead to wasteful tension and fighting. And offended parties will resent and perhaps seek to undermine the state.

The DEPENDS Approach

The ingredients of just development combine to make the acronym DEPENDS:

development of infrastructure
economic growth

poverty alleviation
equity
natural resource base protection
democracy
social justice

The DEPENDS approach is as appropriate for governments, for the World Bank and for other official aid agencies as it is for NGOs, and it is even more important that they adhere to it. Of course subscribing to a formula of words in itself is useless. Development agencies should objectively assess whether their actions match up to those words.

The World Bank has deepened its concern for poverty issues in recent years. Its 1990 *World Development Report* stresses the importance of "labor-enriching growth," increasing investments in the social sectors and agriculture.[15] It certainly embraces poverty alleviation, and more recently the protection of the environment alongside economic growth among its principal aims. However, although it recognizes the importance of equity, the Bank is hesitant to discuss income and land distribution, and refuses to put issues of human rights and democracy on its agenda, since these are seen as the internal affairs of sovereign nations.

It is true that no aid agency can impose these things, but there are many ways in which they can promote them, even if not altogether welcomed by the government in question.

A donor can require a certain degree of popular participation and consultation in the design of projects, and withhold funding if these are blocked. Where governments steadfastly refuse to move in the direction of just development, aid could be cut off and diverted to use elsewhere, for example through the country's NGOs.

It is time to rethink the meaning of sovereignty. As Larry Diamond argues:

> True sovereignty resides not with the regime in control of the state of a country, but with its people, and when the people clearly indicate their rejection of the ruling regime, democratic governments and organizations are justified in offering them assistance to realize their political aspirations. This is not a carte blanche for democracies to overthrow regimes they fear or dislike, but rather an argument for popular legitimacy as the fount of sovereignty, and for reading unambiguous signals of the illegitimacy or delegitimation of an authoritarian regime as due cause for no longer according it the full respect and privileges of sovereignty.[16]

David Korten develops this theme to argue that international cooperation should be predicated on the basic human right of the people of any country to organize, to access information, to undertake development activities of their own choosing on their own initiative, to express views on policies, to participate in any international exchange and to receive financial and other assistance from foreign and domestic contributors.[17]

> Sovereignty is inseparable from democracy. There is, of course, a danger in this argument: who determines the democracy "litmus test"? Wrongly applied it could be a slippery slope towards a new form of colonialism.

Two current trends in international affairs add nuance to the debate about sovereignty.

First is the dawning realization that we live in an interdependent world. National boundaries are not hermetic seals. What goes on in one country can have profound effects on others. Acid rain, ozone depletion, the spread of AIDS and drugs, increasing numbers of refugees from war or repression, fallout from nuclear accidents and the ramifications of religious fundamentalism are all illustrations of this. Spaceship Earth has many cabins. The occupants of each must allow fellow passengers in other cabins a modicum of privacy, but not a *carte blanche* to damage the craft itself. The greatest challenge to any state leader today is to forge a consensus on the minimum rules of good planetkeeping necessary for the survival of our ailing spaceship. This involves an environmental code of conduct, but it also involves agreement on minimum standards of human rights and democracy, and procedures for eroding the maldistribution of wealth, both between individuals and nations. Northern governments can expect limited cooperation from the South regarding their newfound concern for tropical rainforests and other environmental issues unless they are prepared to compromise on the debt crisis and other economic injustices. Leaders of vision will realize that real progress will only be made by major concessions all around. The North has squandered its own environment and consumes perhaps 80 percent of the world's resources. It is in no position to give lessons to the South about ecology. Concessions desired will only be won if the North gives ground on the issues the South feels to be most pressing. Likewise, the North is likely to scorn talk of wealth maldistribution between nations from presidents who lord over the most polarized economies in the world.

Second is the trend in development assistance toward conditionality. Though structural adjustment has been hotly criticized by voluntary organizations it is, in at least one respect, a step forward. Conventional development aid has largely failed the poor partly because the projects supported tend to serve the interests of a minority, but chiefly because they fail to address the political causes of maldevelopment. Structural adjustment lending wades in where other aid fears to tread—inducements to make reforms which the donors believe correct maldevelopment. Unfortunately, structural adjustment has focused only on particular categories of reforms such as removing impediments to wealth generation posed by governmental inefficiency and liberalizing markets. Adjustment funders are right to want to foster an environment more conducive to entrepreneurship, but there are other causes of maldevelopment which are much more important. Unless the full range of DEPENDS goals are drawn into adjustment conditionality, then the results can actually be damaging to the poor, as critics of adjustment have demonstrated. The conclusion is not necessarily to scrap structural adjustment but to reform it: a theme of future chapters.

3

What are Voluntary Organizations, and Where Have They Come From?

A Brief History

Though voluntary organizations in different guises existed well before the twentieth century in both North and South, NGOs as they are recognized today have a more recent history. The early Southern NGOs typically arose out of independence struggles. For example, the Gandhian movement in India had many offshoots that still flourish today, including handloom centers and other appropriate technology initiatives, schools concentrating on functional education, People's Courts that use nonviolent citizens' pressure to achieve justice for the lowest castes and campaigning organizations for land reform and other aspects of social justice.

The first Northern NGOs to enter the stage did so just after the First World War—such as the Catholic Church-based CARITAS and Save the Children Fund. They gained strength toward the end of and immediately after the Second World War, Hence OXFAM started in 1942, Catholic Relief Services in 1943 and the Cooperative for American Relief Everywhere (CARE) in 1945. Initially these NGOs were engaged in relief work, primarily in war-torn Europe. They gradually shifted their attention to the Third World and also broadened it to include welfare activities—a natural extension of relief.

During the 1950s and 1960s the number of Northern NGOs multiplied and their focus moved progressively into development activities. They saw that relief attacked only the symptoms of poverty. To attack deprivation itself necessitated helping the poor increase their capacity to meet their own needs with the resources they control. The shift of location from the refugee camps, feeding centers and hospitals to the villages and slums

29

where they set about establishing their projects opened the Northern NGO's eyes to the full reality of poverty. In the first locations the symptoms of poverty are apparent, in the second its root causes.

At the start of this period their development work fitted into a conventional "modernizing" school of thought—helping poor communities to become more like Northern societies by importing Northern ideas, Northern technology and Northern expertise. They were initially oblivious of their Southern counterparts, of village committees and other indigenous structures. They set up their own projects, with their own staff. But gradually many of them came to criticize the negative effects of the traditional development model and to question seriously their contribution to it. They started to shift to a new role, that of providing a service to the popular grassroots organizations and self-help movements. This work was characterized by its small scale, its local (or at least national) leadership and its support for economic and political independence of the poor.[18]

By 1961, for example, Oxfam UK had made a policy decision to move away from financing missionary organizations and other Northern implants and to switch funding to support indigenous efforts. Many of the earliest organizations it funded have gone on to become significant NGOs in their own right.[19] The increased funding opportunities from Northern voluntary sources led to a mushrooming of Southern NGOs. Many of these grew rapidly to become national-level institutions (albeit made often in the image of their Northern funders) which served as intermediate organizations, channelling assistance from the Northern NGO to the grassroots level.

New political concepts emerging from Third World intellectuals, such as the theology of liberation, also greatly influenced NGO thinking during this period. Development theory, once dominated by Northern practitioners, was becoming an indigenous process, led by the people themselves.[20]

In the "early days" there was a homogeneity among NGOs. They more or less pursued a common agenda. But by the 1960s there had been a considerable fanning out. Some remained with their traditional activities, others progressed to new activities and analysis at different rates. And many Southern NGOs became more assertive. Up till the 1960s the NGO community was almost exclusively a Northern preserve, thereafter it has become increasingly a shared ground, initially shared with Southern NGOs created by their Northern "partners."

In the 1970s the spectrum broadened. Many NGOs engaged in self-help activities came to realize that there was a limit to how far self-help activities could go, governed by the vested interests of the political and economic elite. Development was increasingly viewed as a *process* of liberating the poor, both from their physical oppressors and from their own resignation to poverty. New approaches were called for. Brazilian NGOs (particularly inspired by the ideas of Paolo Freire) pioneered the approach of "conscientization"—a combination of political education, social organization and grassroots development—designed not just to improve living standards, but to help the poor to perceive their exploitation and realize the opportunities they have for overcoming such exploitation through mass organization. Conscientization, it was claimed, would also liberate the oppressors! NGOs in other countries developed similar approaches to empowering the poor, for example through adult and functional literacy programs in the Indian sub-continent. To those who are brought up to believe that, because of their caste, they are born inferior and therefore destined to be illiterate, it is liberating to discover that they have the ability to learn to read and write.

Throughout much of the Third World, NGOs concentrated on fostering structures to help the poor in their struggle against injustice. Social development came of age. The resulting grassroots organizations were rapidly shifting, often informally constituted, and sometimes unrecognized by their governments. Northern NGOs often could not fund them directly but had to channel their support through the nationally based intermediary organizations.

That development is a political process proved an uncomfortable analysis for some NGOs, especially for those who had come to depend for their funds on governments or on a conservative constituency. Some stood still. Some took the step and attempted to communicate their reasons to their support base in the North, and perhaps suffered a declining income as a result. Some took the step, made little effort to communicate this to their supporters, and have lived with the contradiction ever since.

The gradual realization throughout the 1970s that poverty is political in nature also gave birth to advocacy as a new activity. It was clear that some of the vested interest groups which bear down on the poor are Western based (governments and companies). It is pointless to tackle this in the South alone. The battleground had to be the West itself. NGOs began programs of development education, public campaigning and parliamentary lobbying in pursuit of political changes. Again, a conflict of interests became apparent. NGOs which were dependent on government funding or a conservative donor base were shy of this advocacy role. How could they be seen to be knocking the establishment of which they were a part? Some, at least in the United Kingdom, judged that they would be proscribed from advocacy activities by charity law.

This compromise is unsatisfactory. Although the advocacy NGOs—especially the specific issue campaigning ones—have made an important mark, few can claim much direct Third World experience. They often borrow analysis from the leftist critics of orthodox development (sanitizing the language to make it more broadly acceptable), data from official development sources (reinterpreted accordingly) and snatches of experience from those who have worked in the Third World (to add color, a human dimension and "street credibility").

The 1980s saw an important leap forward in advocacy work on two counts. Firstly some of the Northern NGOs with overseas programs began to lose their inhibitions and started to speak out, being goaded to do so by their staff and their overseas partners. Though their advocacy work may be more timid than that of the specialist lobbying organizations, they have achieved a great deal because of their credibility with the public and with governments. Secondly, and most importantly, a number of parallel advocacy groups have emerged in the Third World. North–South networks of advocacy groups have increased the authenticity, analytical strength and power of NGO advocacy by several orders of magnitude. The first such network to make its mark was the International Baby Foods Action Network. This was set up in 1979 by seven NGOs, rapidly grew to about 150 NGOs from all parts of the world, and led the successful campaign for international governmental agreement on a code of marketing for baby foods.

The more progressive Northern NGOs with Third World programs have supported the evolution of these networks, have often funded them, but have tended to take a backseat role. This is partly because of a residual concern about their public image and legal status, partly because they have few staff strong on the skills needed for advocacy and networking and partly—in spite of the rhetoric—because of an organizational half-heartedness.

As development economists cannot resist using GNP indicators as their measure of progress, so too NGO leaders are preoccupied by their organizations' turnover. Intellectually they are well aware that money spent does not equate to development achieved, that all problems cannot be overcome through projects, but they also know that the public, the media and even their peers judge the worth of their organizations by this single, narrow measurement. When choices have to be made the preference is for raising money rather than public consciousness.

In fact, advocacy and fundraising need not be in conflict. During the height of public concern about the famine in Ethiopia in 1984, Oxfam UK came to hear that the British government was planning to cut its overseas aid budget. This story, when it became public, caused massive public and parliamentary indignation and the opposition called for a debate. Oxfam UK commissioned a leading market research company to conduct a survey on public attitudes to government aid that revealed an overwhelming opposition to any cut in the budget. Oxfam UK placed advertisements in all the major newspapers on the eve of the parliamentary debate, releasing the results of the public opinion poll. The government withdrew its plans to cut the aid budget, but the debate still took place, with some of the MPs citing the opinion poll and other Oxfam UK evidence during the debate. The advertisement releasing the results carried an appeal for funds to support Oxfam UK's relief work as a footnote. It proved to be one of the charity's most profitable advertisements during this period.

Oxfam UK also conducted an opinion poll of its own donors to ascertain whether they were put off at all by the advocacy work the organization was doing. At the time there was considerable criticism of the organization in the conservative press on account of this activity. The results, in fact, showed the opposite. Donors said they would be *more* prepared to give if they felt the organization was doing *more* to address such work.

A more recent NGO trend is influencing change in Southern official structures. David Korten[21] calls this "micro-policy reform." Official aid agencies have, through structural adjustment, positioned themselves as primary actors in the promotion of macro policy reform, in the conviction that more effective and sustainable development is only possible given a conducive policy environment. Equally, if not more important, are the reforms in local government structures and institutions.

Some of the more thoughtful NGOs have come to realize that their projects by themselves can never hope to benefit more than a few chosen communities and that these projects are only likely to be sustainable when local public and private organizations are linked into a supportive national development system. The prevailing local or national policy environment may actively discourage the self-reliant local initiative. Some NGOs have therefore attempted to increase substantially their development impact through muscling in on policy debates as catalysts for appropriate micro-policy reforms.

In some senses macro-policy reforms are relatively easy. A government can alter the exchange or interest rates, remove bureaucratic barriers, and increase producer incentives through action at the political center alone. Micro-policy reform involves action throughout the country, the creation of new institutions (for instance, to provide credit to the poor), mammoth retraining exercises (for instance, to redirect agricultural extension services) and wholesale changes in attitudes (for instance, to dismantle the barriers that hold women in a second-class status). To achieve this is a gargantuan task—more possible in some countries than in others, but the potential benefit for the poor is revolutionary.

An early example of this comes from the milk cooperatives of Gujarat, India. The Kaira District Dairy Cooperative is an NGO which grew rapidly in the 1960s. It helped women and the landless to acquire milch stock and organized daily collection from villages throughout the district, paying good prices for the milk. Helped by funds from Northern NGOs (and later from official sources, including the World Bank), it introduced technological innovation in animal feeding and the use of milch-buffalos. Its success was such that it was able to invest in the construction of a factory producing a wide range of dairy products under the brand name Amul, which became a household name throughout India.

In the mid 1970s the EEC, embarrassed by a mountain of surplus dairy products, offered some of this surplus to the government of India as food aid. The government willingly accepted with a view to reconstituting the skimmed milk powder and butteroil into a range of dairy produce for sale to meet the nation's rapidly growing demand for such goods.

The leaders of the Kaira District cooperatives were alarmed. They saw that the market that they had built up over the years could be swept away overnight. They responded by putting forward an alternative plan and entered into negotiation with the Indian government to promote it. Their argument was that the EEC aid would not come forever more; it would be better to use it as a pump-primer, to reconstitute it as whole milk (not other dairy produce) and use the income from the sale of this milk to finance dairy production throughout India on the Kaira model. The government eventually agreed and Operation Flood was launched.

The scheme has had many difficulties and drawbacks which are not relevant at present (though it provides an interesting case study of the problems encountered in attempting rapid replication of village structures). The point here is that a local NGO initiative became threatened by an insensitive policy decision. Rather than accept the new, more hostile environment, the organization lobbied successfully for a reform of that decision. Furthermore, it has helped the government, through training at all levels, research and drawing up alternative plans, to pursue its reformed objectives.[22]

NGOs Today

NGOs do not comprise a tight community but a broad spectrum—too broad, perhaps, to leave the term with much meaning. It embraces multi-million-dollar food aid managers and trade unions of peasants and street hawkers, lawyers advocating the environmental cause and illiterate barefoot midwives.

NGOs, reflecting largely their historical evolution, can be divided into six schools.

1. *Relief and welfare agencies,* such as Catholic Relief Services, various missionary societies and so on.
2. *Technical innovation organizations.* NGOs that operate their own projects to pioneer new or improved approaches to problems, and which tend to remain specialized in their chosen field. Examples

include the British Intermediate Technology Development Group, the international Aga Khan Foundation and the Grameen Bank of Bangladesh, 6-S in the Sahel.

3. *Public service contractors.* NGOs that are mostly funded by Northern governments and that work closely with Southern governments and official aid agencies. These NGOs are contracted to implement components of official programs because it is felt that their size and flexibility would help them perform the tasks more effectively than government departments. Examples include CARE and the Emergency Social Fund (in Bolivia).

4. *Popular development agencies.* Northern NGOs and their Southern intermediary counterparts that concentrate on self-help, social development and grassroots democracy. Examples include the seven independent Oxfams (in different fundraising countries), Bangladesh Rural Advancement Committee (BRAC), Centro Ecumênico de Documentaçao e Informaçao (CEDI) and Federaçao de orgãos para Asistência Social e Educacional (FASE) of Brazil.

5. *Grassroots development organizations.* Locally based Southern NGOs whose members are the poor and oppressed themselves, and which attempt to shape a popular development process. They often receive support from PDAs, though many receive no external funding at all. Examples include the rural workers' unions of Brazil, the Self Employed Women's Association (SEWA) of Ahmedabad, credit and savings groups in the Indian sub-continent and movements of the landless in many countries.

6. *Advocacy groups and networks.* Organizations that have no field projects but that exist primarily for education and lobbying. Examples include the Freedom from Debt Coalition in the Philippines, the Third World Network based in Penang, environmental pressure groups in North and South and Health Action International (campaigning for reforms in the marketing of pharmaceuticals).

The spectrum doesn't divide precisely into separate primary colors. Most (including some of those cited as examples) are mixtures, a blend of several of the colors on the pallet, though one may predominate.

Such categorization is not intended as a value judgment. An NGO in any school can be good or bad. All have an important role to play and all can make a contribution to just development. Whether the NGO does its job well is determined largely by its success in integrating all the DEPENDS elements into its work.

While this might seem more natural for popular development agencies than public service contractors, say, it is by no means impossible for the latter. Research institutes, for example, which are routinely contracted by official aid agencies for specific projects, have on occasions brought about a fundamental redesign of those projects based on insights into their social implications, and have in this way acted as conduits of social concern. Similarly, NGOs contracted to help implement official low-cost housing schemes have insisted on establishing community councils so that the intended beneficiaries can influence the direction of the project.

The good NGO should have a clear mission statement which guides all its activities, from its field work to its fundraising techniques to its advocacy roles. The mission statement should describe the NGOs development philosophy (along the DEPENDS line), define its own potential contribution to this process and set out its strategy for realizing this potential through its various departments.

While it is not vital that the mission statement be a formal document it is important that everyone in the NGO is broadly aware of what the mission is and their individual role in achieving it. An organization that runs as much on idealism as on financial resources (and whose staff may accept low wages in return for a high sense of purpose in what they do) risks great tensions if it makes little attempt to define clearly what that idealism is and to achieve broad support among its staff and supporters for that idealism.

Conflicts between the operational and fundraising arms are the most frequent manifestations of the tension. One NGO worker, for example, criticizes European NGOs for the images they used in their fundraising advertisements during the African famine of 1984–85. He describes these as "starvation pornography . . . despite the constant reminders from Africa about the long-term disasterous consequences of using such degrading images, reinforcing prejudices which are often racist."[23] Conversely, NGO fundraisers frequently feel that the program staff do not recognize the difficulties of raising money, and do not feed them with the information which would make the task easier.

Both sets of staff are acting idealistically but are pursuing different missions, probably because the organization as a whole has neglected to provide the right guidance. A clear organizational mission statement might ease the conflicts between different departments, create greater unity and coherence, and provide motivation for staff and supporters, through painting an exciting vision of what it is that the organization is striving for.

The mission statement would position the NGO's project work in the context of macro-development issues—showing how it at times supplements and at times opposes trends in the latter. Its advocacy work would arise from the tensions between its own development mission and the macro-development trends—in other words, it is located as a natural extension of its field work. Likewise, the fundraising would be designed to maximize public and institutional support for the NGO's mission (not just for the NGO itself), with money donated being a major, but not sole, indicator of success.

Having a mission statement is an ongoing rather than a one-time activity. It requires the NGO to invest in ongoing analytical work, both to be better placed to seize the opportunities for forwarding the development process it has defined, and to bring together the various departments of the NGO in a spirit of common endeavor.

Neither Left Nor Right—But Radical

Popular development agencies and advocacy groups have something of a left-wing image in Northern societies where they may be based. It is probably true that the majority of their staff and often of their most active supporters have left or liberal views. But it would be a great mistake to compartmentalize the major issues with which they deal under the conventional labels of Left and Right as defined by the domestic political divides. "Progressive" or "radical" would be more appropriate labels.

Grassroots movements and popular development agencies in the Third World are mostly pursuing struggles that lie outside the divided territory of Northern politics. Pressure to allow more democracy within development planning, to challenge the second-class status afforded to women, to resist the unsustainable "mining" of the environment on which poor people depend and to encourage land reform in the South has also been supported by many on the right. Such causes—and many others championed by advocacy groups—are radical causes but not necessarily left-wing. Some could even be said to be free-market oriented. Pressure to allow the informal sector, and women in particular, access to credit uses as its chief weapon the evidence from NGO experience that the poor use credit wisely and repay promptly. In other words, such pressure seeks to make the marketplace *more* free. It exposes the prejudice that obstructs market principles and economic reality.

There is, however, a growing political tension within the NGO sector centering more on their practical role than on their political orientation. It cannot be described as a left–right tension so much as a polarization between the radical and non-radical NGOs. The latter would claim to be politically neutral. This claim would be refuted by radical NGOs who argue that no development intervention can be totally neutral and that any action which does not seek quite deliberately to transfer power and authority to the people is supporting the *status quo* and so is antiprogressive.

A message that the radical NGOs have learned is that development is fundamentally about taking sides. Some achievements are possible by improving services and economic activities for the poor, but the most significant changes depend on redistribution—increasing not just the incomes of the poor and their access to productive assets, but also their democratic power. Such redistribution is highly political and controversial.

Radical NGOs—North and South—see the non-radicals as a considerable threat. They compete for donations, capture government funds and distort development work.

The radicals are trying to change the images by which the Third World is conventionally portrayed in the North. They are trying to inject images of dignity rather than despair, self-help rather than beggaring, active struggle rather than hopelessness and ingenuity rather than ignorance. These they see as very much more honest images than the classic charity portrait of the Third World—the amorphous sprawling concentration camp of pot-bellied children and sunken-eyed, starving mothers. The progressive portrait is more complex, however, and not so effective at triggering immediate response—like writing checks. Other NGOs, including some of the resource-abundant evangelical charities such as World Vision, suffer nothing of this inhibition. They go straight for the artery connecting heart and wallet. No image is too harrowing for them; no technique too tacky. This, coupled with the rapid rise of mass media evangelicism, particularly in the United States, leads to a very steep growth curve for these agencies.

Questions of Integrity

Though most people would agree with the familiar adage that it is better to teach people to fish rather than to hand out fishes, when it comes to giving money the private donor wants to keep on paying for the fishes. It is always the famine appeals which bring in the money. Raising funds for development is never as lucrative.

Official funding of NGOs may be increasing but it is not possible to decipher from the figures how much is channelled for purposes designed freely by the NGOs rather than by proxy on behalf of the official agencies. Public service contractors will often tailor their projects and indeed their organizations to suit the official aid agencies who fund them. They are happy for the project initiative to come from governments and for their role to be that of a subcontractor implementing a component of another's project. And they are equally content to act on strong hints they receive from official donors that the latter would welcome funding applications for a particular type of project in a particular country. It may well be that "free" official funding is actually decreasing, as some suggest is the case in the United States.[24]

The carry-over effect of these trends is that local development efforts in the Third World are being distorted towards the interpretation of the non-radical NGOs. The immense funding of these spawns local partners anxious to meet the job descriptions defined by the funders, who in turn draft those job descriptions mindful of the interests of their major donors. This amounts to a neat reversal of bottom-up ideas of development and can be disruptive.

Non-radical NGOs are increasingly seen as preferred partners by many major official aid agencies and Southern governments. In response, some radical NGOs have advocated drawing up an NGO charter or Code of Conduct to define the responsibilities all NGOs ought to accept toward promoting more democratic, equitable values in the South and greater public awareness and political debate about development issues in the North.[25]

How Much Do They Give?

NGOs are generally seen as worthy and efficient but negligible on the scale of development needs. This may be true individually, but collectively NGOs now constitute one of the major channels of finance from North to South.

In 1989 they shifted US $6.4 billion to the South—about 12 percent of all Western aid, public and private. In terms of *net transfers*—and in the age of debt crisis, when the cashflow of developing countries is all important, this is perhaps the most important measure—NGOs collectively contribute more than the World Bank. (The Bank invests more each year in the Third World, but when the debt service for past loans is deducted from the gross figure the resulting net transfer is smaller.)

The NGO role measured in money terms has expanded greatly in recent years. In 1970 they handled less than US $9 million. Measured in real terms (at 1986 prices) their resources have doubled from 1975 to 1985 (during which time Western official aid rose by 39 percent). The lion's share of this increase has come about, however, not because they have persuaded the Northern publics to give more, but because their governments have contributed more, as Table 3.1 demonstrates.

As can be seen, private contributions reflected concern for the famines in Africa in 1973 and 1984–85 but have otherwise been rather constant in real terms. In fact, total official aid has grown faster than private contributions, which is sobering news for those who berate their governments for failing to increase their aid to the UN target of 0.7 percent of GNP. Table 3.2 shows this pattern more clearly and demonstrates how official contributions have evened out the fluctuations in private contributions and enabled more steady growth in the NGO sector.

Table 3.2 illustrates that from 1975–83 OECD aid rose on average 3.5 percent per annum while private contributions to NGOs rose by just 1.8 percent per annum. The increases in official funding, however, meant that total NGO aid increased by 6.1 percent per annum in this period.

Table 3.1 Voluntary (private) and Official Contributions to NGOs (US $billions at 1986 prices)[26]

Contribution	1970	1972	1973	1974	1976	1978	1980	1982	1984	1985	1986	1987	1988
Private	2.7	2.7	3.1	2.5	2.5	2.3	2.7	2.8	3.2	3.5	3.3	3.1	3.4
Official	0.04	0.1	0.1	0.2	0.9	1.1	1.2	1.4	1.6	1.8	1.9	1.7	1.8
% Official	1.5	3.6	2.8	7.1	26.5	32.4	30.8	33.3	33.3	34.0	37.1	35.0	35.0
Total	2.74	2.8	3.2	2.7	3.4	3.4	3.9	4.2	4.8	5.3	5.2	4.7	5.2

Source: OECD.

Table 3.2 Total official and NGO aid (US $billions current and constant, and as a percentage)

	1970	1975	1980	1982	1983	1984	1985	1986	1987	1988
OECD aid	7.0	14.3	27.7	28.2	28.1	28.7	29.4	36.5	41.6	48.1
at 1986 prices	22.2	26.0	31.7	34.2	34.2	35.6	36.1	36.5	36.0	38.7
% of previous	—	17.0	22.0	7.9	0.03	4.1	1.5	1.1	-1.4	7.5
NGO private	0.86	1.35	2.39	2.32	2.32	2.60	2.88	3.34	4.0	4.2
as % of GNP	0.041	0.034	0.032	0.029	0.029	0.038	0.041	0.35	0.3	0.3
at 1986 prices	2.73	2.44	2.73	2.81	2.82	3.22	3.54	3.34	3.1	3.4
% of previous	—	-10.6	12.0	2.7	0.4	14.5	9.8	-5.7	-7.2	9.7
NGO total at 1986 prices	2.77	2.64	3.93	4.21	4.25	4.86	5.35	5.29	4.7	5.2
% of previous	—	-4.7	48.7	7.3	1.0	14.4	9.9	-1.1	-11.0	10.6

Source: calculated from OECD and World Bank GNP figures.

From 1983–86 OECD aid rose on average 2.2 percent per annum, private contributions to NGOs by 5.8 percent per annum and total NGO aid by 7.5 percent. In other words, private grants increased slowly in the first period (half the growth rate of OECD aid), but rapidly in the second (almost three times the growth rate of OECD aid). However, if official contributions to NGOs are included then NGO growth over both periods is rapid and sustained.

Some governments are very much more prepared than others to support their NGOs, and the form of their support varies. The US government is by far the largest funder of NGOs, contributing almost half of all official funding of the NGO sector. However, the largest proportion of this is in the form of food aid rather than cash, and to a large extent the US government uses NGOs as subcontractors in its own aid program. A relatively small share of its support is cash contributions for projects submitted by NGOs.

Measured as a percentage of the official aid program contributed to NGOs, the league table is:

Switzerland	19.4	Sweden	4.6
United States	11.1	Italy	1.9
Canada	10.8	Japan	1.6
Netherlands	7.0	United Kingdom	1.3
Belgium	6.6	France	0.3
West Germany	6.5		

Of all OECD countries, only Australia, Austria and France contribute a lower proportion to NGOs than the British government, yet Britain was one of the first countries to start giving public support to its NGOs. In 1971 the United Kingdom contributed about 8 percent of all OECD official funding of NGOs, by 1979 this had fallen to 1.6 percent, and by 1986 to 0.6 percent. Other governments rapidly *increased* their support while the British government did not.

Official funding of NGOs can be a double-edged sword as is particularly apparent in the United States. The government, through its aid ministry, USAID, has been able to influence greatly the shape of the NGO community and mold NGO objectives to fit its own foreign policy and aid objectives. One indicator of this is the wide variation in support which the government gives to different members of its NGO community, as Table 3.3 shows.

There is growing concern that the government is increasingly telling the NGOs what projects to submit for funding.[27] It is feared that NGOs are starting to plan projects based on the interests of the funders, projects which are likely to be more oriented to the wealthier elements of Third World societies.[28]

A warning signal was given as long ago as 1982 that NGOs could find that they prostitute themselves in the quest for official funding. Jan Pronk, then Deputy Secretary General of the UN Conference on Trade and Development (UNCTAD) and former Dutch aid minister, warned on opening a UN/NGO conference.

Table 3.3 US support to its NGOs[29]

| US NGO | Contribution (US $Millions) | | |
	government	private	% government
Agricultural Cooperatives Development Institute	5.882	0.149	97.5
Pathfinder Fund	5.472	0.796	87.3
Catholic Relief Services	333.0	61.9	84.3
CARE	127.0	25.0u	83.5
Church World Service	8.8	29.5	23.0
American Friends Service Committee	0.018	18.0	0.1

Source: Fox, 1987.

> The corruption of NGOs will be the political game in the years ahead —and it is already being played today . . . NGOs have created a huge bureaucracy, employment is at stake, and contacts in developing countries are at stake. It will become impossible for them to criticize governments for decreasing the quality of the overall aid program. NGOs will lose in the years ahead . . . they will be corrupted in the process, because they will receive enough money for their own projects but the rest of the aid program will suffer.[30]

It is often suggested that one of the advantages NGOs have over official aid agencies is their flexibility owing to their smaller size. Today, however, several of the larger NGOs handle funds of similar orders to many of the official aid agencies. For example, in 1985 the aid from Catholic Relief Services was US $437 million compared with US $426 million of Belgian government aid, that of CARE was $274 million (compared with Austria's US $258 million, and in 1989 the budget of Oxfam UK was US $119 million, higher than that of the New Zealand government's aid budget (US $104 million).

At the same time that the size of many NGOs is increasing rapidly, there is a mushrooming of the numbers of NGOs, especially where governments are disposed to funding them.[31] In the United States this is not just the case in the development field. Total private philanthropic contributions amount to about 1.75 percent of GNP (about 2 percent of which is for Third World causes), and if public contributions are included the "private voluntary organizations" handle approaching 5 percent of the country's GNP (close to total defense spending of 6 percent GNP). In the United Kingdom, private contributions to charities amount to about £2billion, or 0.58 percent of GNP, of which about 6.5 percent was for the Third

World. In the United States there are some 500 development NGOs, in Canada over 300, in the United Kingdom about 100 and in the OECD as a whole over 2,000 (of which some 200 account for 75 percent of the funds).

One writer on NGO issues, Hendrick van der Heijden, estimates that Northern NGOs work with 10 to 20,000 Southern NGOs, which in turn assist some 60 million people in Asia, 25 million in Latin America and 12 million in Africa.[32] A similar estimate has been made by the Club of Rome.[33]

It is also important to point out that a great many Southern NGOs receive no Northern funding whatsoever. A recent World Bank study of NGOs active in the health sector in six Indian states indicated that four-fifths of them receive no foreign funds.

NGO projects vary in size from a few dollars to several million. For example, CARE in Liberia has a program to build 100 schools, and Catholic Relief Service has a joint food-for-work project with the World Food Program in Lesotho, which has created half the roads in the country.[34]

4

Magic or Muddle?

Strengths and Weaknesses of NGOs

The media love NGOs. The world's public—at least those who have any compassion for the struggling poor—love NGOs. And increasingly official aid agencies and many Third World governments are courting them. Is the glowing image realistic? Can NGOs deliver all that is expected from them?

The Northern media—with its zest for drama, for simple stories and for clear heros and villains—find NGOs "good copy." True the whiffs of misdemeanor or inefficiency are also eagerly pounced upon, exaggerated, turned into generalizations and politically dressed up for the scandal-loving public. But the bias is overwhelmingly pro-NGOs. After all it is *governments* that we, the public, love to hate; *non*-government organizations can't be suspect. It is large bureaucracies we mistrust; small, voluntary organizations are our friends. It is the profit-motive that we find vulgar; altruism is noble.

The media project Northern NGOs as virtuous Davids fighting the Goliaths of famine, hostile climate, government inequity, slavery and oppression. They provide success stories in an arena—the Third World—which is mostly gloomy. They perform modern day miracles by turning modest donations into hope for the hungry millions. Their staff make great sacrifices and confront personal risk daily in selfless service of the poor. Their projects allow crops to grow abundantly where previously there was desert. Their relief arrives on time where governmental emergency supplies remain tied up by red tape, or succour only the well-off. Their people talk in an everyday language, not the indigestible gobblede-

45

gook of "experts." In short, their business is magic. That is the media view and the one the public wants to hear.

It seems, then, rather churlish to ask, but how effective are NGOs really? The very question rings of cynicism but it is well placed for three reasons.

Firstly, there is surprisingly little objective reporting of NGO projects. Northern NGOs' own writings generally concentrate on the success stories and, being aimed largely at their supporting publics, serve a propaganda purpose. The NGOs tend to commission few objective evaluations, as we shall discuss below, and so may not even know much about their successes or failures. Their intermittant evaluations are rarely published and are usually kept confidential, even inside the NGO. When academics evaluate NGO work they generally seek advice of a Northern NGO on "good projects" to look at. "Good" here means that they contain interesting lessons about successful small-scale or participatory initiatives, about flexibility, about the bypassing of governmental structures or about how an official aid program might be strengthened. The studies would also usually need permission from the project agency, hence the weaker projects tend to avoid scrutiny.

Until recently there has been little pressure on donor NGOs for more disciplined evaluations. Most contributors have an implicit faith in the "NGO approach" which they don't want rocked. After all, one doesn't scrutinize magic too closely, otherwise it loses its charm. This era may be passing, however, as NGOs are emerging as significant players on the development stage and as an increasing share of their funding derives from official sources. NGOs will more and more be challenged to say why they are confident about the approaches they adopt. Accountability is the other side of the publicly contributed coin.

Secondly, there is at present a dramatic mushrooming of NGOs, particularly in the South, and their credentials deserve to be questioned. Those set up by Third World government ministers, which work essentially with government departments and which receive their funding from official aid agencies are hardly *non-governmental* (this is not to say that all the above are necessarily *bad* agencies). Neither are Northern-based agencies, financed overwhelmingly by their home governments and operating projects in conjunction with Southern governments. Furthermore, agencies whose primary motivation is religious or political, or which don't aim to help the poor, are not "true NGOs."

These quasi-NGOs take up a great deal of the time of the more established NGOs. The latter are called upon to give advice, and they are drawn into endless debates about the legitimacy of these newer organizations. It is in the interests of NGOs to be ahead of the game in defining what are acceptable or legitimate NGO activities.

Thirdly, NGOs must constantly be questioning where their real strengths and weaknesses lie in order to find ways of improving their performance and to remain confident about the approach they are pursuing. This is particularly important in an age when official aid agencies are offering large sums of money for collaboration with NGOs on projects defined by the former.

Strengths That Hamper

Serving the Poor

While governments and official aid agencies juggle with a wide range of objectives and target groups, an NGO generally has the advantage of being able to concentrate on just a few activities relating to the needs of the poor. Its physical base, therefore, is usually close to concentrations of poverty and it is likely to be trusted by the poor (though the motivation and funding sources may remain puzzling to them) whereas the poor only know of official aid through their governments, of whom they are probably suspicious. NGOs often work in remoter areas where perhaps no government official is seen from one year to the next, though this isn't always the case. There are few NGOs, for example, in the Central African Republic or Northern Sumatra, and in India NGOs are more concentrated in the Southern states than in the poorer Hindi belt. Likewise in Kenya NGOs are more active around Nairobi than in the famine-prone areas populated by pastoralists.

Even for NGOs it is not easy to reach the very poorest and some, unfortunately, make little effort. It is easier to work with people who start with some assets, some confidence and some skills of farming, crafts, numeracy and literacy. It is relatively easy for the NGO to help increase the productivity of those assets and the application of those skills. For example the provision of credit, irrigation or market outlets to small farmers is easier than the provision of land, farming skills and confidence to the landless. Meaningful development (as opposed to welfare) with the disabled and destitute is even more taxing.

Some researchers into NGO work conclude that the NGO rhetoric of working with the "poorest of the poor" is overstated, that NGOs may be successful at reaching poor people but have yet to demonstrate that they substantially benefit the poorest. Judith Tendler,[35] for example, undertook a major study on US NGOs, based on seventy-five project evaluations. She concluded that beneficiaries were often in the middle and upper ranges of the income distribution and suggests that NGOs have in fact moved away from a poverty focus over the years in their gradual transition from relief and welfare schemes (which are carefully targeted) to development focusing on those who have some assets or marketable skills.

Some would argue that NGOs should not be over-anxious about reaching the very poorest. Though the trickle down theory is much discredited —the rich being very skillful at annexing wealth creation—there is considerable experience to show that helping the *poor* will enrich the communities in which the poorest live and all will benefit from this. The fourth quintile (i.e. not the poorest 20 percent, but the next band up) may be easier to help and more prepared to experiment with new ideas. Successful development with this group would make it easier in the future for parallel efforts with the poorest.

For example, Cinci wa Babili in Northern Province, Zambia, has a very successful scheme to encourage the use of ox traction in farms in an area where such technology was previously almost non-existent. Cinci breeds the oxen, trains the animals and the farmers in plowing and provides credit for purchase of both animals and equipment. The uptake has been impressive but at the outset appealed mostly to the slightly larger farmers. In 1987, Cinci organized a plowing competition which proved to be very popular. The spectators—farmers of all classes—enjoyed the day out and also saw how easily new land could be prepared for planting. After this many of the poorest farmers—including women—applied for oxen, and as a result were able to double the area of land they cultivated. Since land is in plentiful supply this has clearly been a very positive development but it is unlikely that the very poorest would have taken the plunge without having witnessed the positive experience of their stronger neighbors.

More generally, research in rural India conducted by the International Food Policy Research Institute[36] has demonstrated that a large proportion of wealth generated by development schemes remains in the project area. The families who benefit tend to spend their increased income within the village, so strengthening local craft industries and trade. Employment on the land increases. Local beer shops open. Barbers, potters and perhaps tailors set up business, and other trades start to arrive. Unfortunately the same does not yet appear to be the case in most African countries. New wealth tends to be spent on consumer goods imported from the cities—and often from abroad—and so the rural poorest benefit little by improving the fortunes of those slightly better off. Rural infrastructure is not sufficiently established to cater to the demands stemming from economic growth.

While reaching the very poorest should be the ideal, NGOs should not regard a project as failing if it reaches mainly the fourth quintile, providing parallel measures are introduced to try to accelerate the "trickle down."

Popular Participation

The Brundtland Commission concluded that one of the main prerequisites of sustainable development is "securing effective citizen's participation in decision making."[37] This sentence sums up the central tenet of progressive NGOs. However appealing the project, it is likely to come to little unless it is well understood and desired by its intended beneficiaries. An NGO credit scheme, for example, is likely to attract plenty of members, but unless the mechanisms for raising capital, allocating loans, charging interest and recovering debts are understood and accepted then the scheme is unlikely to be durable.

A project, to be sustainable, must address problems and aspirations identified by the poor and must have a management and decision-making structure in which they have confidence. This does not relegate the "outsider" NGOs to an easy, passive role. They must ensure that the discussions and conclusions reflect the views of the poorer and less confident members of the community (particularly the women), rather than those of the traditional community leaders. This entails fostering a new cadre of leadership from among the poor—which is likely to be jealously resisted by the traditional leaders.

For example, the peasant leaders of Samata—a highly effective and localized peasant movement in Pabna district, Bangladesh—have been brutally beaten by hired thugs and have frequently been imprisoned pending trial for ludicrous charges of rape, murder or theft lodged by the landlords.

NGOs must help the poor to make sure that the priorities identified are realistic ones and to spot where the difficulties and backlashes might occur. They must inform the people of relevant experience elsewhere and train them in the skills necessary for execution. They must avoid entering a community with preconceived ideas, but on the other hand they must have the breadth of experience to know what can and cannot work. In other words they must be non-directive, up to a point.

The balance is a fine one. Few NGOs would support credit schemes which lend for wedding and funeral celebrations, though these may well be the primary reasons for borrowing from traditional money lenders. NGO workers also have to be mindful of where the real commitment and enthusiasm of potential new community leaders lies.

One pair of NGO workers living in a very poor district of a Copperbelt town in Zambia painstakingly recorded the concerns and wishes of the poor. A list of some fifteen possible project targets was drawn up and then carefully prioritized, following a further series of meetings with the compound's residents. The whole process took two years. Top of the list was water supplies, job creation, health care and education. Bottom of the list was sports and recreation. In spite of this, the very first project undertaking was the leveling of a piece of ground for a football pitch and the provision of football kits. The NGO realized the expediency of responding to a priority of a small group of lively, determined youths who were clearly emerging as community leaders. The compound now boasts its own football team, which plays against others in the Copperbelt league. This has no doubt strengthened community spirit and helped combat the drabness of life for the urban poor and it has also increased the people's confidence in the NGO, which has since gone on to provide valuable help in the sectors originally identified as priorities.

Probably the most important skill in allocating NGO funds is that of discerning "the right people to back." Successful projects are usually built on imaginative and determined leaders. It is doubly important that the people themselves, rather than the NGO staff, select the leadership—the project objectives will be better attuned to local aspirations and the people will feel greater confidence.

True development is about removing the barriers which restrain people from achieving their full productive capacity. This is threatening to those who come to see the erosion of their status, and they are likely to fight back. The only socially neutral course of action is to do nothing. Any intervention alters power balances. NGOs' business is, inescapably, political. It is about taking sides, siding with the poor against those who comprise the barriers to just development.

Participation—a favorite NGO term—should be seen as two-way: involvement of the poor in the project design and execution, but also participation of the funding or intermediary NGO in the poor's struggle for equity, human rights and democracy.

How representative is such participation? The term has been much devalued by schemes such as Harambe in Kenya in which people are coerced by local authorities to make a "voluntary" contribution to some community undertaking. The poor may have little desire for the undertaking—for example the construction of a new village hall—but are expected to give some cash or their labor in the spirit of "participation." Almost all NGOs claim to involve the poor in all aspects of their projects, but this may be overstated. One study by Tendler[34,35] of seventy-five US NGO projects suggests that there is a confusion of terms between participation and "decentralization." Most decision making, the study concluded, is decentralized but dominated by NGO staff and local elites such as village headmen. In that the elite have a vested interest in the outcome of the projects, a paternalistic, centralized approach might be preferable to an elite-led decentralized style. In fact, one of Tendler's most striking findings was that projects which reached the poorest were usually designed by well-meaning outsiders.

This study, which has been influential in subsequent US writing about NGOs, may not be representative, focusing as it did on large-scale projects which received funding from USAID, but it should serve to remind NGOs to look closely and objectively at their operations and ask whether their practice really lives up to their rhetoric.

An advantage of the close proximity many NGOs, particularly indigenous ones, have to the poor is local knowledge—an understanding of the true nature of poverty and of how macro trends or locally planned large-scale initiatives are likely to affect the poor. They are also well placed to act as facilitators to expose relevant decision makers to those best placed to articulate the concerns of the poor, to act in a sense as channels for local democracy. This is a relatively new and exciting task for most NGOs but unfortunately few engage in it substantially as yet. It is likely that this will become a more mainstream activity in the future, demanding new partnerships between Southern grassroots organizations and Northern advocacy NGOs.

Innovation

NGOs are less subject to the straitjacket of development orthodoxy than are official aid agencies and governments. Their staff normally have greater flexibility to experiment, adapt and attempt new approaches. This is partly because the numbers involved in decision making are smaller, because local officials will probably not be as minutely involved, because scrutiny from outside is slight, because the consequences of failure are much less and because the ethos of volunteerism encourages the individual to develop her or his ideas. This same factor could be cited as a problem—namely amateurism. It fosters idiosyncrasy, lack of continuity and poor learning abilities. It should also be said that many NGOs are far from innovative, but prefer to apply well-tested approaches to new constituencies.

A number of NGO innovations have crept into the official development menu. For example, the pioneering work of the Kaira District dairy co-operatives in the 1960s (Gujarat State, India), which placed a particular emphasis on women and the landless, has grown into the India-wide Operation Flood or White Revolution program. The provision of credit to the very poor by the Grameen Bank of Bangladesh provides a model for credit schemes throughout the world (including even the USA) and has demonstrated more than any other scheme that the very poor are indeed a highly bankable proposition. And Oxfam UK's water harvesting experimentation in the Yatenga District of Burkina Faso, borrowing ideas from the Negev Desert in Israel, is now being adapted and applied by many agencies, including the World Bank, in arid regions throughout Africa.

In such cases NGOs often play a catalytic or seeding role—demonstrating the efficacy of a new idea, publicizing it, perhaps persuading those with access to greater power and budgets to take notice and then encouraging the widespread adoption by others of the idea.

More controversial innovations, such as the use of courts and the law to demand justice from unwilling governments or officials, are spreading rapidly but by their nature are likely to be restricted to the more radical end of the NGO spectrum. In India, for example, environmental and tribal rights groups successfully used the courts to halt the construction of a dam in Silent Valley, Kerala. And the Self Employed Women"s Association of Ahmedabad used the Supreme Court to force the local authorities to allow poor women hawkers to set up their stalls in the municipal marketplace.[39]

In some sectors NGO innovations have been more successful than in others. These include development projects for women, work with pastoralists, credit schemes for the poor, primary health care, soil and water conservation, income generation programs, functional literacy, relief programs and work with tribal and ethnic groups.[40] They have also proved effective as early warning agents during the onset of drought, in describing problems associated with resettlement schemes and in pointing out conflicts of interest between national development objectives and the well-being of indigenous people.

A common characteristic in the above list is activities based on a close relationship with the poor and on a high degree of popular participation.

Small Scale

Participatory programs become highly problematic when they become large. Decision making becomes complex and there is greater chance of the benefit being hijacked by local elite. The majority of NGO programs avoid these difficulties by remaining quite small.

However, small projects benefit few people. How can the precision of small scale be retained while multiplying the outreach? One approach is to subdivide the project into large numbers of relatively autonomous units. The Grameen Bank of Bangladesh has been especially successful at this, remaining with cells of just five people who receive credit and decide which of their members should get the first loans. The cells are linked into village, district and regional structures but the basic grassroots decision making unit has stayed the same as the scheme has expanded to 230,000 members.

A frequently stated disadvantage of small-scale activities is the disproportionate administrative costs when NGO staff handle large numbers of small projects. But it would be wrong to see grassroots NGO workers simply as administrators. They also give advice and help to build confidence among poor communities.

One field worker employed by Oxfam UK in the mid-1980s to assist small groups in the tribal belt of Gujarat, India, had a very low productivity if measured solely in terms of funds disbursed. For example, he made several visits to one village where the tribal forest gatherers (*adivasis*) wanted help with marketing to overcome their exploitation by the local middleman. The merchant paid the government stipulated price for the leaves, nuts, fruit, spices and so on, collected in the forests, but he used weighted scales, reserving one set for purchases and one set for sales—each 10 to 20 percent off in the favor of the merchant. The *adivasis* knew they were being cheated and contemplated setting up their own marketing cooperative, sending produce regularly to be sold in the nearest town.

In discussing the proposal with the field worker over a series of meetings they realized their idea would not be cost effective. They opted for a less ambitious idea: they bought a set of scales and set it up outside the merchant's house so that anyone could check the weight of produce they were buying or selling. Oxfam UK gave a grant for the scales—a full $50—and immediately the merchant had to stop cheating. The tribals' real income went up more than 20 percent overnight and they gave employment to one lad to operate the scales.

At one level the degree of staff time cannot be justified for such a small grant but it had a powerful galvanizing effect on the community. The group went on to organize their own successful credit scheme and acquired a government grant for irrigation.

Commitment of Staff

NGO staff are generally highly committed to their work because of widely shared values and a belief in the social change mission inherent in their work. They are often prepared, therefore, to work long hours for low pay. The commitment is often to the work rather than to the organization itself, particularly in the case of Northern NGO program staff.

As David Brown has observed,[41] unlike a company which produces things from raw materials within the boundaries of the organization (in the core), social change organizations are involved in transformations outside, that is, the core is at the periphery. NGO staff closest to this transformation process are involved with external constituencies and often appear relatively uninterested in the NGO itself and its organizational effectiveness, unless it starts to impede their own work.

Social change theories are central to formulating work strategies, though these are often not well defined or articulated coherently by the NGO. Moreover, the dominant theory can change with time and vary greatly from country to country in an NGO that works internationally.

The commitment factor can be a double-edged sword. It may be difficult to persuade periphery staff to follow approaches and procedures agreed centrally by the organization since those staff prefer to receive their work signals from colleagues at the periphery—colleagues they are usually able to choose for themselves. It may be that experience and ideas generated locally are more valuable in determining a locally appropriate development strategy but this feature of NGOs tends to obstruct the evolution of a coherent approach to new priorities—such as looking at gender issues—and to obstruct institutional learning through the widespread uptake of ideas proven to work in one part of the world.

Committed staff also tend to have strong ideas of their own which they are keen to express. While it seems natural for a Northern NGO to adopt at home the same principles of popular participation that it advocates overseas, this can lead to extremely cumbersome and inappropriate decision making. Participation within a small group of people whose background and knowledge is roughly similar and whose accountability is just to themselves is very different from participation with in a large organization employing diverse specializations and complex and varied accountabilities.

Naturally an organization of principled and committed workers will function best if staff feel respected and listened to. Where all the strong views push in the same direction the sailing is clear, but when, as is usual, there are tensions (such as between the fund-raising and fund-spending departments), then decision making can suffer. Lengthy staff debates may lead to consensus compromises in which participants are careful to guard against any decisions which affect their own work plans. This sort of negative decision making results in organizational planning that is conservative and more concerned with avoiding things that could prove wrong, than with creating opportunities for doing something right. Such an organization risks loss of coherence and risks becoming a loose partnership of the staff it employs (the extreme of idiosyncrasy). The NGO loses all advantages of size in becoming atomized, but it retains the disadvantages.

Pillars of Weakness

When practice fails to live up to the rhetoric, the stated strengths start to resemble weaknesses. In the words of Sheldon Annis, a prominent American analyst of NGO performance,

> in the face of pervasive poverty "small scale" can merely mean "insignificant," "politically independent" can mean "powerless" or "disconnected," "low-cost" can mean "underfinanced" or "poor quality," and "innovative" can mean simply "temporary" or "unsustainable."[42]

An NGO may describe in its literature the goal of helping the poorest of the poor, but in practice puts little effort into targeting or sampling to ascertain whether the benefits of its work are really the "poorest" or merely the "poor." It is as if to state noble objectives is sufficient.

Nowhere is the gap between rhetoric and practice starker than in the field of women and development. NGOs will describe at length the importance of this subject, however one (probably typical) analysis of NGOs' practical work with women (Yudelman[43]) indicates that NGO projects tend to enhance their domestic, not productive, role. They typically concentrate on teaching sewing and cooking and nutrition while women's contribution to agriculture seems to suffer most neglect.

Yudelman quotes the example of an NGO in Africa which started by analyzing the position of women within the particular society. It identified a critical role for women in agriculture, crop marketing and processing of the foods grown. The NGO then proceeded to ignore all this and developed a project making earthenware pots. In another, Asian, example, a training program for village women concentrated on strengthening "traditional women's activities" such as health care, child nutrition, family law and sewing, but completely failed to address their active role in agriculture, in spite of many reminders from the women participants that this was their truly traditional activity.

That NGOs often fail to live up to their fine rhetoric can be ascribed to the following weaknesses.

The Legitimacy Problem

In many countries it is easy to set up an NGO. Someone who can write convincingly in a major Western language, and who knows the current donor fashions stands a good chance of attracting funds. Even the most careful donor frequently makes mistakes, and not all donors are careful.

While some funders will support a project for many years, and thereby avoid risk, others will not fund beyond a defined time limit. The latter see themselves as "talent spotters," finding new people with new ideas and backing them. They encourage experimentation and dynamism. But they also lend a faddish, temporary nature to the NGO sector, and can lead to a "supply-led development" in which resources chase new project ideas.

An increasing proportion of NGO funding, as we have seen, derives from official sources, and an increasing proportion of this is being channelled directly to the Southern NGO, by-passing the Northern NGO. Some Southern NGO workers welcome this trend. They find that the alternative funding source affords them a welcome independence from Northern donor NGOs. An equal number of Southern NGOs oppose the trend.[44] They prefer to continue relating to old and trusted Northern NGO colleagues and let these be intermediaries for official agencies' funds, rather than become exposed to the whims and pressures of those agencies directly.

Very frequently, however, the official funding goes not to established NGOs but to new organizations conforming to models defined by, and oriented to, priorities chosen by the donors. This may be the case with the present expansion of official funding for NGOs in Ghana under the Program of Action to Mitigate the Social Costs of Adjustment. In such situations there is a danger of the public sector corralling the voluntary sector, whether or not the services provided are welcomed by the poor. This could not only deflect NGOs from their chosen functions but it could bring the whole sector into disrepute.

Increasingly official agencies are contracting NGOs to implement components of their projects, rather than work with government departments. Southern governments are, understandably, becoming increasingly resentful about this. They see the erosion of their sovereignty; the increasing execution of state functions by staff who are answerable not to them but to foreign governments; the diversion of some of their most skilled labor from government to non-government service; and the gradual takeover by foreign influence, culture and values. The British government and public would react likewise if, say there was lavish Japanese funding for family planning services, with Japanese staff in all key posts and oriented to a peculiarly Japanese approach to contraception.

The "non-voluntariness" of an increasing part of the voluntary sector is the responsibility of NGOs themselves. They are not articulating clearly the NGO principles which official funders should adhere to. They don't always facilitate the official funding of "legitimate" NGOs and they don't coordinate well among themselves. In the fashionable streets of Dhaka, Bangladesh, for example, there can be found a plethora of Northern NGO offices. Many of these will be funding the same Bangladeshi organizations—perhaps without realizing it—and might be receiving money from their own governments to do so.

The NGO community in a given country often puts more energy into criticism of "rivals" than into collaboration. Both Northern and Southern NGO staff characteristically have little praise for counterparts in other organizations. Such emphasis on criticism goes beyond healthy rivalry and can foster isolationism among NGOs—exacerbated, no doubt, by their need to compete for attention and resources.

Leadership Problems

Good leadership is critical to the success of an NGO but NGO staff often resent and impede strong leadership. David Brown,[45] President of the Boston-based Institute for Development Research, identifies a leadership dilemma inherent in the structure of NGOs, characterized by two distinct types of NGO leaders.

1. Charismatic people of deep commitment and vision who lead by inspiration and by their personal qualities but who maintain an ill-defined structure and tend to be somewhat dictatorial in decision making. These are typically NGO founders.
2. Leaders committed to participation, who share influence and functions with other staff and who like decision making to be by a collegial process, within a tight management structure.

Judith Tendler[46] has demonstrated that a common factor in many successful Southern NGOs is charismatic leadership. However, overwhelming demands are placed on the guru-like leaders, particularly during periods of rapid growth. The organizations revolve around them, tend to stagnate rapidly when the leaders are away for more than a short period, are prone to decay and die when the leader moves on, cannot be replicated and are likely to be fixed in their approach, sometimes dogmatically so, being only as flexible and open to new ideas as their leader will allow.

With the second category, NGOs are prone to slow response resulting from cumbersome decision making, are susceptible to paralysis arising from power struggles between competing factions and can evolve conflicting aims as different departments perceive a freedom to interpret their own role without reference to a strongly defined overall mission.[47]

The two styles of leadership—charasmatic or collegial—both have advantages and disadvantages.

Though leadership is critical to the success of NGOs usually little attention is paid to the development of leadership potential or to management training. And, once on the job, leadership skills are rarely fostered efficiently because most NGOs are poor at delegation.

Leadership in Northern NGOs tends to be of the collegial type, often due in part to the staff's ideological disdain for "management" from the staff. An autocratic style simply wouldn't work; the staff require participation. Decision making typically becomes rather committee bound and suffers as a result.

When an organization is being drowned by good ideas, when the paramount problem is insufficient time and resources to take each deserving idea to fruition, then the natural braking power of committees can be a useful counter balance. This, however, is rarely the problem. Usually the brake is more powerful than the engine and this tends to stifle creativity. To handle creative matters by committee is like commissioning a committee to produce a work of art. It might be appropriate for a committee to choose which painting to buy but never to paint the picture.

This tendency to "management by committee" is perhaps related to the "structural amateurism" of most Northern NGOs. While company directors receive top pay, it is customary (obligatory by law in the case of British charities) for voluntary organizations to be answerable to boards of trustees who receive no remuneration whatsoever. This reflects the voluntary ethos, but it also distances highest level decision making from direct experience of the organization's work.

The NGO board may comprise excellent, highly committed people—perhaps the best brains in the country on specific topics. However, this does not necessarily mean that the board is well equipped to run the aid program. Its members cannot travel frequently to see the projects, nor spend time working alongside the program staff, and indeed attempts to do so might be seen as an unwelcome intrusion. How can such a body be expected to make strategic decisions as do a company's board of directors? Yet its members may well be much more personally accountable for the body's decisions than in the business world. Under British charity law, trustees are personally liable for inappropriate use of funds whereas company directors are protected except when a crime is involved.

Achieving the right balance between strong leadership which ensures the resolute pursuit of strong ideas, and openness of style which ensures all staff feeling properly valued, is the greatest management challenge for NGOs particularly as they grow in size. It is a problem that few have cracked.

Staff Problems

The more non-governmental the NGO the greater the problems of staffing. An organization which works closely with government structures—both Northern and Southern—will probably maintain a staff, reward and even organizational structure similar to that of the public sector and indeed it is common for there to be regular exchange of staff, particularly in Southern NGOs. The staff tend to "know their place," see a clear career structure in front of them, and be well isolated from debates in other sections of the organization. They are also likely to be paid on a par with public sector workers. In the case of Southern NGOs, particularly in Africa, it is likely that pay will be very much greater than government workers—a subject of considerable resentment by governments.

In the more truly "non-governmental" organizations different problems can arise, depending on the style of leadership. Under charismatic leadership staff often have a weak position. There is a tendency to recruit staff who will follow orders and be in awe of the leader. All new ideas come from the single source of the leader, who is given little stimulation or creative ideas by her or his colleagues. In such situations NGOs do not get full value from their staff, neither are they likely to present much of a career structure.

In collegial Northern NGOs problems often arise from the ambiguous relationship between staff and authority. Staff are recruited who are strongly committed. However, since "the cause" may not be clearly defined by the organization, personal motivation may lead staff off in different, poorly coordinated and sometimes opposing directions. There will be numerous self-determined objectives rather than an overall sense of mission. Staff may obstruct efforts of the management to exert authority and will argue, with justification, that the participatory environment and ideological satisfaction compensate for the meager salary.

Northern NGOs are also ambivalent about decentralization. Investing authority in program staff encourages innovation and locally determined interventions but it can lead to a loss of corporate identity, cliquishness and sometimes stagnation in individual countries or regions. Program staff may identify more with counterparts in other Northern and Southern NGOs working in that country than with colleagues in their own organization. This leads to a weak identification with the organization and a disregard for centrally conceived requests or instructions. There is also a danger of a nepotistic pattern emerging in which funding decisions are made more on the basis of friendship and peer pressure (making grants because it would look bad not to) than on the identifiable wishes of the poor.

Intra-staff tensions may arise between expatriate and local staff, where these coexist in one country. The NGO may be pursuing the laudable goal of shifting to indigenous staff but in the interim the quandary arises of whether or not to pay all staff at the same rate, and if so, whether this should be at the local or expatriate rate. The resolution might be to have three components to field staff's salary: a spending component enough to support a reasonable lifestyle, a savings component paid in the staff's national currency and calculated on the basis of how much the average professional of comparable status might be expected to save per annum, and a dislocation component to compensate for working away from one's home country. The first component should be equal for expatriate and local staff, but the others will be different.

Project Design

Although some NGO projects are truly inspirational, others are dull. Some authors (such as Annis, Brown, Brodhead, Elliott, Fowler, Garilao, Korten and Tendler)[48] have helped describe the most common Achilles' heels:

- Projects often don't really benefit the poor, they focus on those easiest to reach. In particular too little attention is paid to the needs of women.
- Decision making tends to be dominated by local elites; there is often little real grassroots participation, especially of women, in the planning and design of projects.
- They are often not innovative, but extend a tried and tested service.
- They are of limited replicability, being locally specific in task and approach, and being dependent on rare, charismatic leadership.
- Projects are often unsuccessful when they seek to introduce approaches and values from a foreign environment (though some of the greatest NGO successes also stem from such cross-fertilization). For example, attempts at developing conscientization and community animation programs in Africa along Latin American lines have largely been disappointing.
- Projects tend to be disconnected, isolated and conceived in the absence of a broad planning strategy. In particular, an FAO study[49] describes the frequent failure of apparently innovative NGO projects when they are conceived and developed outside of the context of any overall state strategy. It is common to find a plethora of projects in a country or region which neither learn from each other nor attempt to coordinate their efforts. Furthermore, they are likely to have a total lack of relationship with the state.

- Little attention is often paid to making projects sustainable, either economically or environmentally. They often collapse once funding ceases.
- Project staff often have limited technical capacity and therefore technical matters, such as the maintenance of equipment, are often neglected.

Learning Disabilities

The subtleness and complexity of NGO programs indicates the need for careful learning through the experience both of the NGO and of others. In reality however little attention is usually paid to this learning by Northern NGOs.

Isolation and rivalry obstruct the process of learning from others. A resistance to monitoring and evaluation hampers learning from experience. And an idiosyncratic program approach coupled with high staff turnover leads to a short-term institutional memory.

The documentation of experience is often irregular, subjective and geared more to fundraising than to institutional learning. What is viewed as important is field, not centralized, knowledge since it is the program staff who tend to make the operational decisions, not the headquarters staff. To do this they need eyewitness assessments as to whether the project seems to be on the right track, and the opinions of community leaders. Such things are difficult to quantify and tabulate. This dynamic knowledge is stored not in the papers with charts and tables that are favored by stereotypical H.Q. bureaucrats but in the program staff's own memory. The trouble is that this memory leaves when the person does.

Since senior program staff are free, and are often encouraged, to experiment and pursue their own priorities, country programs may transform unrecognizably as staff change. This factor may be reducing now as networks of strong Southern NGOs are increasingly defining the NGO development agenda and as Northern NGOs become more seasoned.

Progressive funders like to see their relationship with project leaders as one of *partnership,* though this term is more used by Northern than Southern NGOs. The latter are only too well aware that the one-sided control of the wallet gives the lie to the equality implied by the term. The former are loath to compound the inequality by insisting on independent monitoring and evaluation. This would appear untrusting, as already the Southern partners are prone to complain about the bureaucratic controls and reporting systems demanded by the funders. Hence funders will encourage their partners to build self-evaluation into the design of their projects but will not press for independent monitoring.

If there is little attention paid to serious analysis of project experience then there is even less attention spared for impact studies or broader research. Few funding NGOs will have any knowledge of projects where funding stopped five or ten years ago. They probably will not even know whether the project survives, nor whether there have been any lasting benefits and if so to whom. Such impact studies are made all the more difficult as a result of weak monitoring and evaluation. The latter rarely study nearby communities *not* affected by the project to provide a control or baseline data. Hence it is impossible, five or ten years later, to do any accurate comparative research to detect lasting benefits.

The paucity of research is not altogether the fault of NGO staff. The project work of progressive NGOs often does not lend itself easily to monitoring. There are no ready indexes for "popular participation," no convenient barometer to chart the "raising of consciousness," and no comparative tables listing the degrees of "empowerment."

Official aid agencies, by contrast, produce volumes of reports on monitoring and research findings. The pressures within these agencies are quite different. Those who award their funds (governments, parliaments and ultimately the taxpayers) do not have the same ready trust that characterizes the supporters of NGOs. They are more likely to have a cynical suspicion that very little of the funds do any good whatsoever. Hence while sober evaluation of NGO performance, however encouraging the conclusions, will reveal some new flaws, official aid agencies have a mixed reputation in the first place. Monitoring is likely to show that, at least *some* of the funds go to achieving at least *some* of the stated objectives. Official aid agencies also tend to finance a small number of very large projects, hence the institution of a serious study of the project neither swallows a disproportionate share of the project's resources nor dwarfs the project. As a result, as Uphoff describes, "information on the state of the art in development projects, then, must be drawn mainly from the research and evaluation outputs of larger donors and academic institutions"[50] rather than from NGOs, who may well, of course, be practicing a different art.

It is a weakness of the NGO sector that, in the words of Biswajit Sen, the "survival of NGOs has become delinked from their performance."[51] He argues that the close relationship between articulate NGO leaders and funding agencies and the resource rich environment in which NGOs work leads to an "absence of pressures for performance for the NGOs [which makes] self-evaluation of their own work a non-priority area."

A way forward which avoids many of the problems might be for the main progressive Northern NGOs to combine forces to fund six or eight Southern based research institutes. These institutes would be commissioned to conduct the necessary evaluations and research. They could either be institutes newly created for this purpose or existing bodies expanded accordingly. Though they would not be able to quantify the unquantifiable they would be well placed to make comparative judgments on factors such as the degree of popular participation. They would naturally have a geographical emphasis but also a sectoral specialism. Hence the India-based institute, for example, might specialize in studying social action groups and so be best placed to evaluate a Kenyan NGO which has such a focus.

These research institutes might be less threatening than a donor NGO evaluation team, more objective than a self-evaluation, and more meaningful than an independent evaluation conducted by academics who are familiar with official aid, not NGOs.

Problems of Accountability

The donors, the general public and the media hold Northern NGOs to account, and the ebb and flow of donations is the result. But this accountability stresses by and large the wrong things. It does not challenge the effectiveness of the projects supported but whether the funds go to where they are supposed to go. The preoccupation with detecting the diversion of funds to the *wrong* purpose inherently assumes that the intended one is the *right* purpose.

Cost effectiveness in this "trial by bankers-order" is measured not in terms of changes in the well-being of the poor, size of population helped or by the durability of the benefits, but in terms of the proportion of funds spent on administration. The money can be thrown away but as long as not too many people are employed to do so the NGO will not attract complaint.

The NGO may be accused of paying salaries that are too high (particularly to the Director) and of having too large a staff, but there is little evident public worry about the danger of having incompetent, inexperienced or untrained staff in charge of NGOs. In fact, many NGOs handle millions of dollars annually, have scores if not hundreds of staff and should be run at least as professionally as a comparably sized company, hospital or school.

NGO salaries should be lower than average, but when they fall too low then professionalism slides. The reduced salary should reflect the "psychological pay"—the opportunity staff have of making a meaningful social contribution. This would be much greater for program staff than for office juniors who are no more likely to get personal stimulation from filing papers on rainforest conservation than on toilet roll sales.

There is, finally, an important question that NGO leaders must address. To whom should they be accountable? To their board of trustees, to their governments, to donors, to their staff or to their project partners?

Most would wish to be somewhat accountable to all these constituencies. Their clearest immediate responsibility is to their boards, though unlike the business world the board members may not have sufficient inside knowledge to ask really difficult questions. They have to be accountable to their government not just for the increasing proportion of funds that derive from this source but also to comply with the provisions of accountancy laws, charity law, not-for-profit regulations or the equivalent.

This accountability is quite rigorous regarding the publicly contributed funds but oriented to protecting the donor, not the recipient.

The accountability to donors, the media and the general public tends to focus on the wrong things, as described above. Mutual accountability between Northern and Southern NGOs is unrealistic given the unequal relationship in which the Northern organization chooses its Southern partners in the first place. And finally, accountability to the NGO's own staff, who are certainly likely to be the sharpest and most persistent critics, is rather incestuous. After all, it is the performance of the staff and the appropriateness of their judgement for which the NGO must be accountable.

Northern NGOs would probably benefit from more rigorous, constructive scrutiny and perhaps they should invite this by making more strenuous efforts to describe to academics, development specialists and the general public exactly what it is that they do and why. Opening up in this way could lead to a valuable debate about the guiding principles and also to a diffusion of these ideas to official aid agencies, Southern governments and the academic world.

5

Relationships Between NGOs and Governments

NGOS ARE OFTEN DISTRUSTFUL and critical of governments and wary of forging close contacts. These sentiments are often reciprocated. As has been described, however, NGOs comprise a broad spectrum and such a generalization is dangerous.

Friendly coexistence between an NGO and a government occurs when the NGO requires of the government little more than the freedom to get on with its chosen task, does not seek to influence wider areas of development planning and where its task is not actually hampered by government actions. A government is happy with such a relationship when it feels neither threatened nor challenged, and when the NGO's tasks are not incompatible with its own objectives. Many of the public service contractors and technical innovation organizations also fit into this category. Government officials may, however, be jealous of the relatively high salaries and access to vehicles which some NGOs enjoy, or suspect the NGOs of being motivated by religious or political agendas.

Tensions between governments and NGOs are not unique to the South, they also arise in the North. This chapter, however, is restricted to the Third World context.

The worst tension arises when an NGO subscribes to a development theory different from that of the government, especially regarding NGOs who stress people's participation, empowerment and democracy. Official structures usually present barriers to this approach. The NGO may choose to keep out of the government's way, or to oppose the state outright. The government is uneasy about such NGOs. On the one hand they may well recognize the economic value of their projects (and indeed wel-

64

come the foreign exchange they bring), but on the other hand they see the empowerment elements as troublemaking.

Progressive NGOs are also likely to view governments as part of the problem—controlled by the elite, biased toward "First World solutions," corrupt and anti-empowerment. This applies whether the regime is avowedly right- or left-wing. The former is characterized as exposing the poor to the injustices of international capitalism and to sacrificing their interests in the pursuit of economic growth. But the state capitalism of the latter is similarly rejected as a political, rather than an economic, monopolization of power, expertise and technology to serve the interests of a few.

While not changing their analysis, many of these NGOs are beginning to change their strategy for relating to the state. This is not a symptom of weakness—of giving in, but of strength: the discovery of political analysis, self-awareness and persuasiveness. Sharpened political analysis enables the NGO to see how various policies of the state deliberately or inadvertently conflict with or facilitate their own development objectives.

Heightened self-awareness disabuses the NGO of the degree to which it presents an alternative development path. NGO projects are important, but they do not by themselves provide solutions to problems on a national scale. As one grassroots development worker from Zimbabwe eloquently puts it, "No nation in the world was ever developed by projects alone, let alone by projects based on borrowed models."[52] Their projects will remain irrelevant to the majority of the needy unless used as beacons to light up pathways for others—notably the state—to pursue. Popular participation on a significant scale will come about only through reforms in official structures, not through multiplying NGO projects.

Increased persuasiveness enables the NGO to convey messages from its political analysis and self-awareness to a broader audience. The NGO learns to position its experience in the context of the main political debates of the day and to discover ways of influencing those debates. It also explores ways of injecting lessons from its successful project approaches into official development programs. In particular it may seek to project its positive experiences of popular participation into efforts to democratize the institutions and development processes of the state itself. As these strengths extend the horizons of NGOs' vision and they explore ways of using their influence on a national scale they have three choices. They can oppose the state, complement it or reform it—but they cannot ignore it.

Opposing the state would mean using whatever channels are available to frustrate any government plan which is negative for the poor. This may mean organizing protests, using the courts to challenge official decisions, joining forces with the political opposition or other popular movements such as trade unions to undermine the government's policies or widespread use of the media and unofficial communication channels.

Complementing the state would mean evolving its own program so that it fills the gaps in the government's services in such a way as to make those services more relevant to the poor and more subject to democratic influences. For example, village nutrition groups which have emerged in parts of Zambia have imposed an accountability on and reoriented the priorities of the official Primary Health Care (PHC) service so that it responds more faithfully to the requirements of the poor. They have also, incidentally, considerably motivated the PHC staff who previously felt extremely isolated.

Reforming the state would mean more deliberate collaboration with government departments with a view to helping those departments improve the services they provide. The NGO would position itself not so much as a co-producer but as a co-director of these services, not taking responsibility for actual service delivery, but helping to strengthen the existing systems. Typically the NGO would provide appropriate training, help improve the planning process, demonstrate how services can be strengthened—for instance by establishing local committees—and introduce problem-solving techniques. It would also vigorously challenge the state to implement policies that are positive for the poor.

These approaches are very different in style but all can be effective, as a growing bank of experience testifies. Even "bad" governments have "good" departments with which NGOs can work. For example, in Ethiopia it is difficult to work with the mainstream Ministry of Agriculture, but the Peasant Association department and the village water supply department both cooperate well with NGOs. Almost no government is so bad that it resolutely refuses to help the poor. The government of Pinochet in Chile had an atrocious human rights record but it was quite progressive in response to NGOs on the baby foods issue, introducing regulations curbing aggressive marketing practices and giving considerable resources to promoting a return to breast-feeding.

As David Korten observes, "over the past three decades the guiding assumption has been that development belongs to government and government alone."[53] This can no longer be the case. Governments can create laws and re-allocate a country's resources, which are important functions but partial requirements for effecting a development strategy. Wealth creation and entrepreneurship are vital ingredients, hence the business sector has an important role in development. Similarly social innovation and voluntary action are required—hence the need for a strong voluntary—or "Third"—sector. Healthy development requires the combined and concerted effort of all three sectors—each contributing its share and each influencing and being influenced by the other.

Governments clearly have a tremendous capacity to do harm and to hamper self-help efforts (as indeed does the business sector) but they are part of the reality NGOs cannot ignore. Often the harm governments do is not out of spite but out of a lack of thought, lack of knowledge or a lack of competence. Strategic NGOs might attack the lacks but at the same time articulate a clear, workable alternative.

The degree to which NGOs choose to and are able to influence governments depends greatly on the social and political context of the particular country. Rajesh Tandon helpfully describes three categories of regimes which afford very different environments for NGOs.

1. Military and other dictatorships (such as China, the Philippines under President Marcos, Chile under General Pinochet, Bangladesh under President Ershad): in such countries, especially those which have had liberal or democratic regimes in the past, NGOs are likely to side with the political opposition or—where opposition parties and trade unions are banned—to *be* the opposition. This "filling of the political space" characterized much of the NGO sector in Latin America until the recent outbreak of democracy. Often the "popular organizations" have been the only vocal challenge to state policies. Many NGOs in Brazil feel that they are only now emerging from the clandestine existence of pre-democratic days. In other regions also, popular movements have played an important role in assisting the evolution of democracies as during the 1986 revolution in the Philippines.

In such a climate there is limited scope for NGO–government collaboration, particularly in addressing externally generated problems. For example, the Martial Law Administrators of Bangladesh introduced the most progressive legislation on pharmaceuticals of all Third World nations. In response to effective campaigning by Bangladeshi and Northern NGOs, the government legislated to restrain pharmaceutical marketing to a narrow range of priority preparations, based on the World Health Organization's Essential Drug List. The government appointed Zafrullah Chowdhury, the director of the leading national NGO working on the issue, to the committee set up to review the entire drug situation of the country. The drug companies (many of which are transnational corporations) were furious and sought to discredit the legislation by impugning the motives and information of the NGOs, but the government—which received considerable international acclaim for its tough stance, stood firm. Activists in the campaign have pointed out that, paradoxically, such a victory might not have been as easy in a poor but liberal democracy. The manufacturers would have many opportunities to head off or by-pass such legislation, both through buying off politicians and civil servants, and through bombarding officials and health workers with "relevant information" to confuse the decision-making process. President Ershad wanted the bill to go through and was able to put his foot down.

2. Other single-party states, usually Marxist oriented (such as Kampuchea, Cuba, Burma, Tanzania and many other countries in Africa): typically the government or the Party assumes the role of "vanguard of the people"; it sees no need for autonomous, independent structures and

therefore has usually not been such a tradition within the country. The government tolerates NGOs only in so far as they facilitate its own program. The rise of indigenous NGOs in such countries is usually very slow or non-existent.

A one-party state may have an overall pro-poor development approach but with serious blind spots. For example, it may place little emphasis on democratic principles or human rights, as in the case of the Zimbabwe government's failure to stamp out repression in Matabeleland. Gender and environmental issues may also be neglected. NGOs can play an important role in such situations, especially where the party leadership becomes divorced from the grassroots. The NGO can be supportive of the pro-poor stance, but also constructively critical. If it is seen as becoming too critical it is likely to be cut off by the government, but if it is quiescent it simply becomes absorbed by the party.

3. Liberal democracies (such as India, Brazil, Senegal, Sri Lanka): here the situation is most complex. NGOs may play mixed roles—collaborating with governments on specific programs, challenging in other areas. Governments may appear to be pro-poor, use populist slogans and sometimes take progressive action, but are usually more attentive to the vested interest groups on whose support they depend. Where the signals are mixed in this way the state may not be monolithic. The Indian government, for example, gives more attention to industrialization and modernization than to poverty eradication, yet specific government departments, such as the National Wastelands Development Board, have a progressive reputation.

It is also likely that an NGO might find sympathy from a central government but apathy or hostility from local government officials.

Like the business sector, NGOs find it easiest to survive in liberal democracies and may even be offered help and considerable endorsement by the state. India's seventh Five-Year Plan, for example, explicitly recognizes the role of voluntary organizations and earmarks 1.5 billion rupees for direct funding. Over-endorsement can bring as many problems as ostracism.[55] NGOs in India are wary that their independence, and perhaps eventually their right to receive funds from abroad, might be in jeopardy.

Many liberal governments are coopting NGO leaders on to various official bodies or commissions. This also is a double-edged sword. On the one hand it gives an important forum for NGO opinions. On the other hand it can dull the sharp edge of NGO criticism and occupy the attention of much of the best NGO talent. Liberal democracies tend to respond to NGO criticism in three ways: they harass and intimidate the NGO; they negate publicly the value of the work done and impugn their credentials (for example by alleging a hidden motive such as evangelism or CIA connection); or they co-opt them, providing them funds and status but subjecting them to rules. This latter option has been made more likely in recent years by the ready availability of official aid for government–NGO collaboration.

Other factors influence the possibilities and nature of NGO–government interaction. Indigenous NGOs tend to be more numerous and strong where the government is efficiently structured and confident. A government which feels secure is more likely to be willing to experiment with the new operational methods suggested by NGOs. Conversely poor, repressive regimes will be most likely to restrict the opportunities for NGOs. Even the most reactionary governments (in the North and South) are coming to see NGOs as efficient deliverers of services and conduits for popular participation.

Political and economic factors influence the government–NGO relationship, but so do cultural factors. Countries which are Western in outlook, in particular those with strong tertiary educational systems, are likely to have strong NGO sectors. Hence Kenya and Bangladesh have more diverse NGO bases than do Zambia and Nepal.

To summarize, the rationale for attempting to influence state policies and services is clear. This avenue provides possibilities both to improve the efficiency and equity of government services, and to democratize state functions. Ignoring such opportunities may render the NGO disconnected and its experience wasted. Many NGOs are for this reason beginning to magnify their impact by stepping into the political and governmental arena.

This "scaling up" can be achieved by setting out to challenge state functions through popular mobilization, by molding the NGO operations to fill the gaps and inject ideas of equity into the government structures, or by working in collaboration with state authorities to reform and improve the government services provided. These approaches are very different in nature.

Risks are inevitably posed for the NGO. Its profile will become higher. Potential conflicts with governments become greater. And it may find it difficult to remain in such intimate contact with its popular base. What is more, tensions between NGOs may grow if they move at different paces or along different paths.

Part Two

NGOs: Impact in the South

6

Scaling Up

AN NGO TYPICALLY STARTS a program in a particular country to respond to a specific need. This may be rural credit, adult literacy, empowerment of the landless, economic programs for women or any of a hundred other options, or it could be an integrated program with a range of diverse objectives.

If the program is successful then a significant number of poor people will be better off as a result. This does not necessarily mean that they will be richer, though that should come in time. It could mean that they acquire new strengths to resist the exploitation they suffer or to stand up to crushing bureaucracy.

The inevitable question following success is, "How can we do more?" Only a complacent organization would be content to continue with the same job in perpetuity when it is self-evident that its contribution is not more than a drop in the ocean, however excellent a drop it may be. The answer might have four components.

1. *How to do it.* How an NGO can act to combat directly and effectively the problems of poverty; how it can mobilize the human, financial and other resources to make that a sustainable intervention; and how it can create an appropriate structure for managing that intervention, for ensuring participation and accountability to the people.
2. *Popular concerns.* What the poor perceive their problems to be, their weaknesses in being able to resolve these problems and their aspirations; how these weaknesses might be overcome and the aspirations achieved through well-structured grassroots action.
3. *Local policy environment.* How the programs, policies and laws pursued, or indeed not pursued, by local and national government

authorities exacerbate the problems of poverty; what windows of opportunity exist for generating changes in policies that would improve the situation.

4. *International policy environment.* How external factors, particularly those generated by policies and actions of Northern governments and the international institutions they control exacerbate the problems of poverty; what windows of opportunity exist for generating changes in policies that would improve the situation.

Each of these categories suggests a pathway for magnifying the impact of the NGO program. The first three indicate an indigenous process, in which Southern NGOs move beyond the project focus with its emphasis on "doing," to a wider role with emphasis on "influencing." Northern NGOs can assist by providing funds or guidance based on relevant experience from elsewhere and perhaps by encouraging their Southern partners to undertake influencing activities, but theirs is a secondary role. The fourth category indicates directions for international advocacy through building coalitions of Northern and Southern NGOs to raise public awareness about and seek to redress inequities deriving from policies made in the North.

The first three pathways are what can be termed "scaling up" and comprise the subject of Part II of this book. The fourth is addressed in Part III. Scaling up, therefore, falls into three types of activity:

1. *Project replication.* Using experience of successes and failures both to increase the outreach of the NGO's own program and to help others establish similar programs.

2. *Building grassroots movements.* Increasing support for grassroots organizations who are campaigning for social change. Using the NGO's local knowledge and local contacts to help foster widespread networks articulating popular concerns and striving for changes in systems which oppress the poor.

3. *Influencing policy reform.* Influencing change in the local policies and practices of governments and official aid agencies, so as to create an environment more favorable to the poor and to grassroots development. Using experience of the conflict between the NGO's objectives and government action at the local or national level to lever for appropriate changes in policies, institutions and laws which would reduce the conflict.

The three activities are not mutually exclusive, nor are the dividing lines clear. The particular scaling-up approach adopted must fit with the culture of the NGO in question. A well established health-care organization which is critical of government services is not likely to be well placed to mobilize mass demands for reforms, but it is likely to be taken seriously if it offers to help retrain government health workers so they can deliver a service more appropriate to the poor.

The scaling-up route must also be appropriate to the country in question.

Project replication is most logical where the following conditions tend to apply:

- NGO resources are plentiful;
- institutions and the government are weak but relatively benign, **or**
- the government is autocratic and there is no realistic prospect for influencing policy;
- there is little evident popular perception of exploitation by local elites, **or**
- the poor are fearful of voicing their discontent;
- there is strong community leadership by members of the traditional elite (e.g. tribal chiefs).

In such situations, good examples are Ethiopia and Zambia, and it is unlikely that the official bodies could be persuaded to provide the services desired or to facilitate the NGO's task of providing these services. There is little alternative to scaling up the NGO's operations (this could include include encouraging official aid agencies to adopt a similar pragmatic approach and even the diffusion of NGO ideas to specific government departments). It is also unlikely that attempts to mobilize grassroots action will be effective in the short run, which is not to say that conscientization activities should not be devised.

Building grassroots movements is apt where the following conditions apply:

- poverty is greatly exacerbated by traditional social factors (e.g. land-lords, moneylenders);
- poverty is greatly exacerbated by institutional factors (e.g. corrupt bureaucracies, repressive legislation);
- there is a strong perception of exploitation and injustice among the leaders of the poor;
- there are potential allies of grassroots organizations (e.g. trade unions, opposition political parties);
- there is at least limited scope for free assembly of poor people outside official structures.

In such situations, for example Bangladesh and Brazil, it is unlikely that desired reforms will result from rational persuasion alone; expressions of mass unrest and publicity embarrassing to the authorities are also required. Traditional NGO project activities have a limited role being in themselves a band-aid response to a deeper set of problems.

Influencing policy reform is signalled where the following conditions apply:

- effective and participatory development is possible but hampered by institutional or governmental practices;
- the authorities respect the contribution of NGOs;
- the authorities are strong and have some liberal traditions **or** the authorities are weak, haphazard and pliant;
- the poor welcome efforts to seek reforms;
- the NGOs have or can acquire the competence needed for policy dialogue.

Where such conditions apply, for example India, the NGO is likely to achieve much more by influencing reforms than by its operational programs. A tactic of dialogue and persuasion rather than confrontation is most likely to secure the desired reform.

The three approaches require of the NGO different skills and cultures which may not easily coexist within the same organization. However, there are a number of necessary skills and disciplines which are common to all the scaling-up strategies. They can be summarized as the "Five Ls."

- Listening, to allies but also to our critics, to understand their position;
- Learning, improving our research and evaluation capacity relating both to our programs and to the macro context;
- Linking, building networks and broad coalitions for effecting change;
- Leadership, in particular fostering leadership from among the poor;
- Lobbying, to influence those with access to much greater clout and resources.

New Opportunities for NGO

The new era of single issue campaigns and of popular movements affords NGOs a new role. They need no longer remain the "carers" of societies, they can become the "changers." Their legitimacy depends on their popular base, and on their potential—through influence with governments or sheer might—to become agents of social change. As conduits for local democracy they have the potential to strengthen civil society and to force institutions to be more accountable and more responsive to the needs of ordinary people. In this way they can strengthen the development process and improve the efficiency of governments, as pioneering NGOs are demonstrating.

Northern NGOs can assist their Southern partners by mounting campaigns in their home countries to persuade the official aid agencies to change their policies so as to support the grassroots causes. Such advocacy is beginning to have real effect, as is recognized by Joseph Wheeler, chairman of the OECD's Development Assistance Committee, in his foreword to a recent OECD book on NGOs.

> The voluntary sector has frequently articulated new policy insights reflecting changes which have been taking place in our societies. Ask an aid administrator why he or she has increased the emphasis on environmental concerns, or women in development, or population. Ask where the pressure comes from for more emphasis on reaching the poor, or on health and education. The answer is that these are the concerns of our populations expressed through our political processes and usually pointed up by what we call our NGOs.[56]

A similar recognition of the advocacy role of NGOs is made by officials of the World Bank. For example, Michael Cernea writes:

> International NGOs—like Oxfam UK, Survival International and others—have repeatedly signalled to the Bank cases when resettlement under Bank-financed projects does not proceed satisfactorily . . . ; such signals have at many times triggered additional Bank efforts and have led to improvements in the standards and conditions of resettlement. . . . Discussions between NGOs and the World Bank on policy issues regarding, in particular, poverty issues and the environment, have contributed to the evolution of World Bank policies in the context of structural adjustment programs.[57]

The Bank's Senior Vice President for Operations, Moeen Qureshi, also gave recognition to the influencing role of NGOs in his speech to the Washington chapter of the Society for International Development.

> In just the last few years, NGO influence on Bank policies has grown. Some NGOs joined with UNICEF and other international agencies in expressing concern that IMF and Bank supported adjustment programs in the early 1980s did not adequately attend to poverty concerns. Environmental NGOs have helped us become more keenly aware of natural resource and resettlement issues. I am grateful to them for that, even though their criticism has sometimes been harsh. . . . Some NGOs can give policy makers important insights about the effects adjustment policies have on poor people and suggest alternatives.[58]

More significant than the increase in official funding is the enhanced credibility NGOs command from official aid agencies.

New Dangers

An NGO may find it flattering to have its views and collaboration sought by the mainstream development agencies such as the World Bank and bilateral aid agencies, but within this new collaboration lurk dangers as well as opportunities. NGOs are usually asked to help improve the design or working of particular components of existing projects rather than to design the projects themselves, let alone to help recast the objectives of the official aid agencies. NGOs are expected to lend their much praised qualities of efficiency, flexibility, enthusiasm and low cost, but not their distinctive analysis of what should be done or how. There is a danger, in accepting such invitations, that the NGOs' own, legitimate agendas become swept away.

This is not to argue that NGOs should resist opportunities to work with governments and official aid agencies. But NGOs should approach these invitations as potential negotiating opportunities to forward their vision of development.

The critical question is whether the overall project in hand is in the interests of the poor. The NGO might well see that it can do a good job making a project component more efficient, perhaps more socially responsive, but it must guard against strengthening a system which works against the poor. Much will depend on who controls the system so devised. If the NGO is able to use its influence to give greater power to the poor in determining how the system operates, then its involvement is likely to be positive.

Such issues are the source of considerable tension within the NGO community. For example, some grassroots NGOs working with people who are to be displaced by the construction of the Narmada Dam in India have agreed to help the authorities implement an effective resettlement program. They have been hotly criticized by other NGOs who are opposing the construction of the dam itself because of the environmental damage it may cause and the particular style of development it reflects. There is no simple solution. Developing countries might need hydroelectric power and large scale irrigation potential and perhaps large dams are a valid way of achieving these in certain circumstances. In the case in point so much money has already been invested in construction that it is unlikely that the dam will be stopped. If this is the case then it is clearly better that there is a proper resettlement scheme. But other NGOs still believe that it is possible to halt construction altogether. In their view popular opposition is defused by some of the NGOs joining with the project authorities in planning resettlement.

NGOs with a genuine grassroots constituency are often understandably reluctant to involve themselves in official aid projects. This can reflect a laudable faithfulness to their mission statements, but it can also be short-sighted.

Small-scale projects, islands of relative prosperity, by themselves will not eliminate poverty. Changes in policies, attitudes, institutions and customs are required, and properly constructed governmental schemes may have more prospect of achieving these changes than NGO projects. Official aid agencies who are sincere in wanting to pursue such changes will need to work with popular structures if they are to have access to the local knowledge they need. They should not be spurned by the very NGOs who urged them to take this new, people-oriented approach and who can act as the channel for this local knowledge. Indeed the NGOs should encourage the search for opportunities to convey lessons from the grassroots to the official development planners. It must also be remembered that the more reluctant are grassroots NGOs to involve themselves in official aid projects, the faster will be the evolution of less scrupulous NGOs oriented to official funding opportunities. Funding will gradually shift from the former to the latter and the former may be increasingly marginalized.

Grassroots NGOs should with considerable urgency draw up a code of conduct for mutual collaboration and persuade official aid agencies to accept it. Elements of such a code[59,60] should require the agency to:

1. Inform host country government of the agency's wish to explore involving NGOs as project collaborators. Make it clear that this could be a condition of funding.
2. Use experienced Northern and national NGOs to advise on appropriate indigenous NGOs who would be potential partners. An important criterion in the selection would be the track record the Southern or Northern NGO has of involvement with poor communities.
3. Invite potential collaborators to participate in the project preparation missions, so that they have an opportunity to influence the overall shape of the project (and not just of those components which the NGO is invited to implement).
4. When collaboration is agreed, delegate authority to the NGO to evolve policy and project design so that the NGO is not seen just as a subcontractor but is enabled to introduce changes in the project in response to changing local needs.
5. Recognize that the NGO remains accountable first and foremost to its own constituency, rather than to the agency, that its contribution to the project is in keeping with the NGO's own style of participation and grassroots democracy.
6. Make available to the NGO all project information relevant to its social or environmental impact or to the project components for which the NGO is responsible.
7. Recognize that the NGO would require the freedom to make available to local populations such project information that has a direct bearing on their lives. Allow the NGO to establish channels for direct

consultation with poor communities who are affected by the project and encourage other project staff to take part in these consultations when invited to do so by the NGO.

The negotiation of such a compact between NGOs and official aid agencies is of vital importance if the former wishes to retain its identity and the latter wishes to bring in the real advantages of the NGO sector and is not just out to cut costs. The urgency of this task is heightened by the rapidly increasing numbers of "government-inspired NGOs" or "government-oriented NGOs" (the GINGOs and GONGOs). In many developing countries government ministers or civil servants are establishing their own organizations without popular bases, and calling them NGOs because they know of the likelihood of receiving funds from Northern governments. In Mali, for example, it is reported that a plethora of so-called NGOs has been set up by state employees who have been laid off by as a result of structural adjustment programs.[61]

Creating Space for "Influencing"

NGOs rarely give top priority to developing the skills of scaling up. The preoccupation with "doing" leaves insufficient space for "influencing." In most cases the management structure and reporting requirements reaffirm the project emphasis and deflect staff from attending to the wider role of the organization. In part because of the need to satisfy their donors, NGOs will require detailed reports on project performance indicating how much money has been spent, providing statistics and comparing actual progress with stated objectives. But few require reports on how contemporary events outside the project, such as government policy shifts, economic recession or environmental degradation affect the project objectives or performance, or how they impact on the poor—as the poor themselves see it.

The project is scrutinized but not the context in which it is located. This is symptomatic of the disease of "projectitis." The sufferer views the Third World as being an archipelago; the islands are the NGO projects and there is little in between worthy of note. In fact the sufferer probably also takes little notice of islands belonging to different clusters, the projects supported by other NGOs.

The opportunity to work with government agencies sometimes helps NGOs collaborate among themselves. Preparations for the social investment fund in Guatemala, for example, called for NGOs to help develop criteria for government funding of NGOs and, in the process, to share experience among themselves about what types of project are working. This led to coordination in the development of NGO strategic plans in the social sectors.

The deep-rooted confidence in their chosen project approach is an inevitable aspect of the courage of conviction necessary for successful innovation. But it is a blessing as well as a curse. The principal strength of NGOs lies in their capacity to experiment, to try out new approaches on a modest scale which may in time become well-accepted development techniques or afford useful lesson for others. This requires staff who are original thinkers, prepared to take risks, confident in their own judgment. But these very same qualities make it difficult for such staff to collaborate with others whose views are fractionally different from their own.

> One of the most serious barriers to expanding the development roles of NGOs may be the difficulties they face in working with one another. Jealousies among them are often intense, and efforts at collaboration all too often break down into internecine warfare that paralyzes efforts to work together toward the achievement of shared purposes. Ironically, it at times seems easier for NGOs to work with governments than with other NGOs.[62]

These tendencies toward isolation may be reinforced by the messages received from the NGO's headquarters or from funding agencies. These messages tend to encourage idiosyncrasy by creating a folk-hero mythology about field staff and project leaders. Northern NGOs are looking for "good copy." The "Robin Hood" or "David fighting Goliath" images are ideal ones to convey to their supporters. And policies of decentralization give free reign for experimentation and for changing established programs. To question decentralization in most NGOs is almost sacriligious. Like kindness, it is seen as a self-evident virtue. But to decentralize without limit is to atomize.

An NGO has a responsibility to set operational norms based on experience garnered from across its operation and from throughout its history. NGOs which neglect the tasks of scaling up are wasting their talent and experience. Conversely, those organizations which have evolved beyond a narrow project focus have frequently demonstrated the immense contribution they can make toward reshaping development and toward amplifying the voice of the poor.

The three following chapters give an account of the three very different approaches to scaling up. The intention is not to present an exhaustive handbook on the theory and practice of the art. It is an attempt to distill some lessons out of a rich base of experience generated by a range of organizations who have all had some success in moving, along varied paths, to a wider, "influencing" role.

7

Project Replication

ALMOST EVERYONE IS KEEN to see successful NGO projects replicated. The poor communities who benefit, NGO staff and boards, the funding partners, official aid agencies and Southern governments all welcome the extension of tried and tested approaches. The likely exceptions are local government officials who fear being supplanted, and sometimes—as in the case of Bangladesh—opposition political parties, some of which see Northern NGOs as agents of imperialism.

With such rare breadth of support it may sound perverse to suggest that replication may not be the best approach. But it is important to remember that what works like a charm in one specific situation may be lackluster in others. The key to the successful project is almost invariably its leadership—people of vision, charisma, courage and stamina are inevitably found at the helm.

Sadly such leaders are few and far between, and no formula exists for replicating them. They can be drawn from other sectors—from government service, academia, business and elsewhere—but this may be at the expense of depleting those sectors which are also important for the healthy development of the country.

One study of NGOs in Kenya and Niger conducted in 1979[63] concluded that reproducing carbon copies of successful NGO projects is not a realistic option, is not a defensible use of scarce human and material resources and is unlikely to produce a comparable impact in most of the new settings where it is attempted. This is probably an over-pessimistic conclusion, but it provides an important caution.

Whether or not a strategy of replication is appropriate depends on the following questions. Is there an adequate reservoir of the human resources required? Will the approach work as well elsewhere? Can a loss of flair in the original project be guarded against? Would it be better to multiply the number of like projects, by helping others to develop the NGO's approach rather than increase the size of the parent project? In particular, can official aid agencies and government departments be persuaded to develop some of the approaches? Can the increased impact required be achieved better through other scaling-up approaches?

In practice, of course—rather than a conscious decision to scale up—the project grows organically, with success being the motive force. News of this success inspires others to try a similar approach. Replication *happens* rather more than it is *planned*.

Experience of successes and failures provide a number of pointers which can help to make replication more successful.[64]

Recruitment, Training and Apprenticeship

One of the main blocks to successful project growth and replication is finding the right people and giving them the right training. Rarely, however, is sufficient attention paid to such tasks.

Where NGOs have developed an active recruitment and training strategy it has more than paid off. A good example is provided by the Bangladesh Rural Advancement Committee (BRAC) of Bangladesh, which started in 1972 during the country's struggle for independence from Pakistan. It is now one of the largest NGOs in the Third World, employing over 2,000 staff under the charismatic leadership of Fazle Abed. It operates projects in primary health care, education, credit, adult literacy and other fields and is widely respected as being a highly effective organization. For example, its credit schemes have a repayment record of over 95 percent.[65]

Abed realized in its early days that BRAC was on a steep growth curve and that it would rapidly come to need skilled and dedicated local leaders and middle managers. Rather than depend on the orthodox job market and employ, when the time came, staff with proven track records in management (but who in all likelihood would be new to the voluntary ethos), Abed took the imaginative decision to home-grow his own management cadre of highest caliber. He actively sought out the most promising Bangladeshi graduates and offered them a "moral contract." The recruits were expected to do a period of field work, during which time they would learn about rural realities and about BRAC's way of working. By this time the organization would have grown and in all probability they would be promoted into the new management post which would be needed. As a result of this forward-looking strategy BRAC now has a widely respected management base.[66] It is true that the middle and junior level BRAC has a very high staff turnover, but this has had a positive spin-off. A large proportion of the most effective NGOs in Bangladesh have been set up by people who once worked for BRAC.

Another Bangladeshi organization, Proshika, has helped strengthen the country's NGO sector by running a special training center which provides excellent courses for both staff and group activists. This is offered as a service to all NGOs in the country. The training covers all aspects of NGO work, from mobilization techniques and legal rights to agriculture and functional literacy.

An important factor which grassroots NGOs must be sensitive to is that when they help develop leaders from among the poor, they are exposing those leaders to considerable personal risk. Even an activity which on the surface appears quite neutral is likely to be viewed by local elites as an erosion of their power base and they are likely to retaliate. Part of the training given should be about the nature of the threats that can be expected and how to respond to them.

Management Capacity

The ethos of most NGOs is idealistic, bottom-up, democratic, flexible, responsive and anti-elite. This can easily manifest itself as anti-management. Staff tend to be demotivated by, and resentful of, hierarchy and bureaucracy within their own organization. However, without strong management the organization is likely to drift and underachieve. NGO project staff are likely to be highly motivated in early years by a charismatic leader. As the project grows the leader may or may not seek to recruit a middle-management cadre. If they do so it may be resented by those staff who now perceive themselves to be one-removed from the leadership; factionalism may evolve centered around the middle managers. If they do not, then overwhelming demands are placed on the leader by the project's growth, and the leadership becomes autocratic and reluctant to take on new ideas. Either course confronts difficulties, as is described by David Brown.[67] The first course faces risks of ideological disintegration, the latter of ideological conformity.

There is no easy path, but it is clear that the organization which fails to evolve management capacity as it grows is not sustainable. Too much depends on one person and a crisis is inevitable when, for whatever reason, he or she is no longer around. The difficulties of installing a management structure can be reduced by a very clear statement of the organization's mission, with authority devolved as much as possible so that a wide range of people share management responsibility for achieving that mission. Brown suggests six priorities for building up capacity:

1. Renew the organization's visions and values. Though potentially explosive it is important to arrive at common ground through "ideological negotiation."
2. Formulate strategic concepts which position the organization with

respect to external constituencies and provide a framework for assessing new opportunities.

3. Build consensus on the organization's plans, including the agreement of external constituencies.
4. Empower the leadership. Leaders must have authority to make decisions, but they must also delegate authority so that their time is free for strategic issues.
5. Match the organization to the agreed tasks and values.
6. Emphasize learning from doing, especially learning from mistakes. A good deal of reinventing the wheel can be avoided by having written manuals describing procedures for dealing with routine tasks.

Some NGOs, such as the Aga Khan Foundation (AKF), are realizing that they have much to learn from the business sector. Management training in financial matters, organizational structures, team building, interpersonal skills, person management, negotiation, objective setting and strategic planning all have relevance to the NGO world.

AKF believes that the government, voluntary and business sectors all have a great deal to learn from each other. By working more closely together and overcoming the deep-rooted suspicions each holds of the other they can all contribute towards creating an enabling environment in which public policy, entrepreneurship and social innovation all work together toward eradication of poverty.[68]

Through careful application of management techniques, AKF has achieved a good reputation in its operation of very large-scale projects. In Northern Pakistan, for example, AKF has recently expanded its Rural Support Program (AKSP) from three districts to four. The cost of this expansion was £2.8 million. The British Overseas Development Administration was impressed by the local institution building demonstrated by the project and so took the unprecedented step of agreeing to fund the undertaking not out of its normal budget for NGOs but out of its bilateral aid program. Such a progression is only possible where the government is sympathetic to both donor and local NGO. The World Bank's evaluation department has done two evaluations of AKSP—its first studies of non-Bank projects. Both were positive about the very successful participatory approach to rural development, but the second asked questions about the program's sustainability.[69]

Decentralization

There is an inevitable conflict between the principles of strong leadership and decentralization when it comes to the setting of objectives. On the one hand these should, through popular participation, respond to the priorities the poor themselves set, but on the other hand the benefit of experience and experimentation elsewhere should not be wasted. The balance indicated is to have clearly defined operational norms (such as the procedures and structures for rural credit schemes), but to facilitate local decision making within this framework on all other matters such as the allocation of credit and the choice of other activities the group wishes to undertake.

One NGO which enjoys international acclaim for such an approach is the Grameen Bank of Bangladesh. This NGO was set up in 1976 with support from the Central Bank. It is quite rigid in its approach, starting with the formation of rural groups of five people who are all committed to making regular savings. The group is allocated a capital sum to use as a revolving loan. They decide for themselves which two members get loans at the outset. No one else in the group can get a loan until the first two start making their weekly repayments. This ensures peer pressure not to default and consequently repayment records are extremely high (97 percent compared with 27 percent for private banks). Six groups comprise a center which meets weekly to discuss wider affairs of the village, typically tree planting, latrine digging and fighting the dowry system. Some fifty to sixty groups comprise a branch which decides on the allocation of revolving loans between the centers.

As of July 1990 there were 735 branches and 770,693 members (90 percent of whom were women) throughout 17,746 villages. Members' savings totalled US$17.54 million and loans US$22.4 million. The most common activities for which loans were made include paddy husking and dairying for women, and purchasing rice for resale for men.[70] A limitation of the scheme is that servicing the groups requires a level of staff time that a conventional bank might not support.

Networking

Building up strong networks of similar NGOs and projects can help to overcome any sense of isolation and provide useful forums for learning skills and exchanging techniques. This linkage can be vertical (in which local organizations are tied into regional federations and are required to follow the rules of that federation) or horizontal (in which the member organizations all operate on the same level and retain their autonomy). A survey of 150 micro-level case studies conducted in 1981 showed that NGOs linked vertically performed better than isolated organizations, but that those linked horizontally fared even better.[71] The same survey showed that in general NGOs linked to governments did worst of all, though there were some outstanding successes in this category.

The conclusion that can be drawn is that projects can indeed benefit from learning from each other, but it is best to avoid the loss of local autonomy. Networking allows for a mutual learning of each others' techniques but just as important is the mutual support and motivation afforded.

Some international NGOs are now beginning to fund the exchange of project leaders between programs in different countries to encourage a wider diffusion of NGO experience. Similarly, international workshops on specific topics which bring together grassroots workers from many different countries are proving effective. For example, Oxfam UK organized an Arid Lands Workshop in 1987 which focused on techniques of arresting decertification, arid land agriculture, working with pastoralists and other important NGO innovations from a wide variety of countries.

Planning Withdrawal

One of the first things an NGO should consider when starting a new project is how it might end its involvement. It is not realistic to expect to be leading or funding the venture forever more and, to be sustainable, the project must become self-running and self-financing. Such foresight is relatively rare, unfortunately.

One NGO which has managed to become self-supporting is Jamkhed in Maharashtra State, India. Its record is particularly impressive since it is in the health sector, in which local mobilization of resources is notoriously difficult. Jamkhed was started in 1971 by a husband and wife team. Its original focus was the mass application of high-tech curative medicine (particularly cataract operations through "eye-camps") but rapidly switched to nutrition and other preventive health-care approaches. The local people welcomed and trusted the services provided and were prepared to contribute a small sum of money each month to pay for the modest costs of the scheme. Jamkhed now offers a comprehensive rural health care to 175 villages, with a total population of 200,000 people.

Diffusion of Experience

Through careful documentation of experience and attention to building up a communications strategy to disseminate that experience, a strategic NGO is able to ensure that its good ideas spread without having to do all the work itself. When those converted to a new approach have access to substantial resources the multiplier effect is enormous.

The Grameen Bank has helped to revolutionize thinking about microcredit throughout the world, and Oxfam UK's Yatenga project has influenced the World Bank and many other agencies to develop water-harvesting schemes throughout the Sahel. Clearly when official aid agencies and government departments are influenced in this way the effect can be particularly great.

However, not a great deal is known about this diffusion since it is rare for NGO evaluations to dwell on it. The fragmentary evidence that does exist suggests that there is a good deal of diffusion, even to government departments. Judith Tendler[72] lists a number of examples including: a village water supply program in Tanzania which was taken over the regional government's water department; a program of village polytechnic schools in Kenya which is now run by the government; a skills-training project for young women in Sri Lanka which is now being copied by the new ministry of youth and employment; an NGO which was brought in by the Jamaican government to train the personnel in its Ministry of Youth and Community Development; and an NGO which was commissioned by the Indian government to do a major survey leading to a large investment in irrigation and rural electrification.

8

Building Grassroots Movements

THE MOST EXCITING PHENOMENON in the NGO sector over the last two decades has been the birth, growth and maturing of grassroots organizations throughout much of the Third World.

Some have emerged from self-help projects which sought sustainability by investing control in the people. Others are entirely indigenous, emerging as local people responded to local problems. Whatever their origins, they have come to revolutionize the thinking of progressive NGOs about development itself. The early notion that "our projects will be more effective if the people understand them better and take charge of their implementation" has given way to the realization that "our projects will *be* better if they are based on the people's own analysis of the problems they face and their solutions."

The social development approach sees the poor not as beneficiaries but as the controllers of the development process itself. The people must *make* the theory. What is revolutionary is not the improved efficiency of projects (though this can be impressive) but the unleashing of new-found confidence.

The poor may well be aware of the underlying causes of their poverty. They may be aware that their vulnerability, isolation, sickness, low incomes, meager assets and their exploitation conspire against them. They remain in poverty because their way out is blocked, partly by lack of resources and by ignorance, but also because they don't believe there is anything they can do about it. They lack confidence.

NGOs' support for schemes devised and run by the poor themselves have shown that the poor can indeed control assets effectively to combat poverty. But more importantly it has demonstrated to the poor that they have, collectively, an ability to take action that radically alters their situation. The starting point may be rather modest—a savings club, a literacy program or a women's income generation scheme—but such minor successes can instill great confidence in the poor, confidence which if skillfully channelled quickly leads to ambitions of tackling much bigger problems through their new-found weapon of collective action.

The key word is collective. Their previous analysis was quite correct. As individuals there is nothing they can do to overcome poverty. They have no assets, no access to parliamentary or legislative processes, no skills they can threaten to withdraw. They have absolutely no bargaining power—except their unity. While initially the poor view the funds offered by their foreign friends as their salvation, they quickly realize that their real salvation lies within themselves, in their solidarity. This isn't always easy for funding NGOs to accept. They are probably anxious to find effective economic projects in which to invest funds—especially as official funding of NGOs increases. They would like to increase their backing for successful groups.

It is a story which should be told with some caution, but the problem of too much NGO funding in some of the more accessible regions of the Third World is as serious as the dearth of funding elsewhere. NGO field staff and official aid agencies gather in such places, eager to fund local organizations. They should be heedful that their support, which is so vital in the early stages, can easily become a barrier obstructing a natural evolution of these groups towards a more permanent self-reliant role. This ambivalent position of the funders gives rise to considerable tensions between different schools of NGOs.

NGOs can also go too far the other way (particularly perhaps the Southern NGOs which experience less pressure to disburse funds). Their enthusiasm for conscientization can obscure income-generating activities, leading to a loss of relevance to the poor. As Charles Elliott says, "empowerment without production is as futile as production without empowerment."[73] If the objective is to help the poor achieve their full potential then a judicious balance is called for.

These issues are demonstrated no more clearly than in Bangladesh. There are numerous examples where tiny sums of money have helped to transform communities of landless people. Many important lessons about the skills needed and practical challenges of grassroots mobilization can be learned from some of these practical experiences.

Lessons From Bangladesh

Start with an activity which the people readily relate to. Many small-scale economic activities inspire community strength and lead to greater things. For example, a revolving loan scheme for the purchase of livestock might generate the unity needed to mount a campaign for landlords to recognize minimum wage laws. When all the poor in one area stick together in this way it is difficult for landlords to refuse.

Build awareness raising and empowerment into the process. Group meetings of the poor can be occasions for debate about the causes of poverty and the possible avenues for overcoming these causes. Functional literacy programs are particularly appropriate. The poor are almost invariably not only illiterate, but convinced that they will never be able to read and write. For them it is immensely liberating to discover that, in just a matter of months, they can become quite proficient in these skills. They become able to read newspapers and information given out by local authorities and to sign their name. They feel for the first time secure from trickery. But the intense courses (typically two hours per night for men, and in the afternoons for women) teach not only the basic skills. Each lesson has a social relevance, with exercises based on legal rights, on the democratic process, on the traditional injustices that oppress women and other important life skills. These ingredients are every bit as important as the reading and writing in helping to raise awareness among the poor about their situation.

Foster strong local leadership. The initial leadership is likely to come from the staff and volunteers of the grassroots organization which encourages the village to establish a group. These are likely to be local people but probably with reasonable education and not from the poorest families. They will probably want to go on to set up similar groups in other villages and so their leadership role is temporary. The village must choose its own leadership from among its members. This choice is the single most important factor in determining success. NGOs can help by giving whatever support and advice the leaders call for, and also by providing the training opportunities and support structures that empower the leaders. GSS and Proshika are two large NGOs which have devised their own impressive residential training programs for local cadres, covering subjects from empowerment techniques and women's rights to agriculture and government bureaucracy.

Tackle internal as well as external injustices. Some of the most impressive savings and credit schemes have been among women. The members diligently contribute their few pennies a week and, when enough has been generated to make a few loans, undertake their first-ever business activity—perhaps de-husking rice for sale in the local market or weaving bamboo mats. In many cases their success has bred the confidence to band together and blockade the houses of local men who are known to beat their wives or threaten divorce with no good reason. This social pressure often leads not only to reform of the errant husbands but to increased respect from the menfolk. In a number of cases this has led to an outlawing of the dowry system, whereby young men demand large sums of money, bicycles and other "gifts" from the families of the brides they are marrying. This practice not only demeans women, it is economically extremely wasteful. It is even a frequent motive for murder.

Encourage groups to chart their own course. Success is empowerment, but success in pursuit of the group's own plans is doubly so. One thriving Women's Savings Club decided to make a loan so that one of the members could hire a lawyer to sue the husband who had deserted her, leaving her without a penny. This type of loan had not been envisaged by the NGO which formed the group. The action was highly successful, the husband (a relatively successful petty trader) made over a considerable compensation and everyone in the group shared in what was seen as woman's victory over man.

Develop action research. In deciding what course of action to pursue a group needs good, reliable information. Since this is not likely to be readily available to the poor, the group has to devise its own research capacity. For example, landless groups have, after their literacy training, delved into local authority land records. These might reveal pieces of land which in theory belong to the community but in practice have been annexed by the landlords. This has led on a few occasions to successful action to demand the return of these pieces of land. Research conducted by BRAC groups into the reasons for the poor distribution of relief food led to the publication of a book describing the horrific nature of the widespread corruption. This generated substantial pressure for reform.[74]

Avoid early failure. While groups must be self-determining, the NGO should help guard against action which is unlikely to succeed, especially in the early stages. One group, less than a year old, had done well in its first economic activities. The members, in discussing their exploitation, became angry that the women had to walk several miles each day to fetch water because the landlord nearby refused to allow them to use his well. They decided to take direct peaceful action. On the appointed day both men and women came together to march, carrying their pots, to the well and started drawing water. The landlord merely sent out his thugs and servants with iron bars and knives to beat the villagers. The landless didn't have a chance. With many wounded and with all their pots broken, they had to beat a sad retreat. Thereafter all the landlords in the area refused work to members of the group. Within a month almost everyone in the group had left. They felt it was too dangerous. This example indicates the need for an accurate assessment of the enemy's strength. Perhaps the group should have delayed action until there was a supportive network of similar groups throughout the locality.

Forge alliances of local groups. There is a limit to the scale of victories any one group can expect, however unified its members. Bigger battles can only be fought by large numbers of similar groups coming together in coalitions and networks to support each others' struggle. For example, several village groups in Khulna District (all part of the same functional literacy program) decided to take collective action to demand the right to fish in a large nearby pond. Their research had shown that the landlord's claim of ownership was had no legal basis. They realized also that there must be connivance of the local authorities so action would be dangerous. They enlisted the help of other village groups who wouldn't even benefit from the fishing rights and staged a mass protest outside the local authorities offices. They also banded together to hire a lawyer and eventually the landlord gave way.

Build up strong communication skills. Group leaders need to communicate effectively not just to mobilize and motivate their members, but also to exchange with others outside the group. This exchange may be to share successful experience so that others might follow suit, or to appeal for support. Several techniques have proved effective, such as theater groups, puppet shows and song—combining entertainment with message. One network of powerful groups held an impressive conference in which thousands of village leaders from a very wide area came together, some travelling for several days to do so.

Seek influential allies. Not all the elite are anti-poor. Where politicians, senior officials, judges, journalists or others can be persuaded to help, the cause of the landless can be greatly strengthened. In at least one case where a landlord refused to hand back land that rightfully belonged to the poor and gave bribes to local officials to win their connivance, a sympathetic politician was able to take up the case with the officials' superior and the dispute was resolved.

Explore the use of state instruments. Though traditionally the poor can expect little justice from the legal and police services, and are wary therefore of attempting to use these, grassroots organizations are increasingly discovering ways of using them skillfully. For example, groups in one area became aware that the authorities were not distributing relief supplies (food and clothing) that had arrived in the district stores. Instead, the clothing was finding its way to the local market for sale. After mounting an unsuccessful demonstration, they decided to take the officials to court. By conducting careful surveys throughout the area they were able to show that only a fraction of the relief goods had been distributed. Journalists reported the scandal and the officials were found guilty in court and made to repay what they had stolen.

Develop a political strategy. The power of grassroots organizations to influence local structures and secure justice is clearly increased if they are able to command positions of power. In some areas with a long and strong tradition of group mobilization, groups are beginning to put forward their own local candidates. This can of course lead to tension with those political parties which consider themselves to be the traditional friends of the poor.

Those in political parties claim that the grassroots development organizations (GDOs) are, with finance from Western powers, squeezing them out from the rural areas. The GDOs maintain that the parties had become irrelevant to the landless and that they are simply filling the vacuum so carelessly left. The party activists claim that the GDOs are doing a disservice in concentrating so much on short-term victories, mostly battles fought against small-time local exploiters—themselves not rich by the standards of the national elite—and are diverting people's attention from the more serious battles for national power that should be waged. The GDOs contend that the parties are too bound by a Marxist analysis concerned with exploitation in the formal sector, that they concentrate on issues of concern to cities, trade unions and students and neglect the issues of concern to the majority of the country's poor. The parties accuse the GDOs of naivety in being devoid of a long-term strategy—citing as evidence their preparedness to be co-opted into governmental initiatives (for example to forward a national program to distribute community land based on the success of some grassroots land struggles). The GDOs counter that victories achieved in this way are not only important in themselves but they are also the confidence-building foundations on which bigger struggles can be mounted in future.

Both sets of arguments have potency. GDOs do need to position their local, immediate struggles in a broader context. Equally, party activists need to learn from the grassroot movements about the importance of fighting battles of immediate relevance to the poor. Resolving the tensions through a process of mutual learning and recognition of each other's contribution could be greatly strengthening all round.

Balance external and internal contributions. External funders should see their role as pump-primers. They cannot continue funding indefinitely, and experience shows that groups become stronger when they develop self-reliance. Credit schemes are more durable, for example, when the bulk of the capital is contributed by their members and when interest charged allows the capital to grow in real terms, even if an initial grant enabled revolving loans to commence.

Expect threats and be prepared to respond. Whenever the poor win a victory, somebody more powerful has lost and reprisals can be expected. In Bangladesh these can be particularly vicious. False claims—such as of theft or rape—are frequently filed against local leaders who are then arrested, beaten up and thrown into prison where they may languish for several months awaiting trial. The group members and local NGO need to be prepared to give whatever defence is necessary, such as legal aid and financial support for families. As the contest heats up there are, sadly, increasing numbers of murders of village-level activists, and some groups have had to arm themselves with sharpened sticks to ward off attacks from thugs hired by the landlords.

Develop where necessary international support. Especially where the reprisals from the local elite are becoming serious, and where the authorities are slow to side with the poor, international attention may help. For example, a British television documentary highlighted the struggle of one group, Samata, to gain rights over a large piece of land which was "accreting" (in Bangladesh, river erosion and siltation constantly lead to land being submerged and new land "coming up"—the latter by law belongs to the landless, though is normally annexed by the powerful). This, and the concern of international NGOs, galvanized authorities into action. The imprisoned leaders were released and victory now looks more hopeful.

These illustrations from Bangladesh are not unique. They are mirrored by similar activities in many other countries, particularly in Latin America and South and South East Asia. This rich bank of experience allows confident conclusions to be drawn that, with good leadership and the right help, popular movements have the capacity to shape national institutions, national politics and development theory. Each of these is achieved by shaping attitudes: attitudes of authority toward the impoverished and attitudes of the poor themselves toward their own situation.

Shaping National Institutions

Where grassroots movements are strong they demonstrate that they can transcend small-scale local activities to evolve their own structures on a national scale and to make major reforms in official structures.

The large numbers of successful credit schemes in countries such as Bangladesh have fostered their own powerful umbrella organizations which are able to channel large quantities of funds from official aid agencies. Sometimes this activity has led to reforms in commercial banking so that groups of people who have virtually no collateral and who may be mostly illiterate become eligible for loans.

Grassroots organizations will typically challenge the system to serve their members. The Self Employed Women's Association (SEWA) of Ahmedabad, India, illustrates this. SEWA was established in 1972 as a trade union of women in the informal sector. These would typically have to borrow fifty rupees every morning from a moneylender. They would use this to buy produce which they would then hawk. At the end of a long day they would have to return fifty-five rupees—sometimes more—to the moneylender. Out of the few rupees profit they would frequently have to pay fines for illegal street hawking, or bribes to the police to avoid such fines. They would have very little left in their hands—perhaps seven or eight rupees if they were lucky. SEWA established its own bank which provides loans at 12 percent interest. Its 13,000 members have seen a considerable rise in their daily incomes as a result. SEWA has also been successful in combating fines. Many of the vegetable hawkers set up their stalls in one particular street every day. Though not officially a market, it had been so in practice for as long as anyone could remember. SEWA applied through the law courts to legalize this practice. The authorities refused and SEWA took their case to the Supreme Court in Delhi. The authorities wouldn't give way but eventually they agreed to something even better. They made available space in the municipal market for the women and promised to build proper structures to house them.[75]

In many areas of Brazil, rubber tappers—who live in the Amazon jungles where the rubber trees grow wild—started to form their own associations to organize resistance against the big ranchers and logging companies who were moving in, cutting down the forests and destroying their livelihood. Sometimes they were able to persuade the tree cutters to avoid certain areas or certain trees, but usually they had little success.

Under the leadership of Chico Mendes the many local associations came together to form a nationwide rubber-tappers union. Their first meeting, in Brasilia, brought together representatives from all over Brazil, which in itself was no mean feat. For one woman this meant a journey of twenty days by canoe, boat and bus. They were able to meet national politicians, and for most of them this was the first time they felt able to talk to those who had the power to save them from economic and ecological destruction.

This didn't bring about immediate change, but the new-found sense of unity gave a great boost to their confidence. It also gave them a chance to explain their case to sympathetic journalists, to the Brazilian environmental movement and to others. Soon their cause became internationally known and the pressure on the government to reform its Amazonia policy grew into one of the major political issues of the day.

Such a high profile, sadly, was not enough to save Chico Mendes. There were almost daily threats on his life such that he required constant police protection. But the assassins needed only one opportunity, and they took it. On 23 December 1988 Mendes was murdered by a hail of bullets as he walked across the backyard of his modest home to go to the outside bathroom. Nothing could illustrate more starkly the constant danger that the leaders of such popular movements expose themselves to. Power and status is not given up without a struggle.

This example also illustrates how a struggle which starts small—at the grassroots—can turn into an international cause célèbre. The news of Mendes' assassination was relayed around the world in a matter of hours. NGOs in many countries sent messages of sympathy and support, and called on the Brazilian government to reform their policies swiftly to prevent future bloodshed. Television documentaries were shown in many countries about the life and work of Mendes and the rubber-tappers union. Mendes' death, tragically, has done more than anything to alert the world to the rainforest issue.

Elsewhere in the world other environmental battles have been fought by grassroots organizations. In Sarawak, Borneo, tribal people were able to stop timber companies from using bulldozers to tear down the forests. In Malaysia the local Friends of the Earth and the Consumers Association of Penang took a Japanese company to court for polluting the waterways from the mining of rare earths and won their case. NGOs in Sri Lanka halted the building of a coal-powered power station in Trincomalee when they came up with their own report showing flaws in the economic appraisal and revealing that the team which drew up the proposal had not even visited the area. They also stopped a forestry project by persuading the Finnish government to withdraw its aid for this scheme. The project was described as conservation but amounted to the opposite, said the critics. It sought to replace natural forest with commercial plantations.

The use of law courts in countries where the judiciary is relatively neutral is an increasingly important tool for NGOs. In some countries the GDOs are taking a less militant approach now that they realize that there is hope of redress through the legal system. For example, in Sri Lanka a former Chief Minister (Mr. Bagwati) has forcefully spoken out in favor of such social litigation, and is giving advice to NGOs on how best to proceed. Following a meeting on the environment and the law, a small group of environmental lawyers has now been formed.

Shaping National Politics

One of the clearest examples in recent times of the shaping (or at least shaking) of national politics by grassroots movements has been in China. The apparently spontaneous uprising by hundreds of thousands of students, backed by intellectuals, journalists and even allies in the police force, the army and the government itself, brought Beijing to a state of seige in Spring 1989.

Democracy once tasted is not readily forgotten. At the time of writing the destination of China's reform path remains uncertain but what is beyond doubt is that the relationship between the people and their state will never be quite the same again. The political leaders know that if in the future they ignore the popular will they can expect the events of Tiananmen Square to be replayed. The popular leaders and radicals will also be confident in their ability to trigger mass protests to confront government excesses.

Elsewhere grassroots movements have similarly helped to shape the political scene. In Chile the influence of NGOs and popular movements throughout almost every community and their sophisticated organization became particularly apparent during the October 1988 plebiscite. Using microchip technology, they were able to give a minute by minute report on voting patterns and to counter false information released by the government to journalists.

In the Philippines the turmoil during and immediately following the downfall of President Marcos revealed a considerable influence of NGOs in raising democratic awareness among the rural and urban poor, and in mass organization. In particular the National Movement for Free Elections persuaded people to register in the run-up to the February 1986 election. Then, having registered, the Movement persuaded people to turn out to vote, and organized protection of polling stations so that voters would not be intimidated nor ballot boxes rigged. The NGO sector, having demonstrated its strength and popular legitimacy, is now prominent in national debates on key issues such as agrarian reform and the debt crisis.

Also in February 1986 grassroots movements played an important role in the overthrow of Haiti's dictator, "Baby Doc" Duvalier. Since then the degree of organization of the peasantry has surprised the intellectuals who had all but written off the rural population as politically backward. The peasant movement has shown itself to be strong, aware and well orchestrated. Their demonstrations in which 10,000 people took part have obliged politicians to turn to the issue of rural poverty and has led to a confrontation with the residue of Duvalier's private army, the Ton-Ton Macoute.

In much of Latin America throughout the eighties the failure of left-wing political parties to win power, resist repression or reflect the day-to-day concerns of the majority of the poor created a political space for popular movements. Throughout the region ordinary people saw their battles being fought not by opposition parties but by popular movements. Communities would mobilize around one or a set of issues to take direct action against an institution, policy or authority which they perceived was at the root of their frustration or loss. While initially reactive—responding to situations created by others—the popular movements have gone on to create the political agenda.

In Brazil, for example, a coalition of NGOs including the rubber-tappers union, rural workers unions, and organizations concerned with the rainforest, wildlife, tribal people's rights and rural development has brought the issues of the Amazon and the environment into the limelight.

The leaders of such grassroots struggles are often assuming important political positions, either as catalysts for change within political parties or as politicians in their own right. In Bangladesh the cause of the landless has been advanced significantly by NGOs and many of the leaders of the landless are now putting themselves forward at local elections. This blending of NGO and political work can create tensions.

In Andhra Pradesh, India, an NGO, AWARE, has made a profound impact on local politics. AWARE has tens of thousands of members and on many occasions has forced local government officials—by pressure of numbers—to implement progressive laws, for example on land reform (which had been promulgated by the central government but largely ignored subsequently). Paradoxically, AWARE is now substantially funded by the government—a sign of the pluralism of Indian politics.

The early demonstrations of AWARE were impressive vehicles for publicizing issues and raising consciousness and confidence, but in moving to carefully targeted specific demands which exploit loopholes in government legislation they have been able to have a major impact on policy and practice. Now they are positioning themselves even more strategically in the political process by putting forward their own candidates in local elections. About 40 of the 200 or so seats in the AP parliament are held by members of AWARE local groups. The supporters of the Northern charities who fund AWARE might pale at the thought of their funds going to an organization engaged in political campaigning. (In fact the election campaign funds are not drawn from the foreign contributions.) However, this does appear to be a successful approach. The poor can be helped immeasurably through winning carefully chosen political reforms, and in liberal democracies there is no more effective lever for pressing home those reforms than the ballot box.

In many countries the popular grassroots movements are shifting from a stance of distance from the formal apparatus of democracy to being cautious participants. They rarely seek to replace political parties but use them as conduits for furthering their causes. David Lehman[76] suggests that Latin American popular movements are demonstrating that their confrontational, expressive style can bring about a gradual reduction in the institutional arbitrariness and oppression of the state. This demands not just reforms in the political and administrative systems but wholesale changes of attitude regarding, for example, discrimination against women or ethnic groups.

This shifting into the political arena has been accompanied by a change in the profile of NGO leaders, particularly in Latin America, as Leilah Landim describes.[77] Many former members of traditional left organizations and church activists find that they can best forward their work for social transformation within the popular sectors. In general they have university degrees and often maintain links with the academic world. Since NGO salaries are relatively attractive the sector increasingly presents a professional career option for middle-class intellectuals. The new cadre of intellectual leadership have adopted a new methodology. Their process is no longer simply to lead a process and to teach but to place themselves at the service of the process and to "learn-teach-learn."

The struggles which have been described in this section are far removed from the stereotype image of NGOs. However, sustainable changes in the system itself are more likely to be achieved by mobilizing popular pressure than by offering improved service delivery.[78] Governments will increasingly recognize that the strengthening of civil society will help make their democracies stronger, their institutions more efficient, their policies better respected. They, too, stand to gain in the long run from democratizing development.

Shaping Development Theory

An NGO may start with a program to improve the prospects of a particular group of poor people—a doing activity—and evolve into an influencing role, carving out some humanitarian space within the political agenda of the country for reforms that attack specific root causes of poverty. The most sustainable reforms are those gained not by sheer force but by winning the argument and so changing the way politicians and the public view the particular issue—changing the theory.

On many issues NGOs have, by challenging the sacred cows or by focusing on areas hitherto neglected by the development profession, contributed greatly to shifting official thinking.

The pioneering work of NGOs has revolutionized ideas about small-scale credit. They have demonstrated that, contrary to perceived wisdom, the poor, and women in particular, are not only trustworthy but also credit-worthy. With appropriate organization the poor are not only able to use credit profitably and manage their books efficiently, but they have higher repayment records than the better-off. Interest subsidies aren't normally necessary. Poor people can afford market rates—in fact, they normally have to pay considerably more than this to traditional local money lenders. They do, however, need help in organizing credit schemes and in providing pump-priming start-up capital.

Frequently, the mainstream suppliers of credit (the commercial banks and state schemes) are having to revise old-fashioned notions about the poor being an unbankable proposition and initiate new programs to respond to an unmet but commercially viable demand. Through such initiatives NGOs are helping to change banking theory.

More generally, NGO projects have frequently demonstrated that the poor are the most efficient users of assets such as land and water rights. This is causing the more progressive people in institutions such as the World Bank to advocate a rethinking of development economics. One of the theories which has guided this institution is that development is achieved by the creation of assets or by improving the productivity of assets. Redistribution of existing assets might be socially desirable but is not developmental in a macroeconomic sense since it does not add to the country's total stock of assets and so does not provide new engines for economic growth.

This logic has provided the rationale for the Bank's policy of not lending for the acquisition of land to distribute to the poor in programs of land reform. In many reports, however, it argues cogently in favor of land reform and it can in certain circumstances lend for the minor, non-land costs of such schemes, but its own rules prevent it from becoming a major actor on this stage.

Experience clearly shows that where grassroots movements have helped secure the redistribution of particular tracts of land, the land becomes more effectively utilized. The poor invest labor, use every square inch of land and are more diligent in use of inputs and avoiding crop losses. Yields may well double or triple. The logic deriving from experience indicates that land reform (and indeed other aspects of agrarian reform) makes economic sense even on the Bank's terms. Investing in the purchase of land from large landowners (at carefully regulated prices) and redistributing that land to the landless should yield a good rate of return providing that there are alternative investment opportunities within the economy which the large landowners can turn to.

The theory that the redistribution of assets does not contribute to development has been demonstrated by grassroots experience to be as fallacious as the notion that redistributing water through an irrigation scheme does not contribute to wealth creation. One only has to look at the impressive economic record of South Korea, where the land reform enacted by the US military government after World War II provided the foundation for the strong economic growth that followed, to see the effectiveness of what David Korten calls equity-led growth. Taiwan, China and Zimbabwe all point to a similar conclusion but from diverse political starting points.

In other fields popular movements and NGOs have also contributed to a modernizing of attitudes and a revising of development directions. The women's movement in many countries is beginning to erode the gender bias which characterizes orthodox development strategies. This erosion stems not just from winning moral arguments but because it is becoming self-evident that any society which, purely for reasons of prejudice, denies one half of its population the opportunity to achieve its full potential, is using its human resources appallingly.

The women's movement also provides a useful caveat to development NGOs about the balance between doing and influencing. Had it rested with a project approach there may, by today, have been many more women's projects, women's research institutes, women-led businesses but perhaps little change in society's attitude towards women and relatively few changes in policy. It may be, indeed, that the paucity of financial resources in the women's movement in early days saved it from diving down the project route which, if not a blind alley, may certainly have been circuitous.

It is interesting to speculate on what response development NGOs would get if they told their supporters to stop giving money but instead to join forces to change attitudes and change policies, and if they admitted that the poverty they and their supporters are concerned with is barely dented by all the NGOs' projects combined. Charitable giving is not the answer to structural poverty, and if it deflects Northern publics from the pursuit of more forceful answers then it does a disservice. In fact, it is unlikely that it does deflect concern in this way. Those most active in campaigns on development issues are also likely to donate to other NGOs. However, no one can tell how many of those who at present give but don't act would switch to action if told that their donations were not the answer.

The environmental movement provides similar lessons. Their campaigns have dramatically shifted the political agenda throughout the world, especially in the North, though the contribution made by their projects has been minor. In the Third World, Northern and Southern environmentalists have joined forces to cajole official aid agencies into rethinking their economic theory. Planning processes which are determined by narrow indicators of economic rates of return have hitherto ascribed zero value to inputs provided free by nature, irrespective of whether the use of those inputs is sustainable. Planners are having to devise new, more flexible, approaches to decision making, considering not just the economic but also the natural resources balance sheet.

This demands modifying the traditional economist's practice of "heavy discounting," whereby the assumed benefits and costs in calculating a project's economic rate of return diminish steeply the longer ahead those costs or benefits are likely to arise. This "buy now, pay later" approach ascribes disproportionately low value to the environmental costs which may take many years to be realized. We must learn to value things we traditionally take for granted, such as the fish stocks in our oceans or the ozone layer which protects our climate from overwarming and our skins from melanoma.

The mass demonstrations and riots which have greeted economic austerity measures in many countries have similarly caused a necessary rethinking of structural adjustment. It is becoming clear that, however desirable it is to have a healthy economy, this is not the sole determinant of a healthy society. Adjustment programs which demand a heavy social cost from those who have least and who have already lost much is neither morally defensible, politically feasible nor, in the long run, economically sound.

The more sophisticated governments are realizing that their projects are more sustainable when the public is well informed about them and when those affected are consulted. Information which is officially withheld, but which then becomes available through leaks, is embarrassing to the authorities. Those affected can, perhaps, take legal action or organize mass protests and slow up or even halt the project. The experience of local people may even be critical for the project's success. On a number of occasions in the Philippines, Nepal and Mexico, for example, local populations warned engineers that proposed dams would not withstand the peak flooding and were subsequently proved correct. The warnings were ignored, the dams were built and were quickly washed away.[79]

In that popular movements are by definition campaigning against the policies and practices of authorities they can easily be seen as anti-state or anti-progress. Often their stance is critical of business, of plans to privatize state functions or of plans for economic growth. They appear, therefore, to be anti-liberalization. An alternative view, probably not popular with the NGOs themselves, would be to see grassroots movements as pressing for the "modernizing" of the marketplace.

When parastatals are dismantled and replaced by a private sector oligopoly in which a few racketeers form a rigid cartel to push down prices post harvest and to bump them up some months later (as was the case, for example, in parts of Malawi), this cannot be seen as a free market. When women are denied loans not because they are uncreditworthy, but because of prejudice within the banking system, this is not a free market for credit. When traders choose not to supply to or collect from remote areas because it is more trouble for them and more damaging to their vehicles, this is not a free market.

NGOs which campaign for reforming rather than abolishing parastatals, which demonstrate by example that women and the poor are creditworthy and that trade to and from remoter regions can be profitable, are in practice truer exponents of the free market system than those who voice monetarist rhetoric but who would hand over that market to a system based on patronage and prejudice rather than principles of fair competition.

9

"The Unreasonable NGO": Influencing Policy Reform

IN *MAN AND SUPERMAN*, George Bernard Shaw wrote "the reasonable man adapts himself to the world; the unreasonable one persists in trying to adapt the world to himself. Therefore all progress depends on the unreasonable man." To parody this maxim, NGOs should not simply adjust their programs to accept whatever strictures authority or convention bestow upon them but should be so unreasonable as to seek to change those strictures when it is clear that they are not in the interests of the poor.

When development schemes go wrong it may be because they were wrongly conceived but it is more likely that the prevailing policy environment simply did not allow them to work. Project approaches which work well in one country may fail miserably elsewhere even when the leadership is excellent and where the need is every bit as great. They fail because of government indifference, corruption of officials, the dead-weight of bureaucracy, the inefficiency of institutions, the hostile attitudes of local elite and a host of other factors. One USAID survey of 277 micro-development projects concluded that 88 percent were negatively influenced by the policy environment.[80] NGOs have to decide whether to learn to live with the obstacles, or to try to remove them. Ignoring them allows progress in the short term but it may lead to unsustainability. These NGOs plan activities—in isolation of the state. Their projects no doubt give vital help to many but are vulnerable to rapid erosion once funding ceases. A recent FAO study revealed how many innovative NGO projects failed because they were conceived outside of the context of any overall state strategy. For example, in Burkina Faso in the early 1980s (then Upper

Volta) a plethora of NGOs set up projects which were isolated from each other, unrelated to the state, and as a result were sometimes diametrically opposed.[81]

The unreasonable approach is to seek reforms in policies, attitudes and practices so as to eradicate the obstacles. This path is lined with danger but it is more realistic in the long term.

NGOs that concentrate on popular participation in their projects should realize the importance of policy reform. Through their work they not only encounter establishment obstacles to their own activities but they are also constantly reminded how state policies can exacerbate poverty. They are well placed to realize that the self-reliant development they aim to promote will be sustainable only if the policy environment allows it to be, hence the need to weed out local and national policies and practices which thwart these ambitions. In their place should be constructed a supportive development system, in which the three sectors—public, private and voluntary—all have an important and coordinated role to play.

It can be daunting, however, to seek to negotiate with the state on policy reform. It may be difficult to find time from the project work to develop the necessary advocacy skills. Or NGOs may fear alienating officials, leading perhaps to their access to foreign funds being cut off for indigenous NGOs, or to expulsion in the case of Northern NGOs. For example, Anand Niketan in India, which has campaigned stridently for the human rights of tribal people to be respected and for reforms in the legal system, has been barred from receiving foreign funds.

These are very real difficulties and in some countries policy reform activities will remain unrewarding and dangerous, but in most countries the potential is enormous and as yet underexploited.

However undesirable they may view the results, NGOs should look to lessons that might be learned from structural adjustment. Most Southern governments, particularly in Africa, have come to accept the "new realism" promoted by the agents of adjustment. They accept that healthy development depends as much on introducing the right kind of policy reforms as on specific projects, and moreover they accept, albeit unwillingly, the involvement of foreign agents in devising these reforms. Until recent years such intervention—meddling in economic planning, weeding out inefficiency and engaging in all aspects of government policy—would have been out of bounds for official aid agencies. Now they are routine features of aid programs.

Some governments have welcomed this. They perhaps were already aware of the need for reforms, as the debt crisis became more and more severe, but shied away because of the political difficulties entailed. They needed a spur and the official aid agencies, under the leadership of the World Bank, were swift to provide it. A considerable proportion of official development assistance has swung round to "program aid," and both the

World Bank (25 percent of whose funding goes to adjustment lending) and the IMF have assumed extremely powerful influence in the planning of national development strategies.

Official aid agencies believe they can multiply the effectiveness of their aid by promoting those economic reforms which they see as conducive to enterprise and growth. They also see a foreign policy advantage in coaxing Third World governments away from the central planning model and toward a Western one. They are also helping ensure orderly debt payments instead of default, and so there is an element of economic self interest. This mixture of motives is resented by Southern governments and strongly criticized by progressive NGOs.

The debate about structural adjustment—its impact on the poor, its impact on stimulating renewed growth and its impact on restoring credit-worthiness of debtors—has preoccupied development thinking in recent years. Official aid agencies have given little attention to what David Korten calls micro-policy reform,[82] though they would probably agree that getting the right policies, the right attitudes of officials and the right institutional capacity at local level is every bit as important as the national level reforms they concentrate on.

The World Bank and IMF assure their critics that the paramount objective of adjustment is the sustainable relief of poverty. If this is the case it is extremely shortsighted just to focus on macroeconomic policy reforms. A leader of a major rural NGO in Zaire recently said, "in my country it is not economic reform the poor need, but political reform." Economic reforms may—if genuinely politically neutral, which is rarely the case—create the necessary conditions for sustainable growth and poverty elimination but not the sufficient conditions. By themselves they may even exacerbate poverty among the very groups they aim to help. For example, increasing agricultural prices in most countries is necessary if rural development is to be promoted. However, if peasant farmers cannot get access to the inputs, credit, markets and transport they need, if little of the price increase is passed on to them and if they have severe land or labor constraints, then they may not benefit at all from the increased prices. The rich farmer–poor farmer gap is likely to widen, prices of goods the poor need to buy will increase and the poor will become worse off, not better.

NGOs are often well placed to observe such processes taking place. They should be able to predict the distributional impact of the reforms included in an adjustment package and to advocate alternative reforms or supplementary measures which could rescue the situation from the poor's point of view. For example, an African NGO might be concerned about the impact of an agricultural sector reform on women farmers. Though the rural sector may be strengthened as a whole, the women may become worse off for various reasons:

- Women do not have the same access to land as do men. The laws of

the country may actually discriminate against women, denying them ownership or security of tenure. Farming rights may be at the whim of local chiefs or village headmen.
- Women find it difficult to acquire credit. Many credit schemes are available only to men, or demand land or other assets as collateral, so compounding the first problem. This may mean that women are unable to acquire the inputs they need to take advantage of the new opportunities.
- Government agricultural extension services are geared to male farmers. Training programs may only be available to men, and there will be few extension workers who are women.
- Agricultural markets will be biased against women. Women may find it hard to sell their produce, either because of the smaller volumes they may produce or because of outright prejudice. Furthermore, it is likely that when they do succeed in marketing produce it is their husbands who get paid the proceeds.
- Women are likely to experience more severe labor constraints than male farmers. This could be because they are the last in the pecking order to benefit from the village's resources of animal traction, because traditional household chores leave them with little time free for farming or because of other factors.

There are many examples of impressive pioneering work which NGOs have supported which have tackled these barriers. NGOs have formed women's clubs which have managed to secure plots of land to farm. They have set up credit programs for women. They run micro-package schemes providing smaller units of seeds and fertilizers than the government or cooperative services deal in and which are particularly suitable for women and others who farm small plots. They have established cooperatives so that a number of small producers can band together for marketing purposes. They have developed special training programs and extension services for women farmers. They have expanded animal traction availability with special attention to women users. And they have helped reduce the time spent on household chores, for example by improving village water supplies and by developing community kitchens and bakeries.

The net result of all such schemes is to improve the situation of many thousands of women, particularly the female family heads. But perhaps a potentially more powerful result is that they demonstrate the economic practicality of such schemes. Women farmers are, on the whole, highly efficient. They have a good record for repaying loans. They are adaptable to new techniques and are hard working. In short, they should not be viewed as the objects of charity but as commercially viable entrepreneurs. Why is this lesson still so rarely heeded!

The NGO experience is almost wasted unless it is used to change the attitudes and practices of decision makers. This entails a deliberate strategy of making time to talk with government servants, aid officials, journalists, academics and others. There may be a window of opportunity offered by structural adjustment. NGOs can, for instance, urge that reform of discriminatory land tenure laws be included as ingredients in adjustment programs. They can urge the central government to apply pressure on the tribal chiefs to modernize their attitudes toward providing land to women. They can advocate reforming credit schemes toward the needs of women farmers, perhaps by suggesting targets or by introducing incentives for the staff who allocate the loans.

NGOs can advocate changes in agricultural extension services, for example gearing the service more to the crops that women tend to grow, the employment of more women extension officers and the provision of special training programs for women farmers. The NGOs might provide training to government employees to facilitate such reforms. NGOs can seek reforms in marketing arrangements, urging that seeds, fertilizers and other inputs be provided in units which are suitable to women farmers. They can call for payments for crops to be made promptly and directly to the women. NGOs can also argue for schemes to help remove the labor constraints which particularly affect women. They can, for example, encourage the government to give priority to village water supplies, to planting trees and bushes for domestic fuel near the villages, to establishing creches and to expanding the availability of animal traction.

Such reforms should be compatible with structural adjustment as they would all contribute to improving economic efficiency. Until lately there has been little history of NGOs' involvement in the planning of adjustment. Neither governments nor the international financial institutions have invited NGOs views, nor have the latter been inclined to sit down with the "architects of austerity." Within the World Bank's current Social Dimensions of Adjustment in Africa project (SDA), however, an NGO window has been opened up. Though this will include recruiting NGOs support for "compensatory programs" designed to dull the pain of austerity, the World Bank has stressed that it welcomes the input of African NGOs into the overall design of adjustment programs. Quite how forthcoming that input will be, and how seriously it will be heeded, remains to be seen.

As the above examples illustrate, micro-policy reforms cannot be achieved purely through changes in legislation and central government policies. As Korten points out, it is also necessary to bring about complex institutional changes, the development of new capacities and new institutional roles and, most critically, changes in attitudes.[83] In comparison, macro-policy reforms are easy. They can be achieved by governments taking action in the capital city alone, for example, making decisions to devalue the currency, reduce subsidies, increase producer prices or liberalize markets. Micro-policy reforms demand central government action but also require action by local government officials, changes in local institutions and careful retraining of all those whose cooperation is required for the reforms to be effective.

NGOs potentially have an enormous role to play in securing micro-policy reforms but this requires building up new skills of influencing and facilitating. They need to have a thorough knowledge of the country, not just the region they customarily work in. They need to have a sound analysis of the economic situation, of government policies and priorities, and of the stance taken by those such as the World Bank who wield considerable influence over the government. They need to build up contacts with academics and others who can help conduct the research needed to strengthen their case. They need to establish close contacts with a wide range of other potential allies for example in trade unions, the business community, international agencies and other NGOs. They also need to have advocates who are skilled at presenting arguments to politicians and officials at all levels.

Planning for Policy Reform

Having worked out a convincing case for the reforms sought, the NGO must consider how it can build up influence. The World Bank's leverage comes largely from the volume of money at its disposal. With NGOs there is no such direct leverage and they must look instead for indirect influence.

The NGOs' first step should be to record carefully its direct experience indicating the need for reforms. This may need to be supplemented by specially commissioned research to establish whether the problems they have witnessed are peculiar to the project area or are general, whether the suggested reforms appear appropriate elsewhere, to survey the literature available on the subject and to identify relevant expertise in the country. This analysis should include a study of the government's present policies in the field.

The next priority for both the Northern and Southern NGOs would be to develop the in-house capacity for advocacy of the policy reforms. At the earliest possible stage it is important to seek allies. A strong network of NGOs calling in unison for reforms makes the case more convincing and provides mutual security against reprisals from entrenched and resentful officials. Official aid agencies should be urged to lend support. Do their projects, for example, provide any relevant evidence? Other allies should also be sought. The case is more likely to be won if it is supported by prominent politicians, respected academics and others with influence.

It may be difficult for Northern NGOs to take a prominent role in such lobbying. This would be resented as "foreigners meddling in our domestic affairs" by governments. They can at least help fund the research, lend advice and experience and help in the dialogue with official aid agencies.

After the case is prepared it is time to seek dialogue with the government. This entails spadework in identifying the right people to approach in the first instance. It is probably best to aim high because in most ministries there is little delegation of power. More junior officials may be able to advise on the best way to take the case forward but more often they will not want to stick their necks out. It may be appropriate to enter into parallel dialogue with officials in local government, parastatals or other relevant institutions.

If reforms are won it may necessitate a revision of the NGO's own programs. The authorities may need practical help to implement the new policies. This can engage the NGO in major new activities. For example, it may be asked to draw up and run a nationwide training program for government officials.

Some Examples of Micro-Policy Reforms

The following examples illustrate policy reforms which have been secured as a result of NGO action. Some have involved campaigning by Northern NGOs and so might also deserve a place in the chapter on international lobbying (10). Some have involved popular mass actions and so could also be quoted as examples of grassroots mobilization. All, however, have involved the direct negotiation between the NGOs and the government or other official body as the principal spur.

Primary Health Care Services, Malawi and Zambia

As health budgets are squeezed by economic crisis, primary health care (PHC) services are often the first to be cut, since it is politically more difficult to cut spending on hospitals in the cities. Though staff may be kept on, other items of recurrent expenditure and capital spending will be hit particularly severely. This leads to an acute shortage of drugs and other equipment, a shortage of vehicles (even bicycles), the cancellation of training programs, poor supervision and low staff morale.

In Malawi there has been increasing pressure on the NGO sector to step up its PHC work. One NGO, the Private Hospitals Association of Malawi (PHAM) which acts as a service for missionary and other NGO health programs, organized a special training program for its primary health care workers. This program broke new ground by concentrating on people's participation in safeguarding their own health. The PHC worker is not so much a technician, bringing cures to those who are sick, but a social animator helping communities resist disease and unhealthy ways of living.

The program was inspiring and motivating for the PHC workers. The government's PHC sector became interested and commissioned PHAM to devise a training program for the entire PHC sector—a considerable undertaking. This program also proved very popular. Unfortunately, the changes in the structure of the service which were hoped for and would have allowed the PHC workers to play a fundamentally different role were not implemented and so the full promise has not been realized.

The PHAM experience, however, was conveyed by Oxfam UK and became an inspiration to health workers in the adjacent Eastern Province of Zambia. They were facing great difficulties as the government service was strangled by budgetary cuts.

Oxfam UK decided to step up its contribution to the health sector in the mid 1980s, but rather than fund an increasing number of NGO projects throughout the country it agreed with the Ministry of Health to explore the possibility of entering into a joint venture in PHC. The double objective was to help strengthen part of the existing health structure (and so make a more sustainable contribution than by creating new, parallel structures) and to bring into the government system some new approaches, such as those pioneered by PHAM in Malawi.

The Ministry welcomed the idea and three districts of Eastern Province were chosen for the collaborative approach. UNICEF was already providing the essential drugs and so Oxfam UK agreed to provide bicycles for PHC workers, vehicles for supervisors and training courses along the PHAM lines. The PHC system had become almost moribund in many of the remoter districts. There were virtually no supplies of drugs or equipment; few vehicles were serviceable; the wages for PHC workers often did not come through and when they did the workers had to make long journeys to the nearest town to collect them and then stand in line for at least a day in order to cash their checks at the bank. The staff were completely demotivated, and many abandoned their posts and returned to their family homes.

It is too early to tell how successful this scheme will be. Working alongside a government service is undoubtedly more frustrating than conventional NGO project work. The bureaucracy works slowly. It often takes dogged persuasion to ensure that vehicles supplied get delivered from Lusaka to their intended destination; and the whole program can easily be jeopardized by the continuing difficulties of getting wages paid promptly. However, there are promising signs of a revitalization of the sector in the three districts. A strong Oxfam UK connection with local nutrition and agriculture groups has helped strengthen the analysis of health care providers and ground the program within the community.[84]

Oxfam UK sees this program as a risk. By NGO standards it is a very costly undertaking with no prospects for the immediate returns which often come from small-scale project work. Also the results, when they come, will not be the highly visible ones which satisfy donors who typically like to hear how many vaccinations or traditional midwives their donation has provided. The consequences of failure are considerable. Not only could the training and vehicles be wasted but it could, at worst, lead to the government abdicating responsibility for PHC in the districts, anticipating that foreign agencies will pick up the tab since they have already invested so much, or to a rift between the NGOs and the Ministry of Health. This is not a criticism of that particular Ministry and there are no signs to date of such difficulties emerging, but they have to be considered as possibilities in any collaborative venture of this nature.

If, on the other hand, the scheme is successful, it will lead to a greatly strengthened health service in the rural areas, to a PHC workforce whose skills are much more carefully attuned to the needs of the rural poor, to much stronger community awareness of preventive health and participation in the health care system, to stronger motivation and an improved career structure for PHC workers, to better planning in the deployment of the scanty financial resources available, and to better cooperation between the public and NGO health sectors. Such a success may inspire similar approaches elsewhere in the country.

These examples illustrate many of the important ingredients of micro-policy reform, namely:

- the need for longer-term planning;
- a wider geographical spread than is customary for NGOs;
- providing support for existing structures;
- seeking changes in existing policies and attitudes;
- less emphasis on delivering and more on facilitating;
- a movement away from controlling the process from beginning to end, toward influencing key aspects of the process;
- developing close working relationships with governments, local officials, other NGOs and others who have a contribution to make;
- the need for strategic management skills and analysis;
- and the importance of training not just to impart technical skills but to teach problem solving techniques and to encourage learning from each other.

Social Forestry, India

Since the early 1980s the government of Karnataka in South India has been implementing a social forestry project, funded until recently by the World Bank and the UK Overseas Development Administration. The objectives were to increase the production of wood for both commercial and domestic use and to increase the incomes of small farmers. The project provided saplings, markets and other incentives to encourage farmers to divert a portion of their land to silviculture (farm forestry). It also made plantations out of common land—that is, wasteland and other land which is used by communities rather than privately owned.

In a country which is facing rapid deforestation these seem to be laudable objectives but many drawbacks were experienced by the poor in the scheme's implementation. Initially there was a very heavy emphasis on planting species of eucalyptus—very fast growing trees whose widespread root system is remarkably efficient at sucking up water. The species has a number of disadvantages (though these are often overstated). Crop yields are likely to be reduced in fields adjacent to eucalyptus plantations and nearby wells can dry up as the trees lower the water table. In Karnataka the eucalyptus harvested was almost all shipped to the local paper and rayon industries and contributed little to household fuel supply, building material, fodder, fertilizer or other domestic needs.

Much of the land which was classified as wasteland was actually an important resource for the poor who regularly used it for grazing their animals, gathering roots and berries and even for cultivation, which was technically illegal since they did not have title deeds but a common practice nevertheless. Once a woodlot had been established on the land the poor were denied access. In the case of land which was classified as common land, belonging to the village, it was agreed that the village would receive the proceeds from sales of produce and would also have certain browsing and wood gathering rights, but this would be controlled by the village councils (*panchayats*) which usually comprise the more powerful members of the community.

The net effect for the poor peasants, therefore, was a switch in farming toward growing trees for industrial pulp purposes (some say at the expense of local food availability, hence leading to food price increases—though the evidence on this is not conclusive), a switch in the use of common lands from purposes in which the poor participate towards purposes which exclude the poor; the physical eviction of many poor people from land which they had been traditionally cultivating, affecting water availability for crops and household purposes, and no increase in availability of forest produce for household purposes.

A consortium of NGOs—the Federation of Voluntary Organizations in Development of Karnataka (FEVORD-K)—carefully documented these problems and enlisted forestry experts to help construct a detailed list of reforms which they took to the project officials. At first they got short shrift but as time elapsed more and more eminent specialists came to see the force of the NGOs' case. Many of the NGOs themselves had impressive track records in forestry projects and so had a considerable credibility. The official funders became aware of the problems (assisted by some Northern NGOs who took up FEVORD-K's case). As a result, in the mid-term review of the project, the funders insisted on certain changes. By this time many of the state government officials were also anxious to see it take a new direction so as to bring it closer to the social objectives declared at the outset.

Although many of the problems remain unresolved there have been major reforms which increase the benefits for the poor. The authorities now buy saplings from peasant cooperatives, thereby affording them a significant new source of income. On common land the emphasis has shifted away from eucalyptus toward trees which provide fruit, browsing, fuel and other household requirements. The project now employs a large number of "motivators" whose purpose is to make the project more relevant to small farmers and the landless. The authorities have declared their commitment to concentrate in future on genuine wasteland, rather than land which is customarily occupied by poor peasants. And they have invited the NGOs to cooperate in implementing some of the reforms.

The Karnataka NGOs' success in making the social forestry project a national *cause célèbre* and in winning some significant reforms has inspired NGOs in Gujarat and other statesto launch similar campaigns. It has also contributed to fanning a national debate on forestry priorities and the need to revise Indian laws on forestry (which remain unchanged from the nineteenth century). This example shows how, with a modest expenditure of time and money, NGOs well versed in a particular sector can influence important changes in official practice which have considerably more impact on the poor than the NGO projects by themselves could possibly have.

Housing for Pavement Dwellers, Bombay

An estimated 100,000 people live on Bombay's pavements with only a rag tent to call their home. These are among the poorest of the poor. Typically they are the most recent migrants from the rural areas—environmental refugees, fleeing from drought and seriously degraded land. By law they have no right to make homes on the pavements and in 1981 the state government attempted to carry out mass evictions without providing any alternative site. Two Bombay-based NGOs took a case in favor of the pavement dwellers to the Supreme Court that was partially successful, determining that the authorities had some responsibility to provide them with alternative sites.

In 1984 a new NGO—the Society for Promotion of Area Resource Centers (SPARC) was established to help the pavement dwellers. The principal aim was to secure better and permanent sites on which the pavement dwellers—particularly the women—could erect their homes. SPARC's first activity was to conduct detailed needs surveys using a participatory research approach. This made it clear that any distant site would be quite unacceptable since it would mean that the majority would lose the little employment that they had. The survey, encouraging people as it did to speak out, had the effect of mobilizing the women. The women leaders who emerged were given training by SPARC and this increased their confidence to take on the authorities.

SPARC has been careful not to negotiate with the government on behalf of the pavement dwellers, but instead to facilitate such negotiation by the communities' leaders. So far the authorities have offered a few possible sites but these have either been too remote, or have required a fragmentation of the communities, which they decided was unacceptable.

Though SPARC cannot yet claim to have won any concrete resettlement, it has established negotiation with the municipal authorities based on the principle that the pavement dwellers have the right to a decent site on which to settle. It has also helped increase the confidence of the squatters and help them resist the early offer of sites which would have proved inappropriate.[85]

Credit For The Informal Sector, Peru

The Lima-based NGO, IDESE, established a scheme providing credit to the informal sector in the Lima area with funding support from European NGOs. The scheme was successful both in helping the poor increase their economic activities and in achieving a high repayment record. Rather than seek to expand the scheme indefinitely, IDESE sought to persuade the commercial banks that the informal sector is creditworthy.

They convinced officials of how effectively the informal sector responds to a modest injection of capital, and the government agreed to introduce a new regulation requiring all banks to allocate a portion of their credit to the poor, against collateral equalling a fifth of the loan. The government was to put up US$10 million for collateral in this scheme but the economic situation deteriorated and the budget line was shelved. The scheme still continues, however, with collateral provided by Novib (a Dutch NGO) and other Northern NGOs.

Compensation For Those Displaced by a Dam, Zaire

The Ruzizi dam electricity project on the border between Zaire and Rwanda displaced 14,000 people in the mid 1980s. The project was funded by the World Bank, whose terms included proper compensation for those displaced. The Zaire authorities made little effort to implement this clause or even to establish the exact numbers of people displaced until after the people had to move. (Though not perfect, the Rwandan authorities were rather fairer to those displaced). The World Bank also made little effort to ensure that its compensation condition was adhered to, and estimated that only 200 people would be displaced.

Careful documentation by NGOs working with the displaced farmers revealed a systematic underreporting of the problem and derisory compensation payments, violating the World Bank's own rules. In Zaire all land technically belongs to the state, hence the authorities decided to assess compensation on the basis of crop values lost. However, their assessment only considered marketed crops, not subsistence crops which were assumed to be of no value but which comprised the bulk of the crops grown on the lost land.

The NGOs submitted a case for fairer compensation to both the Zaire authorities and to the World Bank. They argued not so much for individual compensation, since it would be difficult to locate many of those displaced but for compensating the *communities* affected. At the time of writing, these proposals are being considered by the World Bank and the Zaire authorities.

Irrigation and Forestry in Southeast Asia

The Ford Foundation was keen to support community-based irrigation and forestry programs in Indonesia, the Philippines and Thailand. Rather than establish its own programs, it decided to identify progressive people in indigenous agencies, and then assist them identify and achieve the communities' proposals. The Foundation provided funds for these activities and for research into existing approaches to community resource management. It also held a series of workshops to which NGOs, researchers and the relevant agencies were invited.

This example illustrates the catalytic role that can be played by a funding agency.

Mobilization of Women, Lima

The Peruvian NGO, FOVIDA, was established in 1984 with a particular focus on health care and setting up community kitchens in the Lima slums. For the latter, a large number of poor women join together to cook family meals collectively on a rotating basis. This not only saves a considerable amount of their time, which is particularly important for single mothers and women who work for income, but it also enables a 20 percent saving on the cost of ingredients through bulk buying. At present some 20,000 women take part in this scheme. They organize it themselves and this has resulted in their increased confidence and enhanced status in the city.

Having become organized in this way, the women have joined other causes. Concerned about the nutrition of the young, they urged the government to distribute free milk to children. The government agreed and so a "Glass of Milk per Day" national scheme was instituted, with the EEC providing the milk.

Following this success, the women decided to press for an improved, more hygienic water supply in their slum communities. They strengthened their case by organizing marches and demonstrations. Eventually the authorities agreed to establish some experimental programs along the lines of those suggested by FOVIDA. These are being funded by Japanese aid.

Focal Countries Program on the Environment

The London- and Paris-based NGO, the Panos Institute, has embarked on a major program to increase the capacity of NGOs and journalists to respond to environmental problems in seven countries (Kenya, Tanzania, Zambia, India, Sri Lanka, Bangladesh and Indonesia). Though supported by Southern NGOs, the program was the initiative of the Dutch and Scandinavian official aid agencies who provide the funds. The starting point in each country has been a series of five-day workshops bringing together NGOs, journalists, researchers and others concerned with environmental issues (sometimes including government officials) to review the major programs and then to decide on a course of action which suits the concerns and ambitions of the participants. Panos provides technical help and advice, funding for the agreed plans, information (which is often easier to acquire in Europe than in Third World countries) and news about environmental issues and citizens' actions elsewhere. Although still in its infancy, the program is discovering the need to adopt very different styles of work in different countries.

In Sri Lanka, Panos assisted the local NGOs to establish the Sri Lankan Environmental Congress, bringing together some 170 NGOs ranging from Colombo-based research organizations employing highly qualified ecologists to a rural-based grassroots organization. The Congress started to campaign on several issues (such as opposing a coal-fired power station planned in Trincomalee) and initially adopted a fairly confrontational style. They rapidly discovered that the government was quite receptive to their arguments. The Trincomalee plan was dropped, and now a separate environmental appraisal is required for all major projects of this nature. The importing of hazardous wastes has also been banned, and NGOs have been brought in to implement compensatory forestation programs alongside the massive Mahaweli irrigation and hydroelectric scheme.

As a result of the responsiveness of the government, the NGOs are now adopting a less confrontational stance, and are placing more attention on building up a dialogue with the authorities. The government, in turn, has become more comfortable with the NGOs and has now invited five NGO representatives on to the Sri Lanka National Environment Council. This Council comprises about twenty heads of major organizations and ministries and reports to the Prime Minister on the environmental ramifications of all major development projects.

In Bangladesh, following the Panos workshop in 1987, NGOs and journalists visited the site of a large dam in Comilla District which was funded by the Asian Development Bank. They discovered that important environmental issues had been overlooked, that, in fact, no environmental study had been commissioned and that those displaced had not received the compensation promised. They commissioned a comprehensive study of the issues, including an environmental impact appraisal (with Panos funding). Their report was published in 1989 and, although it was highly critical of the project, the country's Prime Minister presided at the launch.

In some of the other focal countries NGOs have also moved away from organizing mass protests in favor of taking up cases through the legal system. While still a confrontational approach, this entails bringing in an important part of the establishment on the NGOs' side of the argument. Conversely, in some countries the main NGOs are very weak and it has proved more effective to work with journalists (to raise national awareness of environmental issues) and with sympathizers in government. For example, in Tanzania there is now considerably more discussion about environmental issues in the newspapers and in Zambia government officials helped to organize meetings bringing together tribal chiefs. The latter are of pivotal importance in changing public attitudes and in local level planning.

The "push-style" campaigning of demonstrations and litigation is effective in South Asia but would be totally inappropriate in much of Africa today. Conversely the "pull-style," starting with the national elite, is suitable in countries such as Zambia but would be anathema elsewhere.

Some Pointers for the Future

The relatively scanty experience of micro-policy reform activities provide a number of lessons for future planning which would help to broaden NGO activity from funding and service delivery to catalyzing change.

Develop a Strategic Rather than a Tactical Approach

The traditional NGO approach is to concentrate on service-delivery and village-level interventions, often disconnected from a broader, national context. The language of participation and empowerment conventionally refers to the poor's relationship with the project itself and to decisions and practices at the very local level. As the Asian NGO Coalition, ANGOC, says, "questions of development theory and official policy were left largely to the experts."[86]

Increasingly, however, NGO leaders are recognizing that they and the poor themselves have an equal right to be regarded as experts. As the condition of the poor continues to decline it is evident that we need to reshape our ideas of development. NGOs could play a critical role in this revision.

> [NGOs] are now questioning official policy processes, existing development theories, and their own inclination to wholly accept government leadership in setting the directions of national development policy. . . .

Broader effective participation in the decision making process by which
both local and national development decisions are shaped is increasingly
seen by NGOs as the key to future development progress in South and
South East Asia. Development catalyst NGOs must constantly resist the
pressure to be drawn into permanent service delivery roles. Instead
NGOs must support effective resource management in government by
helping to shift greater control and management of resources to the
people, with government assuming an enabling role.[87]

The challenge for NGOs therefore is to learn how to be concerned with
influencing key aspects of a wider development process rather than
seeking to control micro-development projects from beginning to end.
They must learn how to facilitate as well as deliver.

Develop Planning and Management for Change

The strategic way of working demands much longer time frames than do
typical NGO projects, and requires attention to a wider geographical
spread. This necessitates a much broader knowledge of the geography of
the country and of the society and politics. These have to be combined in a
careful planning strategy and demand a management capacity which some
NGOs are inclined to resist. It also requires much greater attention to
training, with emphasis not so much on the technical aspects of
development, but on building up capacity to analyze, to plan, to
communicate, to negotiate, to set objectives and other skills normally
associated with management in the business sector rather than the NGO
world.

Strengthen Existing Structures

Official structures may be inefficient, inequitable, even corrupt, but they
are usually widespread and permanent. Alternative structures created by
NGOs may be paragons of virtue in comparison but they are likely to be
severely limited in outreach and temporary in nature. Their scale is
determined by the numbers of dedicated and effective staff they can
recruit, and their lifespan determined by the length of time they can
secure funding. If the NGOs were resolute in describing their projects as
illustrations of a different way of doing things, as *beacons* based not on
magic or charisma but on a *methodology which others could follow,* then
they might find more opportunities for influencing existing structures.

Planning withdrawal is inevitably more difficult for NGOs than planning
growth, and few do it. Those relying on foreign funds experience the
familiar problem, namely that donors prefer to fund new ideas rather than
old ones. Some, achieve permanence through generating the funds
required locally. Many evaporate once funding becomes difficult to secure.

The middle path between transience and immortality is seeking redundancy—the highest ambition of development workers. Redundancy can come about by the state fully taking on board the lessons taught by, and the services provided by, the NGO.

Establish New Allies

There is a tendency toward insularity within the NGO sector, but influencing policies and practices clearly necessitate forging new working relationships with government officials at both national and local levels. This may require changes in the NGO's own staffing. For example, Northern NGOs should consider employing nationals rather than expatriates as their representatives as government officials are more likely to heed what they say. NGO advocacy representatives should also not be identified with any anti-government factions and should appear politically mature.

Those who are well connected to senior decision makers or who command broad public respect are important allies in micro-policy reform. The NGO, if it has an open mind, may also find that the issue of concern is not quite as clear cut as it seems on the surface and that it has a lot to learn from others who know the issue or the country well.

These factors indicate the need for NGOs to build much broader coalitions than they are accustomed to, working closely, for example, with the academic community, with the business sector, with politicians, trade unionists, religious leaders and others who have access to the ears that need bending or to the knowledge that the bending process requires.

Avoiding dialogue because this risks compromising one's position is unrealistic and immature. Social change is about compromise because it is about balancing opposing forces—typically the tension pulling toward reform versus the resistance of the *status quo*. A pressure group which achieves a significant reform may be well satisfied with the progress—and say so publicly—even if only 20 percent of their demands have been met. This does not imply that the group has dropped or lost faith in the remaining 80 percent, rather that it considers it politic to consolidate the initial gains.

Negotiate a New Role

Strategic NGOs need to convince others at the development stage of the validity of their new influencing role. They must seek to be consulted on policy issues and be prepared to serve on government commissions. This process can have major ramifications for NGO leaders. In some countries they have been persuaded to leave the NGO sector and to move into government. They are not "selling-out" but are developing a more effective platform on which to make the NGO case. As Eduardo Garilao says, "Third World NGO leaders will begin to enter into public service and politics because, in addressing the structural problems of poverty, it is the logical next step."[88] Likewise with official aid agencies, NGOs must maneuver into a closer relationship so that they can help formulate policies and project design.

Some within the official agencies are advocating this new relationship. Cernea points out that a World Bank impact study of twenty-five projects concluded that the principal reason some Bank projects failed to be sustainable was non-involvement of grassroots organizations.[89] When local organizations were involved the projects endured. Evidence such as this is leading many aid officials to recognize that allowing NGOs negotiating space, in particular to introduce ideas of popular participation, will strengthen their own projects.

Develop New Partnerships

NGOs, like businesses, are moving into the information age. The "software" of their trade—ideas, research, empowerment and networking—is rapidly becoming more important than their "hardware"—the time-bound, geographically fixed projects, such as wells and clinics. In this new age, information and influence are the dominant currencies rather than dollars and pounds.[90] A failure to recognize this is likely to lead Southern and Northern NGOs into an anachronistic relationship.

Just as they must take on new responsibilities in order to preserve their relationships, Northern NGOs must also relinquish others. The "crucial issue is the transfer of power" to Southern NGOs.[91] In particular, decisions over project funding should increasingly be transferred to Southern specialists. It is lamentable that, as the century draws to a close, there is a colonial residue which still believes that decisions concerning poverty alleviation in India can be better made in London or New York than on the spot, where the real expertise lies.

The North–South NGO partnership must not be a jealous one. It must allow room for others. It is important to build new alliances with environment, human rights and women's groups, with consumers' associations, trade unions, professional bodies, academic institutions and others, all of whom have an important contribution to make toward influencing. Northern NGOs must be prepared to move to a more secondary place. If the influencing role is to become significant then the closest partners of the Southern NGO must be indigenous institutions and the government itself, rather than Northern NGOs, as is usually the case at present. The latter, as Garilao says, must help Southern NGOs to define what they want to do, rather than define the agenda for them.[92] They must look beyond their traditional resource–transfer role to invest in the capacity building of their Third World partners.

This relegates Northern NGOs to a lower status in the devising of the grassroots development strategy. However, in other areas a much higher profile is called for, particularly in the field of international lobbying to supplement the case being argued by the Southern NGOs. The reluctance of many funding NGOs to adopt this enhanced advocacy profile is leading to a shifting allegiance within the NGO community. Many Southern NGOs are moving away from their traditional partners who fund them and striking up closer bonds with Northern advocacy organizations such as the environmental pressure groups. For example, grassroots NGOs working with indigenous tribal people in India and Brazil are coming to identify more closely with human rights organizations such as Survival International and with lobbying organizations such as the Washington-based Environment Defense Fund than with their longer standing Northern funders. They are one step ahead of their funders in recognizing that well-placed pressure for international policy change is a more precious development resource than money.

Part Three

Redefining Development

10

International Lobbying

Don't Just Do Something. Stand There!

Most Northern NGOs spend a small portion of their budgets on development education—to influence their own societies about Third World issues. They seek to give a more accurate impression of the Third World, particularly to school children. The commonplace images of perennial starvation, mass ignorance, scorched earth and beggary are challenged by images of vibrant cultures, ingenuity and self-reliance. Discussion of the problems faced by developing countries emphasizes the social, historical and political factors.

Though with schools NGOs avoid overt bias, NGOs are adopting a more propagandist, action-oriented approach with the general public, calling on their supporters to join in advocacy or lobbying campaigns. They quite deliberately seek to influence decision makers into changing some aspects of policy or practice.

A two-pronged approach is needed. No matter how well researched their case and articulate their presenters, significant political change is unlikely unless there is a groundswell of public opinion demanding those changes. The converse is also the case. If a campaign skillfully mobilizes public opinion but does not have a watertight argument, the decision makers will find it easy to dismiss it as little more than hot air. Hence an NGO needs skills of both lobbying and public campaigning. Their supporters must be informed about the issue in question, invited to join the lobbying (for example by raising the issue with their local elected official or by writing letters to decision makers) and asked to help mobilize public opinion (for example, through publicity stunts or writing letters to newspapers).

Effective lobbying affords a powerful and increasingly important means for NGOs to multiply their impact on significant development questions, ranging from the design of specific World Bank projects to the debt crisis. Such lobbying on the international stage has been largely dominated by Northern NGOs until recently, with Southern NGOs concentrating their efforts on influencing decision makers within their own countries. This is beginning to change quite swiftly.

Northern NGOs are increasingly being challenged by their Southern partners to put more resources into education, campaigning and advocacy. An international meeting of Southern NGO leaders in June 1989, for example, called on their Northern counterparts to monitor and campaign on issues such as official aid and multinational corporations (the Manila Declaration). African NGOs meeting at the UN Special Session on Africa in 1986 drafted a declaration which, *inter alia,* called on Northern NGOs to "reorientate their activities" toward development education, advocacy and information flows, and in particular to attack "policies of their governments, corporations and multilateral institutions . . . which adversely affect the quality of life and political and economic independence of African countries" (The Declaration of NGOs on the African Economic and Social Crisis). In 1989 a larger gathering of African NGOs and officials meeting in Arusha made similar points.[93] And many Latin American NGO leaders have called for a new relationship with Northern NGOs in which influencing is the shared goal. For instance, Mario Padron criticized the majority of Northern NGOs for their reluctance to spend money on development education, saying that they "accept too easily the idea that funds are only for the poor."[94] A new, genuinely two-way relationship between Northern and Southern NGOs, in which development education in the North is a shared responsibility, is essential, he argues, for moving "from development aid to development cooperation."

Southern NGOs are saying that it is not enough to give money, what is needed is political action to help them in the struggle to get the Rich North off the backs of the South's Poor. As Larry Minear points out, in effect they are saying, "Don't just do something. Stand there!"[95]

All but the most unobservant NGOs working with the poor must have experience of international factors exacerbating problems of poverty. More often than not, however, they fail to take action on them. This could be because they don't see it as their job to do so, because they distrust the anecdotal nature of their own evidence, because they feel powerless to effect change or because they fear reprisals from indulging in political action, both from host governments and from donors. The dangers and drawbacks are valid but can be surmounted.

Not The NGO's Job

The NGO decides its own work objectives—these haven't been handed down from a higher power. For instance, the NGO will move from hospital-oriented to primary health care when convinced of the superiority of prevention over cure. It should equally be prepared to take up "preventive development"—that is, lobbying to eradicate impediments to just development. This does not mean giving up conventional project work ("curative development") but instead seeing advocacy as a natural extension of its project work.

Many Northern NGOs have assumed the role of ambassadors for the world's poor. With this goes a responsibility to represent the political concerns of the poor, to be a conduit for popular democracy. This entails helping to make the political and economic institutions of the world more broadly accountable, injecting the voice of the traditionally voiceless into international decision making and facilitating the two-way flow of information that might both improve decision making and improve the capacity of the poor to influence those decisions.

Progressive NGOs may agree with this in theory, but in practice neglect to act. Advocacy may be seen as *important* but it is not *urgent.* Consequently it is easily squeezed out by the day-to-day dilemmas and crises arising from the project activities, from donor pressures and from media enquiries.

International factors are not necessarily the most important root causes of poverty but they are ones which Northern NGOs should not ignore. If they do so they must expect to be viewed with increasing suspicion by their Southern partners. The latter are making it increasingly clear that they want a more equal partnership. As donors expect regular financial and progress reports from the projects they fund, so Southern NGOs are starting to ask their donors to report to them on the action they are taking to educate Northern publics and to tackle the international causes of global poverty.

The question should not be whether international advocacy is the job for a Northern NGO. It is whether NGOs which neglect this role should have a job at all.

Anecdotal Evidence

When pitted against great volumes of statistical data, evidence that an NGO may have of the impact of a particular policy on the poor living in one community may seem insubstantial and anecdotal. This lack of confidence is unwarranted.

To get a portrait of a city there are two approaches. The first is to charter an airplane and take photographs of the city from the air. This shows the main housing areas, the industrial complexes, the principal buildings, the main communication routes and the physical terrain. It is a complete view but it only allows guesses to be made about the condition of life in the different quarters. The alternative approach is to visit particular communities or workplaces, talk to the community workers or residents and stay with them long enough to appreciate their concerns and aspirations. This gives a more accurate portrait of the human condition, but a patchy view—a snapshot of a few streets, districts or ethnic groups.

Since development is essentially about the human condition, the street view is at least as valid as the aerial view and one in which the NGO has unchallenged advantage. The street view is perhaps less scientific but it may reveal serious problems and important issues which are not picked up by the aerial view. Whether or not these issues are general or unique to the community studied is important, but the uncertainty should not prevent the NGO from making its experience known. NGOs should make little apology for the somewhat anecdotal nature of their evidence, infuriating as development economists often find it.

For example, in 1987 through its work in two poor districts of Malawi (Phalombe and Mulanje), Oxfam UK became concerned about the costs to the poor of closing down the agricultural parastatal's marketing depots. As part of the World Bank-funded structural adjustment program, the government of Malawi had agreed to start dismantling a number of parastatals, including the Agricultural Development and Marketing Corporation (ADMARC). There is no doubt that some changes in ADMARC were required, since it was losing money heavily. However, most of the losses were on its estate management and food processing operations. The "bread and butter" task of basic agricultural marketing was widely regarded as one of the more efficient examples of state marketing operations in Africa.

Traditionally, ADMARC bought cereals after harvest, sold some to the cities and stored the remainder in its rural depots. Some months later the rural poor would have run out of the food they kept back after harvest for their own use and they would engage in wage-labor activities. They would then purchase food back from ADMARC depots. When the World Bank-inspired program of market liberalization came in, licenses were given to private merchants to buy and sell cereals and other crops. In the regions where it was felt that there were sufficient private traders to fill the gap, the ADMARC depots were closed down. ADMARC was to be reduced to a trader of last resort.

From its contact with poor farmers in these areas, particularly with female-headed households, Oxfam UK became concerned that the valuable food security role played by ADMARC would be lost. Oxfam UK relayed these concerns to the World Bank, however the closure of depots continued. Come the harvest, most of the sales in Phalombe and Mulanje were to private merchants. As the NGO had predicted, when, a few months later, farmers came to buy back food, they found they simply couldn't afford the prices. Whereas traditionally the buying price would be about 20 percent higher than the sale price at harvest time, the merchants were charging up to 700 percent of the sale price. It was proving more profitable to sell the food in the nearby city of Blantyre. This resulted in immense difficulties for the poor in that region.[96]

When this fresh evidence was presented, the Bank became responsive. It investigated the claims and found them to be accurate in certain districts of the country. Generally, they maintained, the new system was working well but they did admit that mistakes had been made which should be corrected by strengthening the food security role played by ADMARC in vulnerable regions.

This is an illustration of how NGO evidence, based on day-to-day contact with poor people in a dozen villages in one region, revealed a problem which had been overlooked by the aerial view and led to the authorities pledging to take corrective action.

Powerlessness to Effect Change

It is true that one NGO acting by itself has little chance of bringing about significant change just by presenting its evidence in isolation. But when the well-argued case is strengthened through an effective campaign strategy a much greater force can be generated. Northern institutions take very seriously criticisms from the media, from politicians and from figures of authority. A campaign which engages numerous NGOs—all of whose supporters are, say, urged to write to their elected officials, generate articles in their local newspapers or take other action—may attract the interest of the media and politicians and become a *cause célèbre*.

In this way combinations of NGOs and public opinion have initiated major policy changes by Northern governments on a number of issues including:

- a code of conduct for the marketing of baby milk;
- the drafting of an international essential drugs list;
- removing restrictions on the importation of certain clothing manufactured in the Third World, such as shirts from Bangladesh;
- establishing an emergency reserve so that EEC food surpluses become more readily available for famine relief;
- concerted action on international environmental issues such as global warming and rainforest destruction;
- affording special debt relief to poor African countries; and
- the imposition of sanctions to combat apartheid.

If it were possible to assess the value to the poor of all such reforms, they might be worth more than the financial contribution made by NGOs. Yet only a tiny fraction of NGO resources are directed to such work.

It may be possible to win the support of Northern or international institutions such as the World Bank when it proves impossible to influence a

Southern government in question. For example, after two years of campaigning, Indian NGOs found that they had little success in persuading the authorities to plan a proper resettlement scheme for the 80,000 people who are to be displaced by a major dam on the Narmada River. They enlisted the support of Northern NGOs to help take their case to the World Bank, which was to fund a large part of the costs of the hydroelectric and irrigation project. After protracted campaigning involving NGOs throughout the world, the Bank agreed to make its funding conditional on a carefully worked out resettlement scheme being put into place. Although the Indian authorities agreed to this, at the time of writing many of the promises have not been fully honored and the future of the loan still hangs in the balance. If, eventually, a genuinely progressive resettlement scheme is implemented this will set a precedent which will greatly strengthen the future prospects for some 2 million Indian people who are scheduled to be displaced by projects already on the drawing board.

NGOs do have enough influence to effect change but only when they act together and plan strategically to maximize their power.

Political Reprisals

NGOs which engage in lobbying can expect trouble to follow. If they don't experience a backlash it indicates that their lobbying is ineffective. Winning change in favor of the poor will inevitably be at someone's expense and those parties will seek to fight back, usually in ways designed to discredit the NGOs.

Risks can be minimized by careful campaign planning. NGOs should broadcast why lobbying and campaigning is an essential part of their work, why they feel that it is their duty to share with their supporters and the general public the evidence they accumulate from their direct experience. They should ensure that their case is well researched, free from prejudice and that political conclusions drawn are restricted to those which really do stem from the NGO's direct or indirect experience.

In the United Kingdom, charities who have done this has have helped moderate the government's line. The recent White Paper[97] makes it clear that seeking to influence policy changes by means of rational persuasion is considered by the government to be a legitimate activity, so long as it is ancillary to the charity's main concern. And in the United States there was a change in tax laws in the 1970s which facilitates lobbying by voluntary organizations.

It is important to build strong networks of NGOs and perhaps avoid any one NGO being identified as the leader of that network. This affords security of numbers to guard against reprisals from offended governments. NGOs should also seek allies in other quarters. The more people of clout outside the NGO sector who add their voice the more difficult it will be for the authorities to dismiss the lobby as an unrepresentative fringe.

Who Should Lobby

Until the 1980s most lobbying on international issues in the North was by specialist advocacy groups such as the World Development Movement in the United Kingdom and Bread for the World in the United States. These NGOs were typically run by politically minded people from the churches and development NGOs, and partly funded from those sources. But they remained independent and increasingly funded by, and answerable to, their own memberships, comprising largely well-read, liberal activists. Operational NGOs produce occasional reports on contentious policy issues but would rarely follow these reports through with concerted lobbying. Their advocacy was largely confined to arguing for increased official funding for their own activities.

For example, War on Want in the United Kingdom produced the first published report on the baby formula controversy in 1974 but left it to specialist campaigning groups to lobby on the issue. It was not until 1979 that War on Want together with the Baby Milk Action Coalition and Oxfam UK mounted a successful public campaign to win British Government support for a proposed code of conduct to restrict the marketing activities of the manufacturers, though by that time there had been considerable campaigning in other countries.

Operational NGOs have been slow to move into lobbying. Until the early 1980s their educational activity (e.g. the house newspaper, leaflets, slide sets, films and so on) tended to emphasize the NGO's own project experience rather than the political issues of development. And their development education work in schools avoided an action agenda, though it frequently dealt with controversial issues such as the actions of multinational corporations. They did little public campaigning. This is unfortunate because they are well placed to influence Northern governments. The public at large knows them, trusts them and has faith in their motives. Politicians and "experts" respect the field-level evidence they bring. The media like the first-hand nature of their experience. Official aid agencies want to build closer programmatic connections and so are disposed to listen carefully to what they have to say. And celebrities stand ready to be identified with their causes.

Experience of numerous campaigns shows that a modest input of time and resources can lead to quite significant policy shifts. In spite of this, the largest NGOs, especially in the United States, have put very few resources into such activities. Throughout the 1980s, however, this began to change and operational NGOs started taking slightly more courageous steps toward lobbying. Their principal umbrella organization, the International

Council of Voluntary Agencies, has drafted a policy briefing, "Making Common Cause Internationally," to help and encourage member agencies to formulate their individual policies on campaigning and advocacy.

Operational NGOs are having to change. They are under increasing pressure from their Southern partners to become more active in both educational and lobbying activities in their home countries. The famine in Africa of 1984–85 demonstrated more clearly than ever the need for closer interaction between NGOs and official aid agencies, and the futility of NGO efforts if not combined with much bolder efforts to change development priorities. And they have seen that the pioneers of NGO lobbying have largely "gotten away with it"; neither their charitable status nor their donor base has been eroded—and in fact they appear to enjoy increased media coverage and public support as a result of these new activities.

What is more, the increasing environmental consciousness of politicians and the general public has heralded a new sense of realism. Conventional NGO project activities are manifestly finger-in-the-dike responses to problems that require nothing short of worldwide and wholehearted governmental commitment to combat. This commitment is only likely to arise from concerted public pressure and hence NGOs have a special responsibility to do what they can to galvanize public opinion.

There are other trends which allow optimism for the future of NGO lobbying activities: the growth of campaigning activities among Southern NGOs, new alliances with campaigning groups outside of the development sphere and the emergence of highly specialized campaign groups and networks.

Southern Campaigning NGOs

Some Southern NGOs have prioritized lobbying in recent years, particularly in Latin America and Asia. Most of their attention has focused on domestic rather than international issues, but this is changing, especially as many of the problems they address have clear Northern connections.

These NGOs may, like their Northern counterparts, comprise highly educated, politicized staff and have a Western outlook and communications style. Or they may be grassroots organizations which have direct experience of the problems. For example, the rubber tappers union and a number of tribal groups in Brazil have led worldwide action for international responsibility for the protection of the Amazon rainforests. And village-level health workers have provided much of the evidence on which campaigns against the marketing malpractices of baby formula and pharmaceutical manufacturers have been based.

Many of these grassroots organizations have long had connections with Northern NGOs but the funding relationship has been the basis for this. They now seek a different form of partnership in which the Northern NGOs lend their name, media skills and contact with people of influence to help champion the cause they are fighting.

New Campaigning Alliances

The increased prominence of Southern NGOs has both strengthened international lobbying and changed its focus. Campaigns for the New International Economic Order, for official aid targets and for commodity agreements have given way to campaigns against environment-damaging logging operations, against marketing malpractices by Western companies and against inhuman adjustment programs. The former set dwell on the unjust treatment of poor nations by rich ones, while the latter set dwell on the injustices done to poor people. The former set demand Northern institutions "to *do* something," implying that their sin has been past *failure to act,* rather than the active causing of damage. The latter set call for harmful practices to be stopped.

These trends have not only fostered new allegiances between Northern and Southern NGOs but have also opened doors to movements outside the development sphere. At the same time, as development NGOs have become more concerned with other social issues, so too various social movements have become more concerned with development and international issues.

International action on hazardous practices in the marketing of pesticides first brought a group of development and environmental NGOs together from the North and South. This was followed by concerted action against careless planning of big dams, and later by the launch of international campaigning on the rainforest issue. Similarly, the analysis by NGOs of the gender relationships in development has engaged the interest of the women's movement. They have helped campaign against male bias in development planning.

Campaigns to reform or scrap projects which involve the displacement of large numbers of people have been greatly strengthened by the support of Northern human rights groups. For example, Survival International and other Northern NGOs have joined forces with Indonesian NGOs against the World Bank-funded transmigration program. In this scheme tens of thousands of people have been moved from the densely populated islands—especially Java—to the sparsely populated territory of Irian Jaya where the culture and environment of the indigenous tribes has become severely threatened. Other campaign issues have brought developmental NGOs together with labor unions (e.g. regarding the conditions of Bolivian tin miners) and with consumers organizations (such as regarding the dumping of hazardous products in the Third World).

Specialist Campaign Groups

Many international campaigns have been successful because they have been led by NGOs uniquely set up for the purpose. Though small in staff terms these have the advantage of being able to concentrate totally on their chosen issue, and to have spokespeople with direct experience of it.

Examples are to be seen in the Canadian NGO Probe International concentrating on environmentally damaging energy generating programs; a number of "solidarity groups" campaigning on specific geopolitical issues such as Nicaragua or the Philippines; and of course the anti-apartheid movement campaigning for international sanctions against South Africa and other action.

Of particular importance are the specialized networks which bring together in an exciting and equal partnership NGOs from North and South, from the development community and from other disciplines. For example, both the International Baby Foods Action Network (IBFAN) and Health Action International (HAI)—which campaigns against the marketing malpractices of pharmaceutical companies—comprise NGOs, health professionals, consumer groups, women's organizations and others. Other networks campaign on the EEC's Common Agricultural Policy, the marketing of pesticides, rainforest destruction, Third World debt, the provision of development aid to Cambodia and a variety of other issues. The important lesson learned from the effectiveness of this networking is that, through coordination, the whole can become more than the sum of the parts.

What NGOs Lobby For

The range of issues has evolved over time as the profile of lobbying NGOs has evolved and the increasing contribution of Southern NGOs to international lobbying endeavors has shifted the focus of this lobbying from the macro concerns of Southern governments to issues which are of more direct relevance to Southern people.

The Seventies

In the early 1970s the major campaigning activities of Northern NGOs followed an agenda which was largely determined by the UN system, in particular by the objectives declared for the Second Development Decade and by the FAO's Freedom From Hunger Campaign. This trend continued throughout the 1970s with attention generated by the World Food Conference in 1974 and UNCTAD IV in 1976.[98] Much of the NGO campaigning was rather untargeted in nature. It sought to bring about more caring attitudes among Northern publics and decision makers, and to describe the immoral contrast between Western opulence and Third World misery, rather than to lever for specific changes or new policies. Where specific targets were set they again reflected the UN offered agenda. Examples were campaigns to reach the 0.7 percent of GNP target for official aid, to increase the multilateral (as opposed to bilateral) component of official aid, to set up specific commodity agreements and to support proposals for the New International Economic Order.

In parallel to these campaigning activities was a more politically charged strand, which attacked multinational corporations for exploiting the Third World. These campaigns were little financed by establishment sources, were usually run by highly committed but inexperienced volunteers and were highly effective at capturing the public imagination. One of the earliest examples of this was a British campaign in which the World Development Movement and War on Want joined forces to challenge the below-starvation wages paid by the United Kingdom food giants to tea pickers in Sri Lanka and elsewhere. This achieved massive media coverage and forced some of the major tea companies to revise their employment practices.

Another British campaign, which subsequently spread to other countries, was the attack on coffee multinationals by the specially formed Campaign Cooperative. This group financed their venture by selling instant coffee they imported directly from a government-owned factory in Tanzania. The coffee also formed the vehicle for their message—"political packaging"—and for action. Their supporters set up stalls to sell the "Campaign Coffee," persuaded their student unions to switch to it, got local shops to stock it and organized coffee mornings using it.

This was an early example of an NGO importing a basic commodity. Similar ventures during the 1970s, particularly in Holland, have influenced an important category of NGOs which are today known as alternative marketing organizations. For example, the Max Havelaar campaign in Holland has now captured some 2.4 percent of the country's coffee market for its own brand name: In this case the consortium of NGOs license the names; they do not import the coffee themselves. Instead, they persuade major Dutch coffee roasters to import from suppliers on a list they provide, offer some collateral to safeguard imports and arrange the advertising and promotion.

The Baby Formula Campaign

In the late 1970s development campaigning became considerably more sophisticated. A landmark was the international baby formula campaign.

The problem of marasmus induced by the unhygienic use of bottle feeds in the Third World had been discussed by health workers throughout the 1960s. However, it wasn't until 1973 that the issue, and its relation to the aggressive marketing of those products in the Third World by the manufacturers, was brought into the public domain by the magazine *New Internationalist*. The following year War on Want (WOW) produced a report called "The Baby Killers." A small Swiss pressure group translated the WOW report into German under the provocative title "Nestlé Kills Babies"—the Swiss-based multinational being the dominant Third World supplier of baby formula. Nestlé filed a libel action which they technically won; however, the outcome was generally seen as a triumph for the campaigners. The judge in summing up made it clear that the moral victory went to the campaigners.

The international publicity generated by this case triggered intense citizen action in the United States. A church group called Interfaith Center for Corporate Responsibility (ICCR) organized pressure from church leaders and shareholders. And a small group of baby formula campaigners, inspired by Ralph Nader's new radical consumer movement, set up the Infant Formula Action Group (INFACT) whose main purpose was to organize an extremely effective nationwide boycott of all Nestlé products.

In October 1979 the World Health Organization and UNICEF organized a meeting of unprecedented composition. It brought together in Geneva for the first time representatives of governments, health professional bodies, the industry and the NGO sector. The stormy meeting eventually agreed to recommend to the World Health Assembly that an international code of conduct be drafted to restrict the marketing activities of the baby formula companies.

An incidental outcome of this event was the physical coming together for the first time of many of the major NGOs—Northern and Southern— which had been active on the issue. Until this time the NGOs had corresponded with each other but few had met. They decided to maintain and broaden this new partnership and so, after the formal meeting closed, representatives from six NGOs held a press conference to announce the launch of the International Baby Foods Action Network (IBFAN). Within a year there were well over one hundred NGOs within the network, including a number of very experienced Southern NGOs.

Thanks to the efforts of IBFAN and its member agencies, the 1981 World Health Assembly was to debate the adoption of an International Code of Marketing of Breastmilk Substitutes—the first global agreement ever to restrict the marketing practices of multinational corporations. The 1981 Assembly—normally a sober occasion—was a hive of lobbying, bribery and intrigue. Confidential telexes to the US State Department were leaked which showed collusion between US officials and the industry in a plan to steer the Assembly away from its course of consensus. And media exposés of the political inclinations of the activists in prestigious journals were shown to have been generously financed by by Nestlé, as part of its orchestrated plan to discredit its critics.

These dubious activities backfired on the industry and served to harden the attitude of delegates in favor of the proposed Code. When it came to the vote only one government, the United States, opposed it. Ironically, this was the country where citizens' action had been most prominent.

Since this momentous Assembly, IBFAN has continued to play a prominent and powerful role. It has lobbied at the national level in many countries for governmental and legislative action to make the code effective and binding. And it has published regular reports describing continued violations of the code by major manufacturers.

Many governments have taken significant action and as a result some of the more offensive marketing practices have been curbed. The politicization of the issue has also prompted many governments to invest heavily in breastfeeding promotion campaigns which have helped to reverse the trend toward the bottle.

Sadly, there has been no evaluation of this campaign. Were one able to calculate the global results—in terms of infant lives saved, reduction in infant diarrhea and marasmus, the return to breast feeding and the wasted foreign exchange saved—it would almost certainly conclude that the combined effort of NGOs, WHO, UNICEF and others has been one of the most cost effective ventures in infant health care ever.

The Eighties

Lobbying and campaigning have continued to become more sophisticated and targeted throughout the 1980s. The campaigns tend to focus on aid, trade, international finance and foreign policy in the governmental domain; and buying, selling, investing and employment practices in the corporate sphere. The major trends have been an *increasing strength* of the NGO lobby, a more *strategic approach* to advocacy, closer *integration* of lobbying and public campaigning/education and more attention to the use of the *media*.

The increasing strength of the NGO lobby comes in part from the substantial resources some of the larger Northern NGOs with overseas operations have begun to put into advocacy activities and from the growing credibility of the NGO sector as a whole.

Learning how best to use democratic channels has led to more strategic lobbying. For example, many US groups and coalitions regularly present evidence to congressional committees and draft bills for individual congresspeople and senators (the structure of the US political system gives greater opportunities for this than in most other countries). In the United Kingdom NGOs frequently submit evidence to select committees or to other parliamentary bodies and distribute briefings to MPs prior to debates on international issues. Furthermore, events on the mainstream political calendar are used more systematically as forums to present NGO concerns (for example the World Health Assembly on the marketing of pharmaceuticals, the World Bank Annual Meeting on "problem projects," the Group of Seven summit on debt).

NGOs have become more forthright in inviting their supporters and the public at large to join in the lobbying. Their publicity materials regularly suggest action in addition to making donations. This, together with public concern generated by the African famine and mounting environmental crises, has sharply increased public support for NGO campaigns. For example, the Fight World Poverty lobby of the United Kingdom parliament in 1985 set an all-time record for the number of people who met their MPs in a single day. Westminster was besieged for the whole day, every meeting room in the Commons was booked for the occasion, some 16,000 people managed to meet their MP and several thousand more took part in other meetings.

NGOs have also formed closer links with journalists and broadcast media. Their causes are, as a result, more likely to be the subject of documentaries and feature articles. And their events are more likely to be planned with a view to being media worthy. Some of the more significant campaigning throughout the 1980s is described below.

Aid. Pressure for increasing official aid, using the UN target of 0.7 percent of GNP, remains a familiar agenda item for Northern NGOs. In some countries such as Finland and Italy, there have been considerable increases in aid budgets as a result. However, campaigns for increasing the quality of official aid (as defined by NGOs this means increasing the benefits and reducing the costs for the poor) have become of greater significance. In the United Kingdom the Campaign for Real Aid (described by the government as the development lobby's most significant venture at the time) was backed by a number of development academics as well as NGOs.

Trade. With a few notable exceptions, campaigning on the economic issue of trade has been relatively unexciting. Most NGOs agree that Trade is a far more important subject than aid. The problems are very clear but the solutions are so intractable. Continuing the style of the 1970s, NGOs loyally make inputs into the agenda set by the UN system (UNCTAD, General Agreement on Tariffs and Trade, support for the Common Fund and so on) but it is doubtful whether this effort is richly rewarded. International lobbying concerning the EEC's Lomé Agreement has been extensive, however, and with some success.

Some specific trade campaigns have achieved considerable prominence—especially concerning trade of problem products from North to South. Baby formula, pharmaceuticals and pesticides have already been mentioned in this context. In many countries high profile attacks have been made on the escalating arms trade and in particular on government subsidies for this. Reforms have been called for to the EEC's Common Agricultural Policy, particularly by French NGOs. And in some countries campaigns for the reform of the Multi-Fiber Agreement have achieved significant success. In the United Kingdom, for example, a campaign led by the World Development Movement succeeded in getting the government to scrap restrictive quotas on the imports of shirts made in Bangladesh.

International Finance. Debt has become an increasingly prominent campaigning item. Though complex, there have been some highly imaginative and provocative ways of presenting the subject to the public, for example the Profits out of Poverty campaign against commercial debt in the United Kingdom and the campaign to Stop the Aid from South to North in Germany. The emphasis has always been on how the debt crisis is at root an unacceptable human or environmental crisis.

NGOs in both the United States and the United Kingdom have formed Debt Crisis Networks to coordinate action (in the United Kingdom this includes environmental NGOs). In Germany, NGO preparations for the 1988 Annual Meetings of the World Bank and the International Monetary Fund gave rise to two coalitions, one oriented to environmental issues, the other to debt. And there is now a Europe-wide network of NGOs designed to plan and carry out common action. This concentrated initially on commercial bank debt.

The main specific issues raised by these campaigns have been the need for special debt relief measures for the poorest countries in Africa; the demand for changes to the orthodox approach to adjustment pursued by the IMF and World Bank; the responsibility of commercial banks to use some of their considerable profits to reduce Third World debt; and the connection between the debt and environmental crises.

Foreign Policy. Geopolitical issues have taken an increasingly prominent place in NGO campaigning. In the United Kingdom, campaigns on Central America and South Africa have achieved massive public support but have had little success in shifting the government's position. The campaign for a review of the West's attitude to Cambodia, conducted by an international consortium of NGOs, has been greeted by rather more concessions. Similarly, the NGO campaign to give increased support to the Frontline States, and to isolate the South African-backed Mozambique National Resistance rebel forces in Mozambique has helped shift the British government's position.

Experience indicates that the major issues of foreign policy are ones on which governments have deeply entrenched views. NGOs have considerable potential for putting a new item on the political agenda, or for changing a weakly held view on a subject on which there has been little debate. But to change a government's approach to an issue on which it has taken a firm stand requires a monumental effort which lies well outside of the NGOs' potential unless they can engage remarkably strong allies.

Corporate Campaigning

The most effective campaigns relating to multinational corporations in the 1980s have centered on irresponsible selling of potentially hazardous or undesirable products in the Third World.

Campaigns on corporate buying practices have been less prominent with two notable exceptions. One is the boycott of supermarkets selling South African produce. This has led many supermarket chains either to withdraw such lines or to have a policy of offering a non-South African alternative wherever possible. The other has been the campaign against unsustainable logging of tropical hardwoods. This has led a number of furniture manufacturers and other wood users to switch to other sources. Some campaigns have attacked the low prices paid to Third World producers for their commodities, such as sugar. This has exposed the low proportion of the final selling price that reaches the farmer or laborer but it has done little to change trade relations.

Campaigning on investment has concentrated on environmental issues and on the role of commercial banks. In Japan, for example, NGOs have attacked companies whose Third World subsidiaries have bad pollution records. And in the United Kingdom the End Loans to South Africa Campaign has mounted shareholder actions against the banks who make major investments in South Africa. Activists each buy a single share in the bank so that they can attend and raise awkward questions at the company's annual general meeting.

Activities relating to employment policies focus on issues such as the exploitative and discriminatory practices with regard to women employees, manipulative use of free trade zones, maintaining appalling standards of health and safety, poor wages and repressive practices by Third World subsidiaries of multinational corporations and racist employment practices and below-starvation wages in South Africa.

Choice of Issues

NGOs clearly need to be guided first and foremost by their experience and in particular by the messages they receive from grassroots workers in the South. But this has to be balanced by an objective assessment of what causes are winnable.

This presents a dilemma. Field-level experience might indicate that what is needed amounts to fundamental, far-reaching changes in North-South relations, for example the cancellation of debts, doubling of commodity prices and a completely new approach to official aid. But "real politik" in most Northern countries relegates such goals to the realm of pie-in-the-sky. On the other hand, setting sights solely on minor reforms which might be winnable risks sidelining an NGO into marginal causes.

A pragmatic course is to concentrate on campaigning for changes which are conceivably winnable in the prevailing climate but to see those changes as stepping stones to more profound reforms. Changes won can be used as precedents to secure similar, further reaching victories in related areas—a case-law approach.

This has parallels with the typical NGO project approach. An NGO may wish, for example, to eliminate the barriers which prevent women's access to credit. It may establish a women's credit scheme in one region. This

amounts to no more than a drop in the ocean, but it reflects the capacity of
the NGO and it might lead to bigger and bolder ventures in the future, and
it should plan for this. The NGO starts with the single project because it
realizes the need to match its work tasks to the resources at its disposal.

An example of the pragmatic choice of targets can be found in campaigning on debt. Most NGOs would like a massive writing off of both official and commercial debt and a considerable reduction of interest rates for
the remainder. After seven years of global concern about the issue, however, we have only seen marginal debt reductions and debt service concessions—and these have been dwarfed by the on-going process of debt
escalation. For Northern NGOs to call for total debt write off, in this climate, is fanciful (this is not to say it is fanciful for Northern NGOs to call
for major debt relief, nor for Southern NGOs to call on their governments
to default).

The campaign of Oxfam UK and others which drew public and mass
media attention in the United Kingdom to the intolerable debt service of
the poorest countries of Africa hit a raw nerve. The slogan was, "The scandal of the money that Africa gave to us. For every £1 we all gave for famine
relief in Africa, £2 came back in debt payments. Don't stop the giving, stop
the taking." It would have seemed unconscionable for Northern governments to ignore such public concern in the aftermath of the African
famine. The Chancellor duly proposed a Group of Seven debt initiative in
April 1987, encouraged to do so by many members of parliament.

His plan—initially resisted by the United States, Japan and West Germany—was eventually modified and accepted by the Group of Seven meeting in Toronto in autumn 1988. However, what was agreed to amounted to
a fraction of Africa's needs. To restore growth and reverse the relentless
increase in Africa's debt burden would require perhaps $3 or $4 billion per
year. The Chancellor's plan amounted to at most $1 billion per year of debt
relief (only countries undergoing IMF-approved adjustment programs
would be eligible). In practice the process of translating promises of relief
into action has proved extremely slow, to say the least. In its first full year,
the so-called Toronto plan has provided only US$50 million of relief, a
twentieth of the original estimate. Several meetings of the world's most
powerful finance ministers and eighteen months of high-level negotiation
between governments was only able to come up with this derisory effort,
amounting to less in financial terms than was contributed to Africa that
year by the United Kingdom's two leading NGOs, Oxfam UK and Save the
Children Fund.

Disappointing as it has been, United Kingdom NGOs guardedly welcomed the launch of this initiative. They pointed out that it set a precedent.
It was the first occasion (other than the translation of past aid loans into
grants) that Northern governments have accepted a share of the burden

of the debt crisis and have accepted anything other than a market-determined path forward. It opens the door to pressure for the scheme to be extended to other poor countries and deepened, as the United Kingdom Chancellor proposed in September 1990 to other finance ministers.

To summarize, experience indicates that when identifying the subject of a campaign, it is important to ask the following questions:

- Is there a clear *link* connecting the issue to the society campaigned in?
- Does the NGO have *direct experience* of the issue?
- Is the NGO seen as a *credible authority* on the issue?
- Is there much prospect of *generating popular appeal?* (If not, then a central lobbying operation rather than a public campaign will be more appropriate.)
- Can *clear and realistic* policy changes be advocated?
- Are there *intermediate goals* that are possibly winnable?
- For Northern NGOs: Would *Southern partners support* the campaign objectives?
- Can the campaign objectives be shown to be of direct *relevance to poor* people?
- For public campaigns: Does the NGO have the information, photographs and so on necessary to prepare *effective campaign materials?*
- Has a suitable *media strategy* been devised, again focusing on human appeal?
- Are there forthcoming meetings, debates or other events which provide useful *pegs* for the campaign?
- Can a *network* of concerned NGOs be formed?
- What *allies* can be encouraged to lend their weight to the campaign?
- Can *pitfalls* be anticipated and planned for?

How to Make Campaigns Effective

The NGO needs to demonstrate expertise regarding both the issue itself and the policy opportunities and dilemmas. It also needs to demonstrate that its field based experience is thorough, convincing and not merely emotive. It needs to have evident widespread and influential support for its cause. And it needs to establish a negotiating relationship with the authorities it seeks to influence.

Valuable lessons can be learned from the experience of Southern NGOs in influencing policy makers (see Chapter 8 on building grassroots movements and Chapter 9 on influencing reform). In addition, there are a number of practical techniques indicated by experience of effective campaigning.

Balance Analysis and Prescription

The foundation of an effective campaign must be a compelling and authoritative analysis of the problem concerned, but this must be balanced by an equally thoughtful analysis of the possible solutions. Authors of a campaign report may put 90 percent of their labor into the main body of the report and only 10 percent into the concluding recommendations, but the attention given by its readers is in inverse proportion.

Many NGOs, however, give scant attention to the specific policies they recommend or to the plan of attack they map out. A wearisome number of so-called campaigns amount to little more than broadsheets or pamphlets in which the NGO demonstrates its knowledge of a subject, presents its own analysis and adds, by way of an afterthought, a few ideas for action its supporters can take. Few will be so motivated, and the "campaign" will enter a lull until the next pamphlet is published.

Such NGOs have been unable to shake off an academic approach. The task of the scholar is to research and to reflect. Their conclusions are presented in a paper or book and they are then likely to turn to fresh pastures, unless another scholar chooses to make a riposte. It is lamentable how few academics seek to encourage decision makers to take note of their conclusions. For most academics, the book or paper is the *end* of the exercise. For a strategic lobbyist it should be the *starting point*.

Scholars can present some justification for shying away from action. Their task is to assist in the pursuit of knowledge, not its application. Their neutrality might be questioned if they became identified with a political cause. And they might feel that they don't have the skills needed for condensing years of research into a pamphlet or a parliamentary bill. NGOs have no such excuses. Their task is action. They are required to have a pro-poor bias. And their constituency is the general public.

The converse of the "academic disease" is naive simplicity. An NGO might spend weeks planning, for example, the shipment of relief food to a troubled region. It knows how complex the operation is, how many things can go wrong, and how important it is to plan for every eventuality. But the same NGO might take just a few hours to prepare a blueprint on changing world structures. An objective reflection should warn the NGO that this is a disservice. It may gain a moment of media attention but it won't change the world and it could devalue its image in the eyes of decision makers.

Plan a Strategy for Presenting the Case

The first people to hear of the concerns outside of the NGO network and close advisors should be those the campaign seeks to influence. It may be that the reception will be hostile but it will certainly be more hostile if the authorities first hear of the campaign through the media or through letter writing campaigns. When this happens the authorities can be forgiven for thinking that the main object is to embarrass them rather than to resolve the problem at issue.

The initial presentation of the case is all important. If too timid and apologetic it will be dismissed as no threat. But if too hectoring and categoric it will be dismissed as arrogant. The lobbyists, in judging their strategy, should think about their own experience: when were they themselves sufficiently persuaded by the argument of another to change their views; how was this argument presented?

Before presenting the case the lobbyists should do enough homework about the institution to be lobbied to know who are the people who have the power to effect the desired changes, and who—in positions of seniority—are most likely to be sympathetic to the cause. Lobbyists should angle to have those people present at the meeting. This might indicate that the lobbyists should engage others in their team who are of comparable status.

Plan When and How to Use Public Campaigning

The NGO has to decide whether it wishes to engage its supporters and the public at large in the campaign, or to take it forward solely by the work of the NGO's representatives. It is tempting to jump to the conclusion that public campaigning is necessary without considering the pros and cons, and without being clear what the people will actually contribute.

The pros are obvious, in terms of increasing the momentum of the campaign, but these will only be realized if the NGO really has the ability to excite a significant number of people. An activity billed as a public campaign, but in which few participate, will signal to the authorities concerned that it is a tired and unthreatening exercise.

To run an effective public campaign also requires considerable investment of time from the issue specialists and they may find that their time is eaten up by giving public talks to the extent that they are not investing enough of it in the direct lobbying work. The effective public campaign also requires considerable inputs of time and money to produce the materials required.

When the public campaigning route is chosen its objectives should be clear. Many so-called campaigns are really no more than educational exercises. Public education is laudable but the NGO should consider whether it is a cost-effective way of achieving heightened public understanding of the issue. It might be more effective to put time into first persuading and then helping a television producer to make a documentary on the subject.

If a public campaign is embarked on, the action the supporters are asked to take should be clear, compelling and realistic. A wide array of options which the supporter is asked to choose from will give the impression that the strategy is unclear and that none of the component actions are really important. Conversely, if the guidelines are too rigid (for example, providing the text of letters which are to be sent to decision makers) then supporters are made to feel like "lobby fodder," and those lobbied resent having to respond to large numbers of identical letters.

Supporters should feel excited by the action they are being asked to take. This means it should be neither daunting nor marginal. And if they receive responses from their lobbying which reveal that the proposals they submitted were unrealistic then they will feel let down by the NGO and become disillusioned.

Action proposals should also reflect the degree of experience of the activists. An effective campaign strategy should be like a ladder. It rests on the ground—which is the level of the bulk of the population: a level of basic human compassion for the world's hungry but no practical involvement and little knowledge of the underlying issues. The ladder should stand there, inviting people to climb on to it. The first rung is an easy step—a simple donation or the signing of a petition. People should be thanked for taking that step but encouraged to move to the second step. The rung might challenge people to learn something about the underlying causes of hunger and to make a commitment to action, such as to take part in a fun-run, attend a demonstration or join a meeting with a member of parliament. At this stage they should be urged to move on to the third rung of deeper involvement and deeper understanding and so on.

This strategy of gradual involvement and facilitating the entry of new blood may seem self-evident, but it is disturbing how inaccessible much NGO literature is to the lay public and how off-putting are the actions asked of them. Such an approach amounts to asking people to jump straight to the top of the ladder—a daunting prospect for anyone.

Reward Supporters

Campaigning NGOs are well aware that the contribution made by dedicated, imaginative supporters is invaluable. A few hours of well targeted lobbying or media work can be worth more than the most generous donation. But on the whole NGOs are poor at rewarding their supporters or confirming the worth of their contribution. No NGO would dream of accepting a sizable donation without sending back a receipt and a note of thanks, and yet the donation of labor to a campaign can go unmarked.

Lobbying NGOs should make a special point of giving out "receipts" to their activists. One NGO which is excellent in this respect is the US-based development pressure group, Results. They have some 150 groups throughout the United States (and some in Canada, the United Kingdom, Australia and West Germany). Results groups are mostly small—four to ten members—but each person is expected on almost a contractual basis to make a very significant contribution of time and money each month. The campaign objectives, set nationally, are to achieve very specific changes, such as an increase in the US contribution to specialized UN agencies (UNICEF and the International Fund for Agricultural Development) or the introduction of a micro-enterprise bill to vote a portion of the USAID funds for small-scale credit.

Results' members are asked to lobby politicians and to get articles published in the state's newspapers. The organization gives excellent briefings, including monthly telephone conferences, which make the members feel valued and professional, and which ensure well-informed advocacy. At major meetings, Results organizers make a point of introducing the audience to the speaker, as well as the speaker to the audience. They will ask all those to stand who have written articles on the subject which were published. Then each person standing shouts out in turn the name of the newspaper which published it. Next, the process is repeated for articles inspired by Results activities but written by journalists. Then for letters printed by newspapers and so on. By the end of this process the speaker is impressed by the commitment and effectiveness of the audience and energized to give a good performance; those standing are proud to have had their personal victory noted and see how it fits into a nationwide campaign which is making a real impact; and those still sitting feel determined that, come the next meeting, they too will be one of those standing.

NGO campaign leaders should avoid the temptation during briefing meetings to spend all the time explaining the issue. Time should also be reserved for carefully explaining the action that is requested and for debating/clarifying it. And, most importantly, time should be made for praising the particularly effective action of specific groups, for summarizing the popular action taken to date (so that supporters feel part of a significant movement for change), and for relaying any significant campaign advances, such as any noteworthy responses or concessions from decision makers (so that the supporters can share in any sense of progress).

A typical NGO spends one-half to three-quarters of its operating budget on salaries. Well-targeted labor is its principal tool. But donated labor is all too often deployed with little thought and little thanks. It might well be more effective to have far fewer campaign volunteers which the NGO staff try to relate to directly and to ensure that these are well used, well supported and well thanked.

Achieve Bargaining Power

Most decision makers in public life are constantly engaged in balancing dynamic forces. The senior civil servant, for example, experiences pressures from high-level appointees, elected officials, other departments, industry, interest groups, the media and from their staff. Each of these pressures waxes and wanes to different rhythms, but the civil servant knows that they must all be reckoned with. The NGO needs to position itself as one such force. It needs to shift from being a body that has something to say, to being a legitimate interest group that knows what it is talking about and that authority feels obliged to negotiate with.

This happens, crudely, when authority cannot afford to ignore the case being made and cannot satisfy it with vague expressions of good will. The NGO needs to have frequent meetings with the relevant decision makers (again, homework is needed to ascertain who these are). One-time meetings can appear constructive, but good intentions may evaporate. Conversely, routine, regular meetings without a very clear purpose will dull the advocacy and serve to draw the NGO into the official camp. The NGO team needs to steer meetings toward clear decisions and to follow them up, such as by asking for progress reports on promised action. It needs to be constantly gathering new information on its case and watch for new developments which present opportunities for follow-up meetings.

The decision makers are more likely to allow a negotiating relationship to develop when:

1. They respect the NGO team. This can mean including eminent experts or influential allies on the team. It can also mean maintaining a cordial style of dialogue.
2. They sense that the NGO listens as well as preaches, that the communication established is two-way.
3. They know that the outcome of the meeting will be noticed. This can be the case when the NGO has good access to the media, to politicians and to others of influence.
4. They know that the campaign is persistent; that the NGOs expect specific action promises and will be sure to follow up on these.

Bring the Issue to Life

The engine driving the NGO cause is moral compulsion. This is revealed not by economic statistics but by the impact of the issue on poor people. It is this *human picture* which will win the case. It is this that the campaign supporters are motivated by, that the media want to cover, that the politicians can include in their speeches and that the decision makers feel obliged to respond to.

Arguments of mutual self-interest (as were developed particularly by the Brandt reports) are important but are unlikely by themselves to change practices radically in the current political climate. Governments which reject Keynesian economics at home are hardly likely to be persuaded to fund a massive program of public works abroad. The NGO also has to recognize that it is not likely to be regarded as a source of credible expertise on macroeconomic analysis, whereas it may well be regarded as an expert when it comes to the grassroots ramifications of the issue.

The NGO can bring this out in two ways: firstly, by careful gathering of human interest stories which illustrate the issue through the experience of poor people that the NGO comes into contact with in its field work; secondly by use of Southern witnesses. Funding eloquent and experienced Third World NGO spokespeople to come over for key meetings, speaker tours or media activities usually proves an excellent investment.

The human interest slant should not be reserved for media work and public audiences. It should also be an essential flavor of the direct negotiation with decision makers. They too will be concerned about the human impact of policies they are responsible for and are most likely to be influenced by graphic (though not distorted) illustrations of it.

Choose an Appropriate Style

The effective campaign must be authoritative, persistent, morally charged and professional but within these parameters the NGO has to decide what style to adopt. In particular it must decide how aggressive or conciliatory to be.

This will depend to some extent on the stage and history of the campaign and the culture of the NGO. A campaign which jumps too quickly to an aggressive style may be excluded from any negotiating relationship and may find that it is no longer given privileged access to information. However, if, having forged a negotiating relationship, action on the issue fails to develop, the NGO should consider a tougher approach (for example, seeding hard-hitting media coverage or tough parliamentary or congressional questioning). Maintaining a cozy relationship with decision makers which does not result in action is not doing the poor any good.

Anticipate the Backlash

The NGO should consider what might happen as the campaign builds up momentum. What steps might the vested interest groups take to discredit the NGO or to frustrate the campaign? How can these eventualities be guarded against by advance planning?

For example, there may be a systematic countercampaign waged to impugn the political motives of the NGO, to challenge its charitable or not-for-profit status, or to press for the withdrawal of foreign funding. To guard against this threat the lobbyists need to ensure that they have influential allies who will testify to the organization's motives, and they need to ensure that everyone within their own organization is aware of and supportive of the campaign.

Build Strong Networks

The advantages of collaboration within networks have been described in earlier chapters. These advantages apply equally to international lobbying endeavors. In addition to mutual fortification and mutual protection, networking on lobbying provides the possibility for NGOs to specialize in areas in which they have individual advantage.

For example, a network may arise because a group of NGOs shares concerns about World Bank funding for a particular dam. Some might know most about the environmental consequences of the submergence. Some might be most concerned with the displacement and resettlement issue. Others might have worries about the social consequences of the changing pattern of agriculture which the irrigation scheme will bring about. Yet other NGOs might have different concerns. Within a network, each can concentrate on its own area of expertise. Similarly, different NGOs might have different constituencies. Their membership may be concerned, variously, with environmental, development or minority cultural issues. Some might have wide, public constituencies, others might be respected by a small but influential academic audience and others might be particularly strong at media relations. Different NGOs might also have access to different decision makers or people of influence. Most obviously, in the case of international agencies such as the World Bank, NGOs can lobby their own government on its voting intentions.

11

New Pragmatism

NGOs ARE AT A crossroads. Never before have they been so powerful, not just in financial terms but also in their credibility with decision makers at all levels. Their practical experience makes them uniquely qualified to comment on how changes in macro-policy affect the lives and prospects of the poor.

In official circles, never before has development assistance been so politically loaded. Over one-quarter of World Bank lending is made not for projects but for adjustment programs, and an increasing proportion of bilateral and EEC aid is given in association with such programs. If adjustment stops, so does the aid. This is called cross-conditionality.

At the same time the architects of development orthodoxy know that economic growth by itself is not sufficient to eliminate poverty. The major development institutions are being pressed to give greater weight to poverty and gender issues. Countries crippled by debt may make strenuous efforts to achieve growth but find that their efforts are futile since debt service obligations leave little to fund their development priorities.

Attempts to correct imbalances by curbing investments and imports are self-defeating in the long term if they give rise to contraction in the country's economy. Cuts in public spending can lead to intolerable social costs and this in turn leads to political instability. Measures to increase domestic investment have lamentably failed. And economically attractive development schemes can be devastating for the environment.

Something is clearly wrong with the conventional development model, though whether or not there is a better one at hand is contested. To say there is a crisis of confidence within official aid circles is going too far, but certainly there is a search for new ideas, if nothing else to reform the increasingly discredited old ones. And most of the new ideas proposed—if they address poverty issues at all—place heavy emphasis on collaboration with NGOs.

This emphasis may be flattering but it can also be unrealistic and disturbing. It is unrealistic because even the combined force of all the NGOs could not play all the various roles suggested by the official aid agencies: delivering social services more efficiently, protecting the poor throughout adjustment, constructing food security systems for the vulnerable, implementing poverty-focused components of official aid projects and so on. It is disturbing because efforts to mold NGOs into the aid agencies' image—and there are plenty of funds available as inducements—can seduce NGOs from their own agenda, and shift their accountability away from the poor they serve to the official aid agencies.

If, however, NGOs remain true to their constituencies and confident in their agenda they might have a profound influence on the shape of development to come. To take advantage of the opportunities and avoid the pitfalls requires of NGOs new disciplines of analysis, research and observation and a rethinking of their position on development policy issues.

This has been a difficult chapter to write. It has been difficult because I am aware that at times it is myself I am criticizing. I have been guilty of some of the oversimplifications I describe below. It has been difficult also because the search for new paradigms can be conflictive. I don't believe my political values have changed over the past decade, but I've changed my ideas about what policies would be necessary to realize those values today. The world has changed. Our ideas must keep up with the times.

A journalist friend recently described himself as "a reluctant convert to capitalism." I sympathize. The experiences of Eastern Europe and Africa have taught the world important lessons about economics as well as democracy. In this chapter I look at lessons such as these, and I question some of the favorite "old chestnuts" of development.

I use, at times, arguments of market economies not because I believe that the Thatcherite free market offers any sort of solution to the problems I care about, but because I think it is a useful discipline, whether a reluctant convert or not, to review periodically how well our old ideas are standing up to the test of modern times. Chapters 13 and 14 will make clear that I am not advocating "free markets with a human face," but rather a more pluralist approach harnessing the creativity of private enterprise but strengthening both the caring and guiding role of the state. Interventionism with a banker's face. The debates I present below are sketchy. I realize I might offend some readers for presenting a caricature of their opinions but I do this to avoid the book becoming a treatise on macro-development issues. I am not seeking to win arguments on the important development chestnuts, but to illustrate that we often debate them in too simplistic a fashion in NGO circles.

Unpacking the Ideological Baggage

NGO workers, in general, are committed to social change, that is to increasing not just the living standards but also the power of the poor. Their starting point will be a political one, and this can strengthen commitment, but also impair objectivity.

Typically the starting point includes the moral conviction that Third World problems stem from colonization, Northern greed, multinational corporations, the IMF and other external factors. Broadly, this is the Neo-Marxist school of thought. It can be compelling, but it is usually too simplistic. True, there is much to criticize about the colonial past. Northern foreign policy does frequently harm the poor. There are copious illustrations of multinational excesses, and there are good grounds for saying that the IMF has helped exacerbate poverty. But this is not the total picture.

Northern NGOs understandably concentrate in their advocacy and public campaigning work on factors relating in some way to their own societies. That is where their major sphere of influence lies. They can aspire to influence their politicians, their company chiefs and their governments, but feel that it is not Northerners' business to influence decision makers in Third World countries. They should, however, convey their organization's objective experience—not use it selectively to substantiate preconceived positions.

Talk to the poor about their problems and they rarely raise external factors spontaneously. They will be eager to blame their own governments, their local bureaucrats, police, landlords and business elite, but they are unlikely to fix on Northern institutions. They may complain about state programs that are supported by official aid, but most of their grievances will be quite unrelated to the North. Listen more carefully and it becomes apparent that on some of their complaints they are actually being supported by Northern institutions.

Poor farmers in Ethiopia will complain that they don't have the freedom to sell their crops to whomever they like. They risk arrest and imprisonment for "smuggling" even small quantities of coffee to Addis Ababa for sale in the market. They complain about the low prices and crippling taxes imposed by the government. They complain about their land being seized for collectivization, about arbitrary arrests, fines, beatings, conscriptions and other violations of human rights. They complain about the cruel inefficiencies of the agricultural parastatals. They might also complain that—in spite of all the aid they hear their government is receiving—none of it is coming to their area, but is all being spent in the cities, in more productive and in politically more strategic regions.

The poor of Zambia have a similar string of complaints. They also bemoan corruption of officials, steep inflation that they have had to endure and severe shortages of even essential items (except at exorbitant black market prices). The women will resent the fact that, even when head of a household, they do not have the same access to land and credit that men have.

The landless of Bangladesh will complain of the failure to enforce minimum wage laws, of exploitation, of rape and brutality at the hands of local landlords—of harassment by the police, and, for women, of brutality by men and callous divorce and demeaning dowry customs.

The poor have a clear-sighted appreciation of the local factors that fuel their misery. A careful and unbiased reporting on what is heard from the poor demands of NGOs a more sophisticated analysis of the root cause of poverty than they are prone to make—even privately among themselves.

For NGOs to maximize their impact in the mainstream development debate the first step must be a disentangling of experience from personal political conviction. An NGO case based on a faithful account of its experience is a powerful one, but when experience is biased toward support of previously held positions this is transparently so to those the NGO seeks to influence.

We need to unpack our ideological baggage and examine each item to see whether or not it is flawed, overvalued or past its sell-by date. Each section below describes a genuine problem area, one in which NGOs can make an important contribution, but one where in the past oversimplifications and sweeping generalizations have risked discrediting the NGO case. In these sections I imply criticism of some Northern NGO workers— myself included! But I reserve far greater criticism for the more numerous establishment-oriented NGOs who fail to use their overseas experience to influence change at all.

Cash Crops

Much NGO literature describes the switch from subsistence to export crops as one of the main causes of hunger. While there is considerable evidence to show that agricultural transition in agriculture can cause serious problems—and these should be looked at much more seriously than they have been to date—the case is usually overstated. With some exceptions, there is generally a reverse correlation. Areas of export crop production tend to be areas where living standards, nutritional status and life expectancy have improved. There is frequent evidence, such as from Nigeria, Ghana and Kenya,[99] that increased export production in colonial times and since spurred an *increase* of domestic food production in those same regions. This illustrates that increasing domestic demand (through increased economic activity and employment) is likely to lead to increased domestic production. This fits with the radical argument that hunger has more to do with the poor's inability to buy food, rather than the inability of the land to grow it, hence the problem demands a political, not a technical, solution.

More recent evidence from Africa illustrates that there is little correlation between food imports and physical needs but there is a correlation between food imports and total exports. In other words, it isn't those countries which need food that import it but those who can afford it, and they can afford it because they have something to export.

NGOs could be well justified to comment on the distributional effects of an agricultural transition, to analyze why, typically, poorer farmers are bypassed. They may also have evidence about the distribution of proceeds within the family which give grounds for concern. And perhaps there are important natural resource base and other concerns which need addressing. But to take a principled anti-cash crop or anti-export crop position is unwarranted by experience.

Commodity Prices

A further argument against a dependence on the export of raw commodities is that the prices of these shows a secular decline in relation to the prices of goods imported in return. The conclusion drawn is that the Third World is being increasingly exploited by Northern consumption and would be best advised to abandon commodity trading. A closer look to commodity price movements suggests a more complicated conclusion.

The net barter terms of trade (NBTT—the ratio of export prices to import prices) has fluctuated wildly in the second half of this century but for most countries until the 1980s it was not possible to discern a secular decline. Some commentators pick two apparently random years and calculate how many extra bags of coffee, say, have to be exported to pay for importing the same truck. Such calculations are usually based on a period which starts with a commodity price peak and ends with a trough. An opposite conclusion would follow by choosing a different period. Some commodity prices, for example for vegetable oil, have remained quite strong.

Four general conclusions can be drawn from NBTT movement. Firstly, commodity prices tend to rise at times of high world growth and fall at times of world recession. Secondly, the 1970s did see for most non-oil exporting developing countries a considerable drop in their NBTT but this was almost entirely due to the oil price rises rather than the actions of Northern governments or companies. Thirdly, the 1980s have seen some further drops in NBTT for many countries which relates partly to world recession and partly to the debt crisis (export-led approaches to meeting high debt service obligations have contributed to the oversupply of some commodities and consequent price slumps). Fourthly, the general problem of commodity trade is not so much the secular decline but the wild fluctuations in commodity prices which make any attempt at long-term economic planning virtually impossible. This fluctuation is magnified by speculation on the commodities futures market, situated in Northern financial centers.

The conclusion is not that commodity trading is fair, but that more care is needed in analyzing whether or not it makes sense for a developing country to turn to particular commodities.

The critical question is what are the alternatives? Relatively few developing countries have broken away from dependence on commodity exports. Some Southeast Asian countries—the Newly Industrializing Countries—have discovered gaps in the market for mass-produced manufactured goods, some countries receive remittances from overseas workers and others get hard currency as a result of narcotics trade, but most developing countries remain dependent on commodity trading. In Chapter 13 we look at alternatives, at building up South–South cooperation, reducing import dependence and reforming Northern markets.

De-linking

Some commentators have called for de-linking, withdrawal from the world market place and pursuing a path of self-sufficiency. China is the obvious example (though the successes of the "closed-door" era are now being questioned). China, however, was a special case and it is unlikely that any other developing country with the possible exception of India would be able to cut off from the world and still prosper. For a country to do this it must be able to supply all its own strategic needs (oil, food, etc.), the technology and machinery needed for production, the intermediate goods, and have a sufficiently large and diverse internal market.

Few countries have attempted de-linking. One example is Burma (now Myanmar) which in 1950 had a similar living standard and infant mortality rate to Thailand, but which is now evidently much poorer and subject to a more repressive regime. Similarly, Albania has fallen well behind neighboring European countries. To urge other developing countries—especially those with few internal resources—to take anything approaching a de-linking path would be irresponsible.

On the other hand, experience also indicates that there are dangers in maintaining too open an economy. The degree of openness is measured by total imports plus exports as a percentage of GNP. Zambia is one of the most open economies in the world and has been since colonial days, when it was regarded as little more than a giant copper mine, exporting minerals and importing virtually all its needs in return. Zambia demonstrates the dangers of openness very clearly. With little state intervention or other incentives to expand production to cater for the internal market or to seek alternative export opportunities, this country has remained the giant copper mine of colonial times and has allowed itself to become extremely vulnerable to a collapse in mineral prices and to world recession, especially as it used copper revenues when the price was high to finance a bloated civil service.

Multinational Corporations

Multinational corporations (MNCs) usually make large profits out of their Third World operations but this may be more due to their operational scale rather than their ruthlessness. As NGOs we must be careful to distinguish whether it is excessive wealth or excessive poverty we find offensive. The generation of wealth by some is not automatically at the expense of increased misery for others. This would be the case in an economy which is static, but where capital accumulation leads to economic growth then it is feasible—likely even—that some groups of the poor will also increase their incomes in absolute terms, even though the wealth gap between rich and poor may grow, and many of the poor will be left out of the benefits.

There may be other, political reasons to be concerned about multinational corporations' Third World operations, such as the naked political influence they sometimes wield, but within a given sector it is likely that the MNC will actually prove to be a better employer in terms of wages and conditions than equivalent national employers. Few MNCs have trouble recruiting the labor they require, and the poor who join the queues in search of work would probably not take too kindly to well-meant NGO pressure to restrict the activities of these companies.

MNCs are frequently guilty of excesses in their overseas operations. Hence it is important for NGOs to monitor MNC activities because they have the capacity to reach the relevant decision makers and to use the media effectively when felt necessary. The captains of these companies have a powerful influence on the peoples of the world and this is a compelling enough reason for charging them to be accountable more widely than to their shareholders. They should also be urged to take more of a lead in opposing customary but exploitative business practices and, in particular, restrictions of workers' rights to organize.

The African Experience

Throughout much of the 1980s—thanks in good measure to the publicity work of NGOs—there has been a dramatic surge in international concern for the famine-prone countries of Africa. This publicity has gone further than presenting Africans as cruel victims of drought and civil war who are in need of charity. It has frequently exposed injustices stemming from the indifference of Northern governments and the hostility of the world economic environment which compounds the suffering of the poor.

Such publicity in Northern countries helped lift the inertia which blocked a substantial emergency food aid program in 1984 from the EEC and other countries who were sitting on mountains of agricultural surplus. It prompted the establishment, by the European Commission, of an Emergency Food Aid Reserve so that relief could be more swiftly dispatched in the future. It helped nudge official aid priorities away from commercial self-interest and prestige projects and toward small-scale agriculture and poverty alleviation. And it cajoled finance ministers into considering special measures for African debt relief.

These results are important but it is time to reflect on whether the pursuit of them led to biased messages which now need revising. Was the image presented one that focused *too* much on colonial legacies and contemporary Western ills and dismissed too readily the failings of African governments? The NGO portrait of Northern injustice aptly counters a prevailing image among Northern publics of corruption, indifference, inefficiency and exploitation by African governments. But the portrait of Western guilt, popular with the media, has—according to some well-placed observers in Africa—helped provide African governments with a convenient scapegoat. Wahome Mutahi, a columnist for Kenya's *Daily Nation,* speaks frankly of the

> monster of African leadership . . . [which] blamed colonialism for all the ills afflicting African countries. . . . So long as there was someone else to blame, all was all right. The result is the present Africa where malnutrition, sectarian violence, plunder, environmental rape, poor health and illiteracy abound.[100]

Generalization is dangerous. Some governments have done all they reasonably can, living up both to commitments elicited by the donor community to reform their economies and to commitments made domestically to help the poor. Others have manifestly failed on both counts. The latter have been most vocal in regaling their publics about the injustices meted out by the North. Indigenous and Northern NGOs have, albeit unwittingly, often helped frame the excuses which so conveniently let the African elite off the hook. It is salutary to ask whether this has undermined the efforts of local organizations, such as trade unions and political opposition groups, or independent academics to call the governments to account.

Paradoxically, those in the North who in effect excuse domestic failings in Africa by focusing exclusively on Northern institutions as perpetrators of injustice are guilty of denying their Third World counterparts the chance to use the very tools of class analysis which are the main weapons in the political armory of the left at home. This is particularly the case with those countries whose governments use the rhetoric of socialism and African nationalism but where disparities of wealth and the elite-bias of government policy are world leaders.

Colonialization has left behind a legacy of suffering in many respects but it is over-romantic to suggest that all was idyllic before that era. Indeed colonialism served to flush out certain traditional injustices, particularly regarding communal or ethnic-based discrimination which have tended to creep back since independence in some countries.

It is true that colonization did little to diversify economies away from a few key commodities, to encourage industrialization or domestic production for the internal market, or to generate a skilled administrative cadre (by 1958 there were, for example, only twenty-eight African graduates in the entire federation of Rhodesia and Nyasaland. By 1979 there were 2,030 graduates in Zambia alone).[101] However, the increased production of those few commodities did in many cases trigger increased food production. In Nigeria and Gold Coast (now Ghana) the production of maize, yams and other foods rose in the cocoa areas in the early part of this century and nutrition improved accordingly. Similarly, in other countries food production in the mining and plantation areas increased, and rice and maize mills started to proliferate.

The increasing food market was rapidly followed by burgeoning markets in other items from kerosene and soap to beer and bicycles. While some of these consumer items were produced locally toward the end of the colonial era this was not encouraged as a priority by the colonial powers. There was, however, a steady emphasis on infrastructure.

Societies underwent rapid transition, becoming more dynamic and more mobile. The elite felt threatened. Their authority, not to mention their supply of cheap labor, was dwindling before their eyes. Hence they often tried to obstruct progress, for instance by trying to block labor migration to the cocoa belt or to the gold mines of South Africa. However, the transition was unstoppable. Nigeria's formal sector increased from just 2,357 in 1881 to 800,000 in 1959 to 2.76 million in 1980.

Post-Colonial Trends

While there is a contemporary tendency to look at Africa as a continent of disasters and failed hopes, there are impressive records achieved by post-colonial Africa which should not be forgotten. Most countries have achieved a faster economic growth (typically 4 percent per annum) than Europe did during the industrial revolution, and agricultural production has generally rocketed. From the early 1960s to the early 1980s agricultural production rose 2.3 times in Ivory Coast, 2.1 times in Malawi, 1.75 times in Tanzania and 1.6 times in Kenya. Yields per acre of domestic food crops typically doubled.[102]

Some countries, however, saw deterioration over the same period. For example, Ghana, Mozambique, Ethiopia, Chad, Uganda and Zaire all faced a rapidly deteriorating economic situation in the 1970s, with declining investments, imports and per capita agricultural production. Many factors should be held responsible, including drought, war, destabilization by South Africa and US foreign policy, but also domestic macroeconomic policy failings.

Declines in export performance are often blamed on the hostile world market conditions but this does not provide a sufficient explanation. While the net barter terms of trade (NBTT—the ratio of export prices to import prices) fell in some cases, the income terms of trade (ITT—the ratio of export earnings to import prices) often fell much more steeply. In other words, lost earnings were due more to dwindling export volumes than to dwindling export prices. This was the case in Senegal, Mozambique, Ghana and Tanzania from 1970 to 1981 where NBTT actually rose. Conversely countries such as Malawi and Ivory Coast managed greatly to increase their export earnings even though the NBTT fell steeply.

Commodities exported by Africa certainly enter a hostile world market, but other countries have been better at weathering the storm. Consequently Sub-Saharan Africa has seen a shrinking share of total world exports from the 1960s to the 1980s. Its share of palm oil slumped from 55 percent to 3 percent, of cocoa from 80 percent to 63 percent, of groundnuts from 85 percent to 18 percent and of bananas from 11 percent to 3 percent. In other commodities which Africa could readily produce, e.g. cotton, rubber and tobacco, its world market share remains minute. Africa's share of world trade in non-oil primary commodities fell from 7 percent in 1970 to under 4 percent in 1985.

NGO workers frequently encounter complaints from smallholders about their derisory income from export crops. They must, however, ask whether this it due to unjust *international* or *internal* market forces. Many governments, seeking to earn revenue to finance their budgetary imbalances, have passed on a declining share of export prices to their farmers. For example, in Ghana farmers received 57 percent of the world market price for cocoa in 1966. By 1970 this had shrunk to 36 percent and by 1978–79 to just 15 percent. Similarly, in Tanzania, although the NBTT increased slightly from 1971–72 to 1982–83, there was a decrease in real producer prices paid for coffee (down 58 percent), sisal (down 57 percent), tea (down 78 percent), tobacco (down 33 percent) and other crops. Over this period the export volume consequently plummeted. In Ivory Coast, in contrast, producer prices for cocoa and coffee were increased both in real terms and as a percentage of export earnings in the same period, and total export volumes increased.[103]

In the provision of welfare services, increasing domestic food production and industrialization to provide for the internal market there has also been diverse performance, as Table 11.1 indicates.

Some countries, such as Ghana, Mozambique and Senegal achieved little if any export growth, industrialization or increased cereal production and the GDP figures echo this. Other countries achieved well on all these counts (Malawi, Kenya, Ivory Coast) and their economies grew strongly. The diverse social performances are reflected in the reductions in infant mortality rates. It is clear, however, that there is not a close correlation. NGOs need no reminding that improved economic and agricultural perfor-

Table 11.1   Trends in Social and Production Indicators[104]

	1981 Export Volume 1960=100	1981–83 Cereal Production 1961–65=100	1981 Index of Value Added 1970=100	GDP % Annual Growth 1960–82	1985 per Capita Calorie suppy	1980 IMR†	% Drop In IMR 1960–80
Ethiopia	1986	128	148	3.2	1704	146	16
Malawi	367	172	184	5.0	2415	172	17
Tanzania	62	293	106	4.9	2316	103	32
Ghana	114	145	85	0.7	1785	103	28
Kenya	165	175	318	5.7	2214	87	37
Mozambique	46	68	—	—	1617	115	28
Senegal	93	118	108	2.7	2418	147	19
Zambia	111	160	139	2.8	2126	106	30
Ivory Coast	496	223	177	6.7	2308	127	27
Nigeria	213	126	338	3.5	2139	135	26
Zimbabwe	—	199	172	3.2	2144	74	3

*† in constant prices
† Infant Mortality Rate

mances by themselves will not improve living standards of the poor. Distributional policies must be pursued in addition. However, it is evident that those countries which have achieved most in reducing infant mortality (Zimbabwe, Kenya, Tanzania and Zambia) have also scored well on all or some of the production criteria. In other words, political commitment to improve living standards is hollow rhetoric without the physical resources to make this possible.

NGOs and Policy Analysis

Economics of Production

NGOs have tended to criticize structural adjustment, but perhaps we should be more prepared to recognize that pressure to increase producer prices, one of its principle objectives, is a key concern of poor farmers. Obviously increasing farm gate prices by itself isn't sufficient to help the poor. Labour constraints in certain seasons and lack of access to credit, inputs (such as seeds and fertilizers) and markets are also problems. Producer price increases may not lead to increased production by poor farmers—particularly by women farmers and those living in remote areas.

NGOs could lobby for an adjustment strategy that avoids these pitfalls and assists poor farmers. This approach would include policy reforms such as increasing producer prices with projects, such as credit schemes, expanding use of animal traction or agricultural extension for women farmers.

An important policy reform would be to increase and make more dependable poor farmers' access to land. In some African countries all land is owned by the state and tribal chiefs have authority to allocate the use of the land to their village members. On the farmer's death the land may revert to the village rather than remaining in the farmer's family. This discourages investment in the land.

This insecurity particularly affects women farmers. They are likely to have poorer quality, virgin land and have less chance of using this land as collateral in acquiring loans. A program of land reform which gives all farmers, men and women, title rights to the land they farm, including rights to bequeath this land to their heirs, would be a massive incentive to increase production.

The left have traditionally resisted such policies, however, as unwarranted privatization of state assets. They argue, with good reason, that such titling might lead to a market for the buying and selling of land, a casino in which the poor would surely lose out. Can the state give land rights while at the same time affording the poor the security they need? Is there virtue in preventing racketeers from commandeering the assets of the poor by ensuring that those assets remain virtually worthless?

Paradoxically in much of Latin America and Asia the left call vehemently for land reform, while in most African countries there is a reverse pressure. Conferring land rights is seen as retrogressive.

There clearly is a difference. In Latin America and Asia it is large landowners who possess most of the land. Land reform means taking from the rich and giving to the poor. In African countries where the state owns the land and the state is the people, land reform entails taking from the people and giving to the people—no apparent social gain.

From the viewpoint of the poor, however, the issue is one of self-determination and control over the productive assets on which they depend. It matters little whether it is a landlord, a tribal chief or a party official who restricts their control over such assets. NGOs should not be concerned about curtailing the wealth of the rich but about maximizing the opportunities for the poor.

The Poor Versus the Elite

NGOs have traditionally attacked IMF inspired austerity programs which make large numbers of government employees redundant. While it is right to attack the *way* such redundancies have frequently been made (in which little or no help has been given to those laid off) perhaps we should be wary of attacking the redundancies themselves.

Unlike Northern countries and even other regions of the Third World, government employees are usually among the highest income earners. Their wages are about 5.5 times national per capita incomes (compared with 2 times in South Asia). These wages have to come from somewhere, from increased taxation, reduced producer prices, reduced capital investment, increased budget deficits (and hence inflation) or reduced spending elsewhere. They are in effect paid by the poor, who derive the least benefit. For example, Ghana built up a huge cocoa marketing bureaucracy employing tens of thousands. To pay for this a shrinking share of cocoa export earnings was passed on to the farmers (down from 57 percent in 1966 to 15 percent in 1978–79). In the mid 1980s, under an adjustment program, a large proportion of these civil servants was laid off with no apparent damage to the farmers who now have a considerably increased income, though obviously the experience was painful to those who lost their jobs.

True, those employed in the formal sector tend to have large numbers of dependents in their extended families. While this indicates the need for care in the making of redundancies—including well designed schemes to help find alternative employment—it is not a good argument against making the redundancies. If, however, the austerity measures just enable higher debt service bills to be met there is no social benefit—just pain.

NGOs should be more ready to criticize the expensive bureaucracy which is a heavy burden on the shoulders of the poor. As one senior aid official recently commented, one of the most unfortunate legacies from colonial times is the expectation of officials that they have the right to enjoy smart suits, high living standards, cars and servants as their colonial predecessors did. But while administrators were relatively few in colonial times, their numbers have multiplied since and so their cost has become an intolerable burden. Peer pressure within the ruling classes has encouraged the creation of jobs for those—the educated elite—who need them, and these jobs are often guaranteed for life. Often there is little pressure to perform effectively and it is common to find whole offices deserted during office hours. It is said in Nigeria that "in most countries you start work when you get a job. Here we *stop* work once we get a job."

Civil servant wages have gone down sharply in many countries in real terms as a result of economic crisis, however this may even compound the problem. The number employed has often been maintained but the higher caliber workers have quit—to move into the private sector or to emigrate. Staff remaining tend to be poorer quality, poorly motivated and always searching for opportunities to make money on the side.

When savings need to be made, the services which the poor depend on should be protected and "adjustments" made elsewhere, such as by cutting subsidies enjoyed mostly by the better off, currency devaluation and curbing inflation by reducing budget deficits.

Such issues are problematic for NGOs. The hardships brought about by austerity measures are highly visible and immediate whereas the benefits, if indeed there are any, are usually indirect and slower. When formal sector workers are laid off, this will be unpopular with the poor (especially the urban poor), partly because of "workers' solidarity," and partly because many have some family member whose job becomes threatened. They have a share in the hardship and are far from convinced that they have a share in any benefits, nor—necessarily—that there *will* be any benefits.

Critics of austerity measures should perhaps consider an alternative strategy: popular education to help the poor understand the actions taken by their government, and formulation of alternative approaches which would better serve their interests. If savings resulting from redundancies were used for poverty-relieving programs (rather than debt service), to curb inflation, and to fund well-constructed compensatory programs to soften the blow for those laid off, then such austerity measures might be better understood and less resisted.

NGOs experience daily the ineffectiveness of most government bureaucracies in Africa. Agricultural extension officers drive around in packs giving advice which is largely irrelevant to the poor. Marketing parastatals are ever slower to pay farmers for their harvest. Municipal offices are empty in the afternoons as the staff employed moonlight elsewhere. State veterinary services are only available to those who can provide transport for the vets, and so the list goes on.

Perhaps NGOs should not be as ready to criticize programs of redundancy and austerity. Both indigenous and Northern NGOs tend to avoid criticizing African governments where they work, and find it easier to blame external factors. While African politicians are keen to seek external scapegoats (such as the IMF, Asian traders, multinational corporations, etc.), NGOs should present a more balanced picture and be wary of cooptation to the African nationalist agenda. They should be more even handed in apportioning blame to the elite both in the North but also in Africa. For example, one of the greatest scandals of Africa is that the President of Zaire, Mr. Mobutu, is listed as one of the world's richest men. He has stashed immense fortunes into family accounts abroad while his people remain in dire poverty, and while corruption in his government is rife. An investigation in the 1970s demonstrated that some 70 percent of the names of civil servants on the payroll simply did not exist. The salaries were being paid but the workers were fictitious.[105] However, it is a widespread phenomenon—since official salaries are so derisory—that government workers such as teachers draw several salaries in order to survive.

NGOs should be careful not to depoliticize the domestic situation in order to unclutter the vilification of Northern exploiters. Such analysis short-changes the African oppressed. Their exploitation may not be as stark as that of the Bangladesh peasants by landlords or of the Latin American poor by military dictatorships but it is every bit as real. The oppressors of the African poor include the unjust international economic system, but also, frequently, traditional leaders, government officials and many of the governments themselves. As Adebayo Adedeji, head of the Economic Commission for Africa, recently said in a meeting with NGOs,

> if in your presentation Northern NGOs give the impression that all of the blame [for the African crisis] is with Northern institutions then you are going too far, and you are doing a disservice. You see, the African elite, too, are a big part of the problem. They see themselves not as Africans, but as part of the elite of London and Paris.[106]

To ignore domestic failings in Africa is a form of racism; rendering the elite innocent, by omission, denies an entire continent responsibility for its action as we might excuse the misdemeanors of delinquent children.

The real political issue—which NGOs should be comfortable with—is the powerlessness of the poor. And so the real challenge which NGOs should take up is to seek ways to empower the poor in their attack on both the internal and external factors which ensnare them in poverty.

12

NGOs and Structural Adjustment

What is Adjustment?

A government, like a company or a household, must at times modify spending and earning patterns in order to balance the books. It has to ensure that its own budget is in good order and that the country's overall balance of payments is in check, meaning that sufficient foreign exchange is being earned to pay for imports and other commitments without having to borrow unsustainably.

At its most neutral, the term "adjustment" merely means the policy measures the government adopts to correct budgetary and current account deficits. Then-President Alan Garcia's attempt to correct Peru's imbalances by setting, unilaterally, a ceiling on debt service was a form of adjustment but it is rarely described as such. Adjustment measures fall into two categories.

Stabilization. This comprises the short-term measures which can be implemented swiftly, usually by central government action alone, to have an immediate effect on the imbalances. Such measures include devaluation, scrapping certain state subsidies, and increasing domestic interest rates. Stabilization, as the term suggests, is usually the response to an economy which has veered off course, perhaps because of a sudden fall in the prices of the commodities the country exports.

Structural adjustment. If the economic difficulties are likely to be protracted, then stabilization by itself will not restore balances (not without wrecking the long-term prospects of the country). Longer term measures are needed, restructuring the economy so as to adapt to the new hostile economic environment. Such measures include government spending cuts

165

to reduce costs and improve efficiency of services, increasing incentives and assistance to exporters and speeding up domestic production—including sometimes attracting necessary foreign investment. Central Governments initiate such actions but, to be effective, they require the cooperation of other bodies. For example, exporters and domestic producers must be willing to respond to the incentives offered, government departments and parastatals must cooperate with the restructuring exercises and the proposed measures may need parliamentary approval.

A typical Third World adjustment package usually comprises both stabilization and structural adjustment measures. Often there is no clear distinction between the two components. Specific actions tend to serve both short- and long-term objectives. Sometimes, however, there is an inherent contradiction between the two components. An across-the-board cut in civil service pay provides short-term savings, but long-run considerations might urge increasing salaries to attract higher caliber staff. Short-term pressures might call for restricting imports to ease balance of payments deficits, but this might scupper long-term plans to strengthen the economy by diversifying manufacturing. Diversification can help both by domestic production of goods which were previously imported and by increasing export potential, but it requires *increased* imports (of intermediate products, energy, machinery, spares, wage goods, etc.), especially in the early phase of such a strategy. The goal of stabilization is to cut the coat according to the cloth available, while that of structural adjustment is to increase the amount of cloth available for the coat required.

The above description of adjustment is neutral and uncontroversial. All governments, North and South, other than the blindest, are continuously engaged in making adjustments in their economic instruments. The reason that adjustment has in recent years acquired a deeply controversial character in the Third World is four-fold.

The depth of the crisis. The imbalances which often fragile Third World governments are having to deal with today are not minor short-term difficulties but major ruptures in the fabric of their societies. The measures necessitated are often painful beyond endurance and without respite. After perhaps several years of searing reforms the imbalances appear as intractable as ever.

Fueling the economic crisis is the painful burden of Third World debt. Throughout the past decade an increasing and intolerable share of the country's foreign exchange and of the government's budget is swallowed up in debt service for which there is no apparent reward. High interest rates, falling commodity prices, reduced market opportunities as Northern protectionism strengthens and other side effects of Northern economic policy affect beleaguered Southern economies seriously. The South is asking with increasing urgency why they alone must bear the burden. Is it not time for structural adjustment in the North too?

The difficult social choices. These become more controversial the more severe the imbalances to be addressed. In essence, adjustment is the government's choice of how to apportion the burden following a decline in national income. There are many ways of doing this—cutting back real incomes of the rich, the poor, the urban sector, the rural, the formal sector, civil servants, businesspeople and so on. And on the income-generating side there are similar choices to be made about who is to be taxed and who offered increased incentives.

The government can cut spending on its services (health, education, agricultural extension, etc.), on its defense spending, or on capital budgets (which may threaten long-term development efforts). Naturally, wherever the government chooses to make savings there will be a backlash. The rich tend to be well connected with the government and so are usually able to safeguard their interests. The urban formal sector workers—usually relatively better off—are also often strongly organized. Their capacity to trigger riots or strikes may frighten the government in question. Frequently, therefore, it is the poor, the social services and the capital budgets which get hit hardest by adjustment programs.

International domination of the adjustment process. Since the early 1980s the IMF and the World Bank have become increasingly active in the shaping of adjustment programs. A growing proportion of their lending is made conditional to a particular adjustment path being pursued. Theoretically the adjustment program is agreed between the IMF/World Bank and the government. In practice, the programs are usually drawn up by the international officials and urged on governments who may resist or even be confused by the measures entailed. There will be consultation with the ministry of finance and the central bank, but other ministries will be left out, even though the eventual adjustment program may have a profound impact on them.

Bank and Fund officials wearily offer the familiar rejoinder to criticisms of "IMF/World Bank adjustment programs" that they are not "their" programs at all, but those of the governments in question. This veneer of self-determination is wearing thin. Many Southern commentators see adjustment as the vehicle which has brought foreign rulers back to their shores. The World Bank has become aware that the heavy-handed approach is not paying off, especially in Africa. It has recently recognized the need for a less dogmatic approach in that continent which allows for greater "internalization" by governments of the adjustment process.[107]

The cost of not adjusting. Harsh though adjustment may be, failing to adjust may be even more painful in the long run. Not only are IMF/World Bank loans increasingly conditional on agreed adjustment programs being pursued, but a growing proportion of other official aid is being tagged to the adjustment program in a similar way. A country which refuses to swallow the medicine kisses goodbye to a good proportion of the aid it would otherwise receive. African countries which energetically pursued agreed reforms received a 19 percent increase in aid in the mid-1980s, while those which eschewed prescribed reforms saw their aid fall by 5 percent.[108] The "reforming countries" did perform better economically during this period than the "non-reforming countries," but the difference can be accounted for by the increased aid they received.

Failure to win an IMF seal of approval makes commercial banks even more wary of rescheduling their loans or making new loans. Even trade credits are denied and the debtor country becomes increasingly cut off from the international community. Perhaps the harshest price of not adjusting is inflation. Maintaining deficits by increasing public borrowing, with central banks printing more currency to meet the demand, is short-sighted and careless. It solves no problems but postpones them and magnifies them for the future. Today's deficit becomes tomorrow's inflation. Confidence in the economy evaporates, black markets and smuggling erupt. In inflationary periods it is invariably the prices of food and essential goods which rise fastest, hence the poor bear the highest share of the burden. While conventional adjustment can hurt the poor, failing to adjust can be even more damaging to them.

The relationship of cause and effect in the above four factors is often difficult to disentangle. Critics of adjustment often fail to consider how much of the deterioration occurred before the adjustment program was launched. Ghana is a case in point. Social indicators have fallen alarmingly, but mostly before the wide-ranging economic reform program was launched in 1985. The reforms may have compounded some of the problems for some social groups, but it is simply unhistoric to hold them responsible for all the increased suffering. Faulty conclusions can be drawn from such oversimplification.

Similarly, the World Bank and IMF are often blamed for prescribing medicine which kills the patient when it might be more appropriate to attack the source of the disease. It is the Northern governments who have constructed an international economic environment which is impossible for most Southern countries to survive in.

The economic crisis is rather like a real-life game of "Monopoly" in which one set of players (the rich world) start with hotels on Boardwalk and Park Place while the others have nothing on Mediterranean Avenue. As the game progresses and the poorer players land on the hotels, the Third World debt mounts. Meanwhile their own rents—the price of the raw commodities they export—fall as the bargaining power of the rich players increases. The latter lend money to the poor players or reschedule past loans to maintain the pretense that the game is playable. But the debts *can't* be repaid, and rescheduling merely prolongs the ludicrous game. Even if the debts were written off at a stroke, given the present inequities, a new debt crisis might evolve within about fifteen years. Each time around the board the picture becomes bleaker for one set of players. It is true they collect $200 every time they pass "Go"—the official aid they receive—but this is increasingly marginal as it becomes dwarfed by the debt service bills.

Of course, it would be wrong to suggest that Northern governments deserve all the blame. Southern governments have frequently pursued shortsighted policies favoring a small group of elite at the expense of the long-term interests of the country and of the poor. And the economic crisis relates in good measure to the protracted problem of recession which gripped the whole world from the end of the 1970s.

NGOs have the opportunity to present a constructive and compelling case for the reform of the current adjustment orthodoxy. This requires, first, a careful review of their practical experience of adjustment, then a detailed critique of the various components of typical adjustment packages.

NGO Experience and Concerns

From the vantage point of poor communities NGOs can see poverty being created at prodigious rates. Long experienced in the need to practice natural disaster preparedness, they are becoming mindful of the need to respond to economic disasters. They see the prices of food and other essentials rise beyond the reach of the poor. They see unemployment soar, and health, education and other services shrink. They see shortages of equipment, fertilizers and other inputs needed by poor farmers. They see a great influx into prostitution and crime as people struggle for survival. They see malnutrition and infant mortality rise again after decades of gradual improvement. And they see escalating violence, rioting and social disintegration as poverty soars and the gap between rich and poor widens. Throughout the 1980s they have seen a decade of "development rollback."

NGOs are having to recognize that no matter how successful the projects they support are, the overall war against poverty is being lost. Poverty will not be defeated just by tackling it at the micro-level, important as that work is for the millions of people who benefit directly from grass-roots development projects. To stem the mounting tide necessitates attacking the root causes of poverty at the macro-level.

In presenting their evidence, however, NGOs do need to reflect carefully on whether their criticisms should be directed at the adjustment program or at the economic decline which preceded it. Where poverty has been deepened, for example, are some components of the adjustment program actually positive? Can the negative components be reformed so as to avoid the damage? To argue, simply, for adjustment to be suspended is not a plausible option. Neither Southern governments nor Northern governments will listen.

NGOs must continue to strive hard for debt cancellation and for "adjustment in the North" but they should not deny the need to correct imbalances. If the roof is leaking, the tenant may be right to criticize the landlord for the bad state of the house, but this is no substitute for covering the furniture to prevent damage.

Close investigation of an adjustment program may indicate that the most negative components have arisen not from Northern insistence but from the government's own choice. Governments frequently find it convenient to use the International Monetary Fund as a scapegoat for their unpopular policies, and a nationalistic press will assist in this. For example, when food subsidies were completely—though fleetingly—withdrawn in Zambia and riots ensued, the government roundly blamed the IMF, and that remains the popular view. The government even organized mass protests to demonstrate public rejection of these, its own, policies. It was true that the IMF had stipulated subsidy cuts as one of its conditions, but had called for a *gradual* phasing out of subsidies on *breakfast meal* only, the basic food consumed by wealthier Zambians. The government delayed action until the last minute and then whisked away the subsidy in such a way that the millers felt they could no longer afford to produce roller meal, he staple food of the poor. This product consequently disappeared altogether from the shop shelves. The poor not only were unable to find their normal staple, but the alternative, more expensive meal had doubled in price—hence the riots.[109]

The IMF and World Bank are frequently blamed for *creating* the economic crisis rather than attempting to manage it. They are creations of Northern governments and they yield enormously powerful influence, but their functions are those of a bank for governments. Just as someone who has recently lost their job and who goes into the red might approach their bank manager for an overdraft, so governments go to the Bank and Fund. When individuals exceed their overdraft limit the bank manager holds back further loans unless they demonstrate they are strenuously reducing spending or increasing income. It would be quite unacceptable for the bank manager to insist that the customers cut their food bill or stop buying clothes for the children. And if thousands of the bank's customers are in a similar predicament a bank manager with any social conscience should do something to persuade local employers or the government to change their policies.

Similarly, the Bank and the Fund should be answerable for what they are guilty of, not for everything. They should be criticized for neglecting the social and environmental consequences of reforms they advocate, for placing undue emphasis on export-led growth and the discredited notion of "trickle-down," and they have certainly not done enough to argue for adjustment in the North, but it is unrealistic to blame them for creating the economic crisis in the first place. In some cases, it is true, the World Bank has funded projects which failed and which therefore contributed to the national debt, but this is a small part of the problem.

It is also true that the IMF and World Bank are in essence institutions controlled and funded by the major industralized countries. They may be *agents* of those powers, but that is not the same as being those powers. NGOs have good cause to criticize Northern economic and trade policies but they should focus their attack on the Group of Seven governments, at individual finance ministers, at OECD forums and at other bodies who have direct influence on Northern policy, not just at the IMF and World Bank.

In conducting research relating to adjustment, NGOs are well advised to concentrate on communities where it works. An action research methodology is effective—in which the researcher has a very open agenda, allowing the communities themselves the chance to give direction to the study—but the NGO should be wary of hearsay evidence or gossip. Most people the world over, given the chance to do so, will readily complain about the government of the day, especially if they think that by doing so they might be increasing the chances of their problems being addressed. On the other hand, in more repressive regimes people will remain silent if they are suspicious that critical remarks will be reported to the authorities.

To be effective the NGO evidence should be thorough, even though limited to a few communities. They should be confident in the street view they are able to offer. For example, in an urban slum an NGO may easily deduce that the poor have found food price increases painful. This is hardly surprising. What might be more informative would be to learn if any benefits from the promised "targeted food distribution" were seen and if so who they went to; whether anyone from the government has talked to the poor about "compensatory schemes," for example, to give training, land and credit to those who volunteer to leave the slums and take up farming; what do they think of such schemes; have there been any changes in the health services, such as the availability of essential drugs at the local dispensary; has the policy of liberalization offered the poor more opportunities for petty trading; has the emergence of a black market affected them at all; what response has the community made to the deteriorating situation they are experiencing; and so on.

Research into the grassroots impact of adjustment programs should also address other questions. For example, have the poorer farmers, especially the women, managed to increase their production to take advantage of farm-gate price increases? If not, what are the constraints they experience and what policy changes or assistance would help dismantle the barriers? Does the adjustment program have any impact on the amount of land allocated to women, the availability of credit for agricultural inputs, the provision of animal traction, help with marketing and the other needs of small farmers? What impact is adjustment having on the provision of the social services and infrastructure that the poor require? Are roads damaged in the rainy season being repaired? Are local primary school teachers disappearing because of non-payment of salary? Are operations at the local hospital being held up because of shortages of surgical gloves, fuel, anaesthetics and other necessities?

Few NGOs have attempted to compile such household-level accounts of the debt and adjustment issue. They are more likely to criticize orthodox strategies by reinterpreting official reports and government-provided statistics.

Where they have offered an alternative street view (e.g. Oxfam UK, the World Council of Churches and its member organizations, IBASE in Brazil), their evidence has been powerful and effective, though this new area of work demands of them new disciplines and skills which they are only just beginning to appreciate. Undoubtedly their early work helped to focus the attention of other more powerful bodies. For example, UNICEF, in its agenda-setting book, *Adjustment with a Human Face,*[110] credited Oxfam and other NGOs with helping to pioneer concern on the issue.

Experience is slow to build up, however. Most direct NGO evidence at present is too cursory to have the impact it deserves. Frequently it is impossible to tell whether the problem identified is adjustment itself or simply the general economic decline, and some evidence appears to be derived from local newspapers rather from the NGO's own experience. It may be more effective for the NGO to commission one or a small group of researchers to make a specific investigation. The methodology for this need not be of an orthodox survey nature. Indeed it should draw from well-tested techniques of rapid rural appraisal and participatory research.[111,112] Valuable models might be the report of Oxfam UK's Action Research Project in Malawi,[113] or a recent social survey amongst poor people in Guyaquil, Ecuador.[114]

A modest investment or research effort is likely to be rewarded by a rich base of dependable information, in the form which makes it immediately usable, not just in the international arena, but also in the country of study. Oxfam UK's first two monographs in its "Debt and Poverty" series, on Jamaica and Zambia,[115,116] were widely reported in the national media of those countries, and discussed both in academic circles and with government officials. If the researcher chosen is from a local institution there may be an added bonus of helping to draw closer links between the NGO and the academic communities.

Evidence which is valuable ranges from a thorough investigation (taking perhaps several months or even years to compile) of the impact agricultural sector reforms have on subsistence crop producers, to a graphic portrait (prepared by a local journalist or NGO worker in a matter of days) of the problems experienced by a specific group of families in one community.

The thorough investigation might look at the response of poor farmers to new opportunities; the consequences of any increased entry into the money economy; the constraints on increasing production; the relevance of agricultural extension services and how these have altered under adjustment; changes in social structures, in particular the impact of reforms on women farmers; the impact of changing agricultural patterns on soil structures and other environmental issues; and the relationship of farmers to the official structures (including parastatals) and to decision makers. On the other hand, a graphic portrait would be less rigorous, but might help remind decision makers that behind the technical issues of economic planning lies a very human drama. It can also provide valuable ammunition for newspaper articles, for NGO publications and for lobbying, and it may also reveal issues which had been overlooked by researchers following more scientific approaches.

A further methodology which is valuable is to study how grassroots NGOs and the communities themselves have devised strategies to cope with the new generation of problems faced by the poor. This might indicate ways in which adjustment programs could be reformed to avoid social damage.

Attention to research and documentation in this way will inevitably strengthen NGOs in their ability to criticize adjustment programs and in the use of their operational experience in international lobbying.

Typical NGO Criticisms of Adjustment.

The most prominent NGO criticisms of typical adjustment programs have been the following:

- Major changes in government policy or government spending practices are introduced with scant reference to their impact on the poor.
- Little or no attempt is made to consult organizations (or sometimes even ministries) which are best equipped to predict the social impact of those changes. For example, experience shows that women are likely to be particularly affected by certain adjustment measures, but there is no effort made to consult women's organizations. Similarly, NGOs, trade unions, peasant associations and other organizations which can reasonably claim to represent concerns of the poor are rarely consulted either by governments or by the international financial institutions.
- Where reference is made to social impact, the poor are generally regarded as a homogeneous group, at best differentiated between urban and rural poor. Experience shows that different categories of poor people are affected in profoundly different ways. For example, increasing agricultural prices is said to benefit the rural sector in Africa and, because most of the poor live in rural areas, such a

change is described as distributionally positive. Work experience in rural areas can enable NGOs to estimate which categories of the rural poor are likely to benefit, which will only benefit if certain additional steps are taken (such as extending credit or marketing facilities), and which categories are likely to lose out (such as landless laborers and those living in remote areas).

- Little or no effort is made to assess the long-term environmental consequences of the reforms. The encouragement of logging or of a rapid transition to non-traditional crops can lead to severe strain on the natural resource base unless corrective action is built in from the outset.

- Conventional adjustment programs favor a particular type of development model whose overriding objective is economic growth. NGOs would argue that, while growth is an *important* condition for sustainable poverty alleviation, it is not a *sufficient* condition. The *style* of growth is a vitally important consideration. In particular, a development model which places excessive emphasis on export-led growth may encourage production for the export market at the expense of production for the internal market. Exclusive emphasis on a few key sectors of the economy may leave the majority of the poor high and dry if they are not engaged in those sectors. The World Bank's rhetoric of the mid-1970s ("redistribution with growth") implied helping the have-nots at the expense of the haves. Throughout much of the 1980s there has been a money-centered emphasis on economic growth and meeting debt service obligations rather than a people-centered emphasis on equity ("adjustment with growth"—taking from the have-not countries and giving to the have countries).

- Many of the reforms appear to relate more to an ideological mission than to a concern to create conditions which foster sustainable development. The IMF/World Bank message is generally hostile to state intervention and enthusiastic about the private sector irrespective of the efficiency of the parastatals in that country or of the sophistication and trustworthiness of the private sector.

- Reforms, when introduced, are usually sudden and sweeping. Unless such measures are explicitly pro-poor, they are likely to be socially damaging. The poor are least able to adapt rapidly to new opportunities and sudden shocks, while the rich are most adept at turning new situations to their advantage. Often adjustment measures could be more helpful or less damaging if they are introduced gradually, with more attention to sequencing—interweaving other actions with the economic reforms, so that the poorer sections of society are not only protected but actually benefit.

- The World Bank has been reluctant to consider any significant redesigning of adjustment packages so as to make poverty alleviation an explicit objective from the outset. This may now be changing. The 1989 special report on the African crisis[117] made clear that early adjustment programs had neglected social spending and the 1990 *World Development Report*[118] calls for a much more sensitive treatment of poverty issues, both within project planning and adjustment lending. The Bank's second review of adjustment lending (March 1990) has gone further. While denying the evidence that adjustment increases "the overall misery of the poor," it concludes that programs in future "should include poverty alleviation as an objective and provide measures to reduce the potential short-run burden on the poor of external shocks or adjustment policies."

Typical Response of the Poor to Economic Crisis

Many grassroots NGOs and community groups are pioneering new approaches, often designed by the poor themselves, to help cope with the new types of adversity they are encountering. For many this entails rapid changes in their programs and sometimes a bewildering range of challenges. When such requests come from the poor themselves or from grassroots NGOs they are sometimes controversial but more divisive are the invitations from official bodies to collaborate in "compensatory programs." The NGO has to consider carefully whether accepting such offers will lead to losing sight of their chosen priorities and losing contact with their chosen constituency.

The following illustrates the vast range of survival strategies in which NGOs are involved:

- NGOs are increasing their work in the urban informal sector, helping those who have become impoverished supplement their incomes through small-scale trading or production activities.
- There are many examples of helping to maintain nutritional levels as food prices soar, through urban vegetable gardens, planting of fruit trees, food purchasing cooperatives, nutrition advice groups and so on. For example, a Bolivian NGO has helped tackle the alarming increase in malnutrition amongst unemployed tin-mining families following the tin price crash of 1985. The NGO has set up a food buying cooperative—buying in bulk so as to get basic food at much cheaper prices.
- Some NGOs are helping newly unemployed people make a new start through training programs, credit schemes, job creation projects and other initiatives.
- Many NGOs have had to decide whether or not to step in and take the place of government health services which have had to close or

which have become emaciated as a result of budget cuts. On the one hand they see the very evident need to maintain services which the poor need, but on the other hand they feel reluctant to pick up the bill for something they feel the state should continue to provide. Similar dilemmas arise in the case of other services such as education, water supply and agricultural extension services.

- In some countries where food subsidies have been abolished, the government has introduced "targeted food distribution" schemes. NGOs are often invited to help operate these and again they see dilemmas as well as opportunities.
- In the agricultural sector NGOs may help poorer farmers (especially women) to take advantage of price increases. For example, NGOs in the Dominican Republic are helping coffee growing *campesinos* to establish their own agencies for direct exporting of their coffee, so by-passing the middlemen and earning more. In various African countries NGOs are establishing credit and marketing services so that the poorer farmers can get the inputs they need and markets they can rely on.
- Where agricultural changes have potentially serious environmental consequences, NGOs are often able to catalog the dangers and help organize local populations to articulate their concerns.
- In many countries NGOs have educational programs to inform poor people about their country's debt crisis and about the adjustment programs. This may lead to discussion groups and perhaps a growing confidence to speak out on such issues.

Adjustment Measures—Unpacking the Package

Adjustment programs usually contain a large number of interlocking measures. The economist will say that the package has to be looked at as a whole, that it is misleading to single out specific measures and consider them in isolation. This view is voiced by the radical as well as the classical economist. The former will point out that the program as a whole reflects a model of development whose foundations are export-led growth, rapid integration into the international economy, private sector exclusivity and unquestioning erosion of state intervention.

To analyze the social costs, however, it is necessary to study the specific measures that comprise the program. This shows how actions which may seem desirable from a macroeconomic point of view can damage particular sectors of society.

It is necessary to look at social benefits as well as costs. For example, increasing producer prices can help small-holders. Some measures are necessary and perhaps inevitable responses to the country's economic situation. For example, a currency devaluation may be unavoidable if rampant smuggling and black marketeering is to be checked. An NGO critique of the adjustment program is not likely to be taken seriously if such factors are overlooked.

There are approximately twenty ingredients which can be mixed in various proportions to concoct a typical adjustment program, as Table 12.1 indicates. The table summarizes the results of two surveys which analyzed the policy ingredients of a range of Bank and Bank/Fund adjustment programs. Though the social cost/benefit analysis will depend on the specificities of the country concerned, it is possible to arrive at some general conclusions regarding the particular measures.

Trade Policy

The major emphasis is on *currency devaluation*. This is an unpopular measure since it immediately pushes up the prices of imported goods and indirectly pushes up other prices. However, it is a mechanism that apportions pain rather than creates it. In a deteriorating economic situation real earnings will inevitably fall. Devaluation can be a relatively progressive way of apportioning that fall. The poor tend to consume much less in the way of imported goods than do the better off. Without controlled adjustment the "natural" way an economy adjusts to lower national income is through price inflation, which hits the poor hardest. Devaluation also tends to favor producers of goods for export or for import substitution. By bringing the currency further into line with a market-indicated level, devaluation also curbs any black market. It should be pointed out that the super-rich tend to be immune from devaluation since they are likely to hold most of their wealth and carry out most of their transactions in hard, rather than local, currencies.

NGOs should therefore be wary of automatic criticism of devaluation. They should, however, study whether intermediate goods needed for domestic production become scarce as a result, whether increased export earnings (in local currency terms) are passed on to farmers and whether essential inputs or household goods needed by the poor and which are imported become scarce or prohibitively expensive. Also, in countries where the poor are dependent on basic imports, they should press for devaluation to be combined with targeted measures to safeguard this access.

The parallel measure of *import liberalization* may be socially useful in that goods which were previously controlled and perhaps only available on the black market or erratically through government shops become more widely available and cheaper. *Tariff policies* can be a better way of regulating the use of scarce foreign exchange than direct control by a government department. The latter attracts bureaucratic delays, inefficiency and corruption while the former offers governments the chance to earn revenue, especially by having high duties on imported luxuries. In this way a

Table 12.1   Policy Conditions of Adjustment Lending

	Percentage of World Bank SALs* subject to this condition	Seven County Study IMF/World Bank adjustment programs	
		Bank	Fund
TRADE POLICY			
Remove import quotas	57	6	7
Cut tariffs	24		
Improve export incentives and institutional support	76	6	6
Exchange rate policy	2	5	—
RESOURCE MOBILIZATION			
Reform budget or taxes	70	5	6
Reform interest rate policy	9	2	7
Strengthen management of external borrowing	49	5	6
Improve financial performance by public enterprise	73	5	6
Current expenditures	—	2	7
Strengthen financial and capital market	—	2	7
EFFICIENT USE OF RESOURCES			
Revise priorities of public investment program	59	6	3
Revise agricultural prices	73	6	5
Dissolve or reduce powers of state marketing boards	14		
Reduce or eliminate some agricultural input subsidies	27		
Revise energy prices	49	5	6
Introduce energy conservation measures	35	3	2
Develop indigenous energy sources	24	3	3
Revise industry incentive system	68	4	3
INSTITUTIONAL REFORMS			
Strengthen capacity to formulate and implement public investment program	86	4	2
Increase efficiency of public enterprises	57	6	1
Improve support for agriculture (marketing, etc.)	57	6	2
Improve support for industry and subsectors (including price controls)	49	4	0

*SAL = Structural Adjustment Loan
Notes: The first column is from a review of World Bank structural adjustment lending 1980-86 by Paul Mosley.[119] The second column is from a study of concurrent Bank/Fund adjustment loans in seven countries: Ivory Coast, Jamaica, Kenya, the Philippines, Senegal, Thailand and Turkey.[120]

government can make some of the earnings previously made by black marketeers on luxury goods.

Improved incentives for exporters can be positive where productive assets are distributed relatively equitably and where the poor are able to produce for export as well as the rich, but it is important to assess whether increased production for export is at the expense of the internal needs.

Resource Mobilization

Reforming budgets is often the most controversial ingredient of adjustment programs. The emphasis is usually on *cutting expenditures* rather than on increasing revenues. This is likely to lead to cuts in those government services that are needed by the poor, though more recently the World Bank has tried to guard against this, for example by advocating the restructuring of health and education services to promote primary health care and primary education, rather than across the board cuts. NGOs are well placed to assess the social costs of proposed spending cuts, but they might also be able to indicate less damaging opportunities for government savings. For example, in Africa many state airlines are heavily subsidized. It is surely offensive that businesspeople, and, for that matter, NGO workers, traveling on the cheapest flights from Europe to Africa, are still being subsidized while health services are being cut.

In a similar way, NGOs could argue for increasing revenues, particularly through increased direct taxation of the better off, rather than cutting services. *Reforming taxes* is usually a positive aspect of adjustment programs, though rarely emphasized sufficiently. Most Third World governments receive a much lower proportion of their revenue from direct taxation than do Northern governments, and indirect taxation tends to be a heavier burden on the poor.

In industralized Western countries, taxes on income and profit account for 9.6 percent of GNP on average. In most developing countries, much less revenue is raised in this way. In 1986 these taxes accounted for just 0.2 percent of GNP in Bolivia, 0.3 percent in Uganda, and less than 3 percent in Bangladesh, Burma, India, Sierra Leone, Ghana and Argentina.[121] In only a few countries such as Togo, Indonesia, Zimbabwe, Botswana, Cameroon, Ecuador and Malaysia are the figures comparable with the Western situation. In fact, in relatively few developing countries do total government revenues or expenditures come close to those in the West, giving the lie to the suggestion that economic problems in the South are simply to do with "too much government." (What is clear, however, is that serious economic and social problems correlate closely with large budget deficits). The reverse case could even be made.

Cuts in food subsidies can be socially harsh and politically unpopular, but not always as negative as they appear at first sight. Most subsidies are universal, not just for the poor, and so they are a very expensive way of protecting the vulnerable, if that is the objective. Often, indeed, the poor don't receive such subsidies. Governments often use free food to supplement salaries for civil servants and the military. To qualify for benefits it may be necessary to register with the local authorities (i.e. to have a permanent address). And sometimes the subsidized food is available only in large units which the poor cannot afford. Either way the wealthier people gain more than the poor. For example, a survey in Morocco[122] showed that the richest 10 percent of the population derived more benefits from food subsidies than the poorest 30 percent combined. In Mexico most of the subsidies on tortillas, bread, milk, beef and eggs have benefited the upper income groups. Only the subsidy on beans benefited the poor most.[123] Inefficiencies can be compounded by smuggling. For example, a very high proportion of subsidized maize meal from Zambia is smuggled across the border into Zaire, where food is not subsidized and is very expensive. This trade is impossible to arrest and means that an immense volume of Zambian public finance is being used to subsidize consumption in neighboring countries and helping smugglers.

But phasing out food subsidies, however inefficient they may be, is socially and politically difficult, and has done more to rock the adjustment boat than any other measure. Riots in Algeria, Egypt, Zambia, Sudan, Venezuela and elsewhere have been testaments to this. NGOs are often very well placed to advise on how and whether a targeted food distribution system could be constructed so that the poor do not suffer if a blanket subsidy is withdrawn.

Other measures in this category are relatively unthreatening to the poor. NGOs may worry that *increasing interest rates* to encourage domestic savings and investment might damage the credit schemes that they are trying to help. They may also question whether this measure would achieve its stated objectives.

NGOs may also question whether "strengthening management of external borrowing" isn't a guarded way of saying "make sure the debts are serviced." They might argue that the international financial institutions should advise debtors to make *less* effort to service their debts. The Managing Director of the IMF has indeed recently cautiously advocated such a line. He suggested in a confidential briefing to representatives of Northern governments that it is time to signal to debtor nations that they should refuse to accept terms from commercial banks which are more stringent than those offered by official creditors, and that they should consider domestic financing needs for restoring economic growth before debt service.

Efficient Use of Resources

Revised priorities for public investment are often needed, but this begs the question of what development model is to be promoted by such investment? NGOs may be able to use any position they attain in the debate about an adjustment program to argue for a development approach which is more in the interests of the poor.

Revising agricultural prices is generally good for small farmers, but not automatically so. The full price increases may not be passed on to them, though they are expected to meet in full increases in prices of inputs. Farmers may well be tempted to increase their proportion of marketed crops only to find, when they come to sell, that the income they derive can buy very little and perhaps they would have been better off to have grown more for their own needs. The urban poor must also be compensated for any increase in food prices which they find impossible to bear.

Dissolving or reducing the powers of state marketing boards is another very controversial measure. Sometimes the parastatals are remarkably inefficient and it is clear that producers would welcome the chance to sell to whomever they choose. This is, for instance, the case with Ethiopian coffee farmers and Zambian groundnut farmers. Where the private sector is controlled by a handful of extremely powerful and ruthless traders it is unlikely that poor farmers will benefit from rapid privatization. The traders are likely to pay low prices and not be prepared to collect from farmers living in remote areas.

Sometimes official aid's enthusiasm for privatization leads to neglect of important social roles played by the state board in addition to simple marketing. The hardship and hunger associated with the phasing out of Malawi's agricultural marketing parastatal is described in Chapter 10.

Reducing or eliminating agricultural input subsidies has an undeniable logic. As with food subsidies they comprise an inefficient way of helping small farmers, and they encourage the overuse of fertilizers and perhaps the wrong balance of farm chemicals. It is usually nitrogen fertilizers that are subsidized but probably lime will not be. This can lead to the use of one without the other and so a gradual buildup of acidity in the soil. Severe soil erosion may result. If the country borders other countries which don't have similar subsidies, then again large-scale smuggling can result. It may be desirable to end agricultural input subsidies, but socially and politically difficult to do so. The pace at which steps are taken is important as well as the sequencing of these steps.

Revising energy prices is not likely to hurt the extreme poor who consume very little purchased energy in most countries. Hence this can be seen as a positive measures from a social perspective, after all why should the poor subsidize the electricity consumption of others? However, the price increases are often detested by the next band in the poverty spectrum, particularly when the price increases include oil and gasoline, and this pushes up fares on public transport steeply.

Energy conservation and generation would probably be socially positive, although great environmental sensitivity is needed in the choice of energy generation. The well publicized and eventually cancelled World Bank loan to the Brazilian power sector is a case in point. This sectoral adjustment loan would in part have financed a major electricity generation drive, concentrating especially on hydroelectric schemes. Many of the dams planned would have proven immensely damaging to the environment and to the tribal communities living in the forests they would have flooded.

Revising the *industry incentive system* gives rise to a number of questions. Do the industries promoted serve the needs of the local populations, in particular the poor? Do they depend on foreign investment and imported technologies? Are the employment conditions acceptable? And have the environmental implications been considered?

Institutional Reforms

Such reforms can be important and consistent with the objective of "institution building," but whether they deserve praise or not depends on whether the development model pursued by the strengthened institutions serves the interests of the poor.

For example, in most African countries there is an urgent need to *improve support for agriculture*. It is common to meet farmers who complain that they were unable to buy the inputs they needed at the critical time or who perhaps brought in an excellent harvest but were simply unable to sell it. However, strengthening rural infrastructure and affording a reliable market may encourage farmers to move further into marketed, as opposed to subsistence, agriculture—whether to supply domestic or export demands. This may not in itself be a bad thing but it introduces new vulnerabilities. If the single supply route becomes blocked for some reason, perhaps because of civil war or a damaged bridge, then the farmers may find themselves suddenly without access to a market. If their produce is an export crop such as coffee, this is very serious as they need to sell their harvest in order to buy food. Similarly, they are at the mercy of fate and merchants for maintaining supply of the goods that they need to buy. Other vulnerabilities arise where the shift to marketed crops leads farmers away from diversified farming into monoculture or where entry into the cash economy alters the power relationship between husbands and wives.

Is Adjustment Necessary, and is it Working?

According to stereotypical arguments of monetarists and Northern governments, developing countries are mostly in a mess because their governments have ignored the need to undergo orderly adjustment, and because they use their resources wastefully. They squander their money on subsidies and on maintaining bloated civil services, they ignore the need to make painful cuts in social services and to encourage investments and savings, they direct too little resources to capital (as opposed to recurrent) spending, they fail to attend to their current account and budget deficits and there is simply "too much government." Though countries such as South Korea—and indeed Western economies—have demonstrated the evident advantages from liberalization, much of the Third World refuses to heed the lessons.

How fair is this view? Using World Bank and other official information we discover three types of flaws.

Firstly, many of the charges Northern governments level against Third World debtors could be applied with more justification to themselves! Low-income countries (LICs) have a more prudent track record than industrialized countries in many respects. They spend a *lower* proportion of their GDP on subsidies (6 percent as compared with 18 percent); a *lower* proportion of their GDP on public sector wages; a *higher* proportion of their government budgets on capital spending (16 percent as compared with 6 percent—though much of this would be accounted for by the repayment of principle on their debts); a *lower* proportion of their budgets on social sectors (8 percent compared with 56 percent); a *lower* proportion of their GDP is accounted for by government spending; and a *higher* proportion of their GDP is directed to investments and savings. Budget and current account deficits may, indeed, be large but they are dwarfed by those of the United States.[124,125]

Northern arguments in favor of opening markets must also be viewed with some skepticism. Northern governments have themselves *increased* protectionism of their own markets throughout the 1980s while preaching liberalization to other countries. There is now more market protectionism in the North than there was in the 1930s. Furthermore, after the Second World War the last thing the troubled economies of Europe wished to do was to remove import restrictions. The oft-quoted example of South Korea deserves closer scrutiny. This country only liberalized after a long period of very strong market intervention and import restrictions which helped build up the industrial strength of the country (around a policy of import substitution) so as to achieve a position of export advantage.

Secondly, the Northern criticisms imply by omission that virtually all the blame lies "over there," on Third World profligacy. They gloss over the fact that their own economic policies have been the principal factor causing interest rates to rise to such dizzy heights. Real interest rates in the 1980s have been the highest they have been in two hundred years. Rather than *receiving* aid from the North, the South is seeing its financial resources extracted at a far higher rate than did Germany through reparations after the First World War.

They also gloss over the fact that the terms of trade have worsened in recent years, again largely because of Northern policies, to the extent that the South is losing US $100 billion per year, three times the level of official aid. They might make reference to the responsibility of commercial banks, but they forget that, at the time, Northern governments were enthusiastic about the banks lending to developing countries, "recycling" the surpluses generated by oil exporting countries in the 1970s. Even as late as October 1981, only months before the debt crisis erupted, and when the writing was clearly on the wall, the UK Chancellor, Geoffrey Howe, described this lending as "practical and pragmatic . . . surely the best form of recycling . . . we can continue to rely on the banks to play a major role here. . . . It is the free market system that has recycled the surpluses and continued to deliver some growth worldwide."[126]

Thirdly, the Northern arguments ignore the fact that the present adjustment approach simply is not working. By the World Bank's own admission, "no country undergoing rescheduling has significantly improved its debt ratios."[127] A Commonwealth Secretariat study[128] reveals that sixteen out of thirty IMF programs under their Extended Fund Facility were cancelled for non-compliance and several more had unsatisfactory outcomes, mainly because traditional short-term performance indicators could not be met. By 1988 only one of these programs was still operating (in Chile). And UNCTAD concludes that "experience to date does not suggest that successful privatization, liberalization and budgetary reform lead automatically to a resumption of vigorous economic growth."[129]

One of the stated key objectives of structural adjustment is usually to achieve export-led growth. However there is little evidence to suggest that this objective is being achieved. A World Bank study of adjustment loans in seven countries showed that only two countries were able to increase substantially their export earnings; the others increased export volumes, but faced declining world prices.[130] A recent World Bank report[131] cited as positive evidence—in support of the premise that "adjustment is working"— the fact that from 1985 to 1987 Africa managed to increase its export volumes by 3 percent per year. However, figures used elsewhere in the same report show that the prices Africa receives for its commodities fell on average by 3.7 percent per annum over the whole of the 1980s. Hence Africa has not achieved increased *income* in spite of its efforts to export more. The same report also fails to comment on whether the 5 percent per annum increase in export volumes from 1976–1980 (after the mid-1970s famine) was also due to the pursuit of favorable policies! If so, then this was prior to the era of structural adjustment. UNCTAD suggests that, in many highly indebted countries, it is now clear that increases in exports have been at the expense of domestic production, not new production.[132]

An IMF staff member quoted in an UNCTAD report[133] has thrown doubt on his institution's method for calculating credit expansion within adjustment programs. He reveals that an economic shock comprising a 10 percent drop in export earnings (due to a fall in commodity prices), a doubling in debt service charges and a complete cessation of capital inflows makes no difference at all to the credit needs of the country according to the IMF model. In reality, of course, such a severe shock would dramatically reduce growth, upset balance of payments and require exchange rate controls. This discrepancy raises questions as to the validity of the IMF's theoretical approach to economic planning.

Though evidence about the macroeconomic validity of orthodox adjustment is mixed, there is very strong evidence that it brings intolerable social costs. The World Bank is increasingly prepared to recognize this, but the Fund denies such a link. One Bank report on adjustment and income distribution concludes that "if contractionary adjustment packages can survive three years of sharply deteriorating social indicators, income distribution will probably improve—but people below the poverty line will probably suffer irreparable damage in health, nutrition and education."[134]

The Bank is particularly concerned about "the urban poor who at present it seems bear a disproportionate share or adjustment costs,"[135] whereas the Fund concludes that "there is no support for the view that adjustment programs generally hurt the poor as a group."[136] The World Bank, however, cites the case of Turkey.[137] Through following a strict adjustment program, the Turkish gross domestic product grew by 3.5 percent annually between 1979 and 1984, while exports grew by a phenomenal 25 percent per year; however for the same period real wages declined by 28 percent overall, at the same time unemployment also rose, indicating, as the Bank concluded, "an increased return to owners of non-farm enterprises."

All parties agree that increased poverty should be avoided. A meeting on Africa's long-term development, chaired by the World Bank President and comprising the World Bank, IMF, UN agencies and others, agreed on a Joint statement saying that

> while substantial economic growth is imperative, it is only the means to the overarching objective of improving human welfare—for example reducing infant mortality, increasing educational opportunities, improving health and ensuring food security. Economic adjustment must lead to the long-term improvement in the quality of life.[138]

The conclusion from the above discussion is not that there is no need for adjustment, but that a different type of adjustment is required—one which involves policy changes in the North as well as the South.

13

Structural Transformation

TODAY'S ECONOMIC ORTHODOXY IS a path not to development but to disaster. It is stripping the planet's mantle of its natural resources and diversity. It is casting millions upon millions into abject poverty. It brings a hemorrhaging of money from poor countries to rich on a scale that eclipses the more naked extraction under colonialism. It is polarizing the already obscene wealth gaps, both between individuals and nations. And it is blind to the multiplying abuses of human rights and cultural integrity.

It is a path to disaster because it sacrifices the weak for the pleasure of the strong, it sacrifices the future for the extravagance of today and it sacrifices moral and spiritual values for the monetary values of the cash register. It exacerbates both greed and resentment, and so sets people and nations against each other, rather than encouraging cooperation.

The global development model has so manifestly failed that talk of adjustment appears farcically inadequate. The very term suggests a fine tuning of a system that is otherwise in good repair. It suggests that it is the countries who face the dual crises of debt and poverty who must do the changing, as if the rest of the world is free of responsibility. It suggests that, through such internal fine tunings, those countries will be able to chart a new course that is acceptable.

The old model has failed. It is not the time for retuning, but for searching for a new order. For this we should speak not of "structural *adjustment*" but of "structural *transformation*"; transformation to a new development model which serves the needs of the people, the planet and peace. The goals would be more than the conventional ones of development and economic growth; they must include poverty eradication, equity, nature conservancy, democracy and social justice. We need a development model based on the DEPENDS formula.

Governments of North and South share a responsibility for structural transformation. It cannot be achieved by the South alone, and the bargain will not be struck unless the North is confident that the sacrifices it is to make contribute to the agreed strategy and are not hijacked by Southern elites.

Reforms in economic management by Southern governments are necessary and NGOs should not deny this. In fact, the reforms required go well beyond the control of money supply, budget deficits and other ingredients of conventional adjustment programs. It is not just good housekeeping that is needed, but a reordering of priorities to ensure that the economic machinery serves the needs of the majority of the people, not just the elite. However, even more urgent and far reaching are the reforms that are needed within the international economic and trading system: the reforms in the North.

Some NGOs believe the latter to be so much more significant that they refuse to be deflected into debates about domestic policy failings of Southern governments. The growing awareness of interdependence makes it increasingly clear, however, that the dual responsibilities of North and South cannot be separated. They must go together, hand in hand. This leads into a critical debate about conditionality.

There is a powerful case for arguing that any actions of the North that increase the burden on the world's poor should be stopped unconditionally. However, simply stopping those actions may not lead to the burden being removed unless parallel measures are taken in the South. In this case, should concessions made by the North be conditional? Is it right for one group of (powerful) nations to impose conditions on others? And can the North be trusted to frame conditions which really serve the interests of the poor?

New Conditionality

One school of thought believes that aid and adjustment is already bound up with too much Northern conditionality, and that this owes more to the export of ideology than to the correction of economic imbalances. It maintains that adjustment is not working because the North is pursuing its own political agenda and allocating too few resources. It advocates debt relief and greatly increased aid, with the barest of conditionality.

This school holds, for example, that tranches of adjustment lending for correcting balance of payments difficulties should depend solely on progress toward meeting agreed targets for restoring economic balance, leaving to the government in question the choice of *how* to achieve the targets. Some might elect to liberalize markets, to reduce state intervention, to reduce subsidies and to increase incentives for exporters. But others might prefer to improve the efficiency of their parastatals, to assist import substitution or to strengthen controls on the private market.

A second school of thought argues that conditionality is an inevitable aspect of North–South relations, that the problem to date is that the *wrong* conditions have been set and that we should call not for "no strings" but for a more visionary type of conditionality which promotes a people-centered approach to sustainable development. This school points out that debt relief given to certain regimes such as Zaire will not benefit the poor at all and may merely assist despotic rulers to remain in power and so be counterproductive.[139]

Current adjustment programs do little or nothing to stem the ruthless repression and denial of democratic and human rights, the legalized oppression of women or ethnic groups, the scandalous laundering of national assets into the foreign bank accounts of the country's elite and the enormous inequalities of wealth and opportunities. Policy-based lending provides an opportunity to encourage reforms designed to improve the human condition, not just the economic condition.

At the very least, this school argues that policy-based lending is here to stay, and that it is rather more realistic to try to persuade the World Bank and others to modify their approach in favor of the poor rather than to relinquish conditionality. Where people have little access to decision making or to other expressions of democracy, and where state institutions are subject to little public accountability, a new form of "pro-poor" conditionality would help redress the situation. The approach may sound paternalistic, but such a risk should be avoidable by ensuring that the new conditions are genuinely those articulated by the poor themselves through their people's organizations and NGOs.

The proposal here is for a concerted effort of progressive Northern and Southern NGOs to construct a common platform. This slate would embrace advocacy for both a DEPENDS style of development in the South and for Northern reforms which would make such a transition possible. The common platform would be that of structural transformation.

Principles of Structural Transformation

Structural transformation requires "good governance" and international justice.

For governments of the South this means more than economic efficiency, it means pursuing a DEPENDS approach to development through:

- Poverty alleviation by improving of social services, policies of food security and other measures.
- Broader distribution of productive assets and income earning opportunities, for example through land reform, credit schemes for the poor and reform of discriminatory practices.

- Creating an enabling environment for individual enterprise, to encourage socially responsible business.
- Matching industrial potential with national needs, through supporting essential industries and ensuring a healthy balance of production for local and export markets.
- Protection of the natural environment, through sustainable resource use and pollution control;
- Ensuring that the government and instruments of the State are publicly accountable, through making information widely available, regular consultations with the people (particularly with those affected by proposed policies or plans) and encouraging public debate;
- Guaranteeing freedom of speech, free press, freedom to worship, freedom to associate in trade unions, political parties or other organizations and full human rights.
- Using United Nations and other external mediators to resolve conflicts peacefully.
- Increasing efforts to cooperate with other developing countries in trade arrangements, regional development strategies, international policy negotiations and the pursuit of peace.

Northern governments can help achieve these goals through sensitive use of carrots and sticks and by removing obstacles. But will they? Northern governments can claim few brownie points for their record of concern for the world's poor. However, now is the time for enlightened self-interest to hold sway in international diplomacy. We all have a stake in promoting good governance and sustainable development throughout the world.

Industrialized countries spend some US $450 billion per year on defense. Now that the "Cold War" is thawing, even though there are military tensions elsewhere, there is a window of opportunity to mount a new type of Strategic Defense Initiative—a battle against environmental destruction, political injustice and poverty. Important Northern contributions would include:

- Elimination of the present net transfer of resources from debt-distressed developing countries to Northern creditors.
- Massive efforts to protect the global environment.
- Removing barriers to the import of processed and manufactured goods from the Third World and supporting initiatives to improve the terms of trade for the South.
- Introducing strict controls on transnational corporations.
- A major global peace initiative.
- Substantial increases in official aid and a reorientation of aid programs toward a poverty focus.

- Use of aid and debt relief to finance and encourage the transition to "good governance" in the South described above.
- Improving governance in the North also, by, for example, democratizing international forums, such as the World Bank and IMF.

Structural Transformation—Tasks for the North

In recent years both Southern and Northern NGOs have given increased attention to debating among themselves and with officials from governmental agencies the changes in the North that are required to make the eradication of poverty possible. For example, in 1987 a workshop bringing together people from NGOs and the UN system concluded that:

> the international community must create the conditions of freedom and solidarity, of peace and self-determination that will help the poor in their conquest of the democracy which is required to obtain a fair return for their production.[140]

Specific policy challenges were voiced by this workshop, including that the North should end and then reverse the present net flow of resources from South to North, through debt write-off, reducing interest charges and pressure on the banks to reduce their debts or debt service. The forum also called on Northern governments to support unilateral action by debtor countries to impose ceilings on their debt service bills when linked to development efforts designed to reduce poverty, and to change the rules governing the IMF and World Bank to allow a rescheduling of the loans of these institutions.

Where loans were made for ill-advised development projects to regimes who are no longer in power and where the loans are tainted by international corruption and deceit, there should be a mechanism for selective repudiation. The International Court of Justice or a specially constituted tribunal should be charged with such adjudication and for allocating the burden to the banks and corporations which have been shown to be at fault. The Bataan nuclear power station in the Philippines is a case in point.

This project was commissioned by President Marcos, built by a US company, Westinghouse, financed by Citibank and a consortium of Western banks and is being paid for, today, by the people of the Philippines. Though the original quote was US $500 million, the final price was more than four times this sum. It is alleged that much of the price escalation relates to corruption and business malpractices. At the time of writing, bribery charges against Westinghouse and another US company are being heard in US law courts and the whole project has been referred to the International Chamber of Commerce for arbitration.

This nuclear power station was built, incredibly, on a seismic fault line in the most earthquake-prone region of the country. In the face of popular pressure, the Aquino government has pledged never to bring the power station on stream. It stands today idle; a monument to reckless planning and a symbol of the country's debt. The interest bill alone stands at US $350,000 per day and in addition four hundred engineers, a hefty proportion of the country's technical brainpower, have to work day and night to service the plant, otherwise the reactor could become dangerous.

Thanks to local NGO campaigning, the government is now scrutinizing all the loans which accumulated in the Marcos era to determine their legitimacy. The NGOs are also researching five other case studies of loans which could be linked to major fraud. The Bataan case will set an important precedent, not just for the Philippines but for other debtors elsewhere.

Concerted international action is also needed to help developing countries recover the funds that have escaped as "capital flight." This requires changes in banking regulations which at present provide a cloak of secrecy, enabling the elite to cheat on their country with immunity. It may be that international determination to hunt down narcotics barons, which requires tracing the routes they use for laundering their money, will set useful precedents.

NGOs have repeatedly called for Northern governments to dismantle the barriers which obstruct fair trade. They argue that developing countries should have access to Northern markets for processed products and manufactured goods, not just raw commodities. Throughout the 1980s, in spite of the rhetoric of trade liberalization, Northern protectionism has actually increased to higher levels than in the 1930s. In 1987 the British Chancellor stated that this increase costs the Third World US $100 billion per year, as much as total debt service.

International agreements such as the Common Fund and commodity agreements are important, but reforms in Northern agricultural, industrial and other policies are even more urgently required for international fairness. Collective international action is also required to curb the abuses of transnational corporations in their employment, investment, marketing and transfer pricing practices.

NGOs have pressed the North to give full support for international initiatives on environmental issues such as tropical deforestation, global warming and marine pollution. Conventions, action programs and new institutions established by international agreement need clout and resources if they are to work, but greater care is also necessary (for example with the Tropical Forest Action Plan) to ensure that they are socially as well as environmentally desirable.

Many NGOs have argued that geopolitical shifts make this the ideal juncture to reduce Northern military budgets and use some of the savings for a global program of poverty alleviation, environmental protection, conflict resolution and the promotion of democracy.

This is the long dreamed-of transformation of swords into plowshares.

A significant precedent has already been set. In March 1990 President Bush announced a US $250 million aid package for Nicaragua, shortly after the election of the UNO government. This aid, he announced, would not result in reduced aid elsewhere, but would be drawn from savings in the Defense budget. He ordered his Defense Chief of Staff to sit down with the Secretary of State to work out the details of this budgetary transfer. It is ironic that the first example of a "disarmament–development swap" (a favorite liberal concept) should come in the wake of this lost liberal dream.

Northern NGOs call, ritualistically, for Northern governments to increase their aid, while in the South NGOs are more likely to criticize how aid is used. An NGO gathering in Manila, 1989, argued that aid placed "responsibility in the hands of foreigners rather than in the hands of the people . . . [so weakening] the accountability of governments to their own citizens." Progressive NGOs agree that the quality of aid is more important than its quantity.

Southern NGOs are therefore increasingly calling on their Northern counterparts to do more to "monitor the plans and actions of development donors, . . . to ensure that the people have access to the relevant information to assess social and environmental impacts and to take necessary actions to protect their interests."[141]

This leads to the debate about "positive conditionality." NGOs are increasingly pressing for aid to support programs and policy reforms that are needed by the poor. All aid is conditional, even that from the most progressive Northern NGO, and it is fanciful to think that Northern governments might be persuaded to drop their selection criteria altogether, although they may be persuaded to modify them.

Much could be achieved by using official aid for projects which enhance equity and for promoting policy reforms which dismantle barriers to just development. This would include rewarding regimes which move to a more broadly democratic approach with increased aid. It would have seemed fanciful to suggest this just a few years ago, but it is now beginning to happen.

While economic reform was the "flavor of the decade" in the 1980s, it is already becoming apparent that political reform will be the flavor of the 1990s. For example, the British government has recently made its intentions clear to put more emphasis in aid policy in future on supporting transitions to democracy and governmental accountability in Africa.[142,143] While this may appear imperialistic, it is very much in keeping with the view of many African grassroots NGOs that political reform is much more important than economic reform. NGOs could play a useful role in ensuring that the democracy introduced is built from the bottom up.

Peasant farmers in Bangladesh and Ethiopia have remarkably similar perceptions about their lack of political power—little accountability of local government officials, arbitrary discrimination they experience without any chance of redress and a dearth of information about government plans that affect them. Those in Bangladesh supposedly live in a democracy, while those in Ethiopia do not. Multi-party democracy is not irrelevant; but it is not all that is relevant. To peasant farmers a higher priority may be local-level democracy.

There is a similar debate about the conditionality of debt relief. Susan George has argued for a "3-D" formula—*debt relief* to finance *development* for the poor and *democracy.*[144] Oxfam UK has similarly proposed that in countries such as the Philippines and Brazil there are strong environmental reasons for giving massive debt relief to finance major programs of land reform. Such countries will continue to tear down their forests while they are obliged to meet huge debt bills, and while family-level debt crises drive more and more peasants off their meager lowland farms to practice slash-and-burn farming in the upland forests. Debt relief is necessary to prevent the former problem and agrarian reform to prevent the latter. International concern about the climate provides the window of opportunity required to make the quantum leap of bringing these two needs together.

NGOs are deeply divided over such ideas of "alternative conditionality," though the same propositions presented under the rubric of "shared responsibility" are much more acceptable.

Southern NGOs are similarly gingerly exploring ideas of such "positive conditionality." The "Manila Declaration" of 1989[145] suggests that "the incentive for successful policy changes toward a sustainable development, including action to reduce population growth rates, should be provided through debt relief rather than through new loans that ultimately add to debt burdens."

As Jan Pronk, Dutch Aid Minister, said recently, it is not just the South that needs good governance, it is needed in the North too. There is, for example, a strong need to democratize international institutions by giving developing countries a much greater voting power in the International Monetary Fund, World Bank and regional development banks, and delinking budgetary contribution from political control within the UN system.

Structural Transformation—Tasks for the South

Though responsibility rests in the North, developing countries must also share the burden. To dwell on the international problems to the extent that it provides an excuse for government inaction in the South does a disservice which the poor and the environment simply cannot afford.

The South must build a new development order from within. This requires efficient economic management to curb imbalances. There are good grounds for blaming the global system for contributing to the problems, but this will not make them go away. Maintaining a high budget deficit and exchange rates well above market-indicated levels are likely to hurt the poor.

However, the right balance must be sought. The welfare and development needs of the poor are too important to be left to the vagaries of the marketplace. Governments should be encouraged to protect and develop economic activities and basic services on which large numbers of the poor depend, even if this means a degree of market protectionism, a slower pace of growth and more cautious economic reforms.

Reforms in the management of human and environmental resources are every bit as important as economic reforms. They are political in nature and are necessary to alter the development course charted.

Bringing these concerns together indicates the need for some reforms which are familiar ingredients of traditional adjustment programs, some which run counter to them and some which are new features altogether.

Common Ingredients

Concerted Action to Reduce Budget Deficits

IMF critics often praise governments which spurn IMF advice, but maintaining large deficits is not progressive—it creates inflation. While spending cuts can be politically and socially difficult, inflation is usually devastating for the poor, as NGO reports on Zambia illustrate.[146] At least with spending cuts the government is able to target the cuts so as to protect the poor, whereas inflation almost invariably hits the poor hardest. Spending cuts should stress the axing of subsidies on goods and services consumed largely by the wealthy, such as air travel or bread (in a country where maize meal is the staple of the poor).

Management of Exchange Rates

Devaluation reduces living standards, but where international economic forces make a reduction inevitable, this mechanism *apportions* rather than *creates* the reduction. Over-valued exchange rates subsidize consumers of imported goods, create difficulties for producers of goods either for the domestic market or for export and generate economic anarchy as the black market becomes more pronounced. Devaluations need to be socially sensitive, however, and gradual enough to avoid throwing the economy into turmoil.

Improving the Efficiency of State-Owned Enterprises

Many parastatals are hopelessly inefficient and provide poor services. This does not indicate the need to abolish or privatize them, but it does mean restructuring them to become more efficient and to be more publicly accountable. This may involve introducing elements of competition, for example giving farmers the right to sell their goods to private traders, or through cooperatives.

Improving the Efficiency and Equity of Government Services

Health, education and other services used by the poor should be strengthened, not cut. This is not necessarily incompatible with reducing spending in the sectors overall. UNICEF[147] describes how savings in national services can accompany improvements in the poor's access to those services, for example by shifting to primary as opposed to hospital health care. While hospitals play an important role, they are often inefficiently run, and so savings may be achievable without reducing services. Similarly it is usually possible to make agricultural extension services much more relevant to small farmers.

Increasing Agricultural Prices

In countries where the majority of the poor live in rural areas, increasing agricultural prices is likely to be a socially positive mechanism. Parallel measures are also needed, however, to ensure that landless laborers and the urban poor can afford adequate food for their own needs.

Increasing Taxes and Tariffs

Many adjustment programs place too much emphasis on reducing expenditures rather than on increasing revenues. In most developing countries there are enormous opportunities for increasing revenues from taxing the better off (with particular emphasis on direct taxes) and for introducing or increasing tariffs on imported goods and taxes on luxuries. In some countries taxes are largely evaded or simply not collected. The emphasis there should be on strengthening the capacity of the government's revenue departments and curbing corruption, possibly even reducing taxes to a more realistic or less punitive level, but ensuring collection.

Improving the Efficiency of the Energy Sector

Reducing energy and fuel subsidies will tend to hit the better off hardest. Increasing domestic energy production (in environmentally sound ways) will save on oil imports. Wherever possible, however, the emphasis should be on energy conservation.

Counter Ingredients

Import Substitution

There should be less slavish emphasis on export-led growth. Third World countries do need to improve balance of payments but not necessarily through exporting more to the North. Increasing exports of a limited range of primary commodities tends to be self-defeating when scores of countries are all trying to pursue identical strategies. Prices plummet. An alternative approach is to reduce the need to import, through well-planned import substitution. Such a strategy may well require a period of state-guided investment for which foreign exchange will be required. A strategy of import substitution alongside selected export promotion was followed by South Korea in the 1960s and 1970s.

Regulation of Foreign Exchange

Government departments which issue import licenses or allocate foreign exchange are often corrupt and arbitrary. For this there is no excuse. However, the answer should not be to abandon all state intervention. A government needs foreign exchange to achieve its development strategy and to maintain the supply of vital imports. Where it is in short supply, it makes sense for a government to have some control over the use of foreign exchange, since it is an essential and strategic resource. In the same way, the war-torn countries of Europe in the 1940s and 1950s pursued careful strategies to ensure that the limited foreign exchange available was reserved for nationally agreed priorities.

Regional Trade Cooperation

Since most Third World economies are small it is important for strong regional cooperation in industrialization and trade. This can strengthen import substitution policies, by avoiding unnecessary duplication. Similarly, coordination on importing, by several developing countries clubbing together to achieve economies of scale and greater bargaining power, could save them an estimated 20 percent on their import bills.[148]

Reduce Debt Service to Manageable Levels

Substantial debt relief, on both official and commercial debt, is essential for any realistic solution to economic crisis in the South. If this relief is not offered voluntarily by the creditors, in particular by the commercial banks, then debtor countries should join forces in agreeing, unilaterally, on their own formulas for determining acceptable rates of debt service. Northern governments should understand, not try to undermine, and even welcome such moves.

Michel Camdessus, the Managing Director of the IMF, privately said as much to Northern governments. He suggested that debtors should refuse to accept terms from commercial banks that are more onerous than those being offered by official creditors, and resist pressure to pay debt service at a rate that is damaging to their economic prospects.[149]

By acting collectively they would be in a position to establish lower rates of debt service without jeopardizing their own situation. A strategy of controlled and coordinated default, while maintaining efforts to pursue economic reforms has been advocated by an ex-Vice President of the World Bank.

Curb Privatization Programs

State monopolies should only be phased out as it becomes clear that the private sector is able to give a better service to the poor. Even then it may be important to retain the parastatals as markets of last resort, to guarantee a market for the weakest—such as farmers in the remotest areas.

Food-First Principles

Agriculture sector reforms should give priority to food security before export promotion. Promoting marketed, as opposed to subsistence, crops requires great care to ensure that vulnerable groups have increased access to basic foods. This involves careful monitoring of nutrition levels, attention to the intra-family distribution of increased earnings and strengthening the local marketing infrastructure to ensure that basic foods are readily available at affordable prices. It also entails ensuring that agricultural wage-laborers share the increased earning opportunities.

Novel Ingredients

Social and Environmental Audits

Adjustment programs and development projects are routinely subjected to economic audits to assess how well they are being implemented, and whether they are achieving the anticipated objectives. They should also be subject to intensive social audits to assess their impact on different categories of poor people, and to assess the seriousness of steps being taken by the government to improve the social condition. Similarly, all projects and programs should be subject to environmental audits. Both types of audits should include, routinely, public hearings so that all who are affected by the schemes proposed have the opportunity to have their voice heard.

Protect the Poor from Further Loss

Sometimes policies will be introduced which may be necessary for the country as a whole but which stand to hurt groups of poor people at the outset. Examples will include the phasing out of subsidies on food or fertilizers, or the building of a dam. Parallel measures should be executed from the outset to ensure adequate compensation. Compensatory programs have often been introduced too late, after social damage becomes evident.

Improve Income Distributions

The objective of development projects and policy reforms should be to increase wealth, but also to distribute it more broadly.

NGOs working with coffee-growing *campesinos* in the Dominican Republic in the late 1980s found that, while devaluation had strengthened the country's capacity to export coffee, the price peasants were paid hardly increased. However, taxes and duties were increased and so they became even worse off, even though the large farmers and wholesalers were doing very well. With NGOs' help, the village associations of *campesinos* set up their own wholesale and export operation, and so captured some of the increased opportunity.

Equity-Led Growth

Policies should be pursued to increase the poor's access to productive assets such as land, water, credit and skills, and to increase the productivity of those assets. Laws and practices which discriminate against specific groups of poor people, such as women, should be reformed.

Guarantee Full Human Rights

Paramount attention should be given to the eradication of violations of human rights. This may include reforms in police services, forest departments, security services, laws relating to detention of suspects and other laws, policies and practices.

Extend Democracy

There should be wider consultations in the planning of projects and reform programs. This should not only include government departments which are frequently left out, such as Health and Environment, but also NGOs, peasant associations, women's groups, trade unions, consumer groups, cooperatives and organizations representing indigenous populations. People who are directly affected should have the right to participate in those decisions. This also means that information about such decisions must be freely available.

The Role for NGOs

Through strategic use of their grassroots experience, NGOs can make an invaluable contribution to development understanding. They can not only demonstrate how present strategies affect poor people, but they can also describe alternative strategies which, while in keeping with national priorities, better serve the needs of the poor. For this NGOs need to strengthen their understanding of the macroeconomic pressures experienced by developing countries. They need to strengthen their research, analytical and other skills needed to draw powerful messages from their "micro-experience" to inject into the "macro-debates." And they need to build up a pragmatic strategy for influencing the mainstream decision-making processes.

They can, for example, use their influence to revise the conditionality of official aid. To avoid Southern resentment or a new form of colonialism, the spirit of this should be one of shared responsibility rather than dogmatic pressure.

It would be naive to believe that Northern-dominated institutions can influence wholesale changes in hearts of Third World leaders merely by changing conditionality. The principle has to be one more of the carrot than the stick.

Reserving a large and increasing proportion of official aid for those countries following a "transformation" path would provide a very real incentive for governments. Those who have no inclination toward land reform will not be swayed by the offer of a US$100 million World Bank loan to support such a program, but, where governments are so disposed, substantial aid or debt relief makes a fine reward, offsetting the inevitable internal political resistance.

Northern governments can expect considerable public support for redirecting their development assistance in this way, and it is up to NGOs to ensure that this message is clear.

Part Four

Conclusions

14

Think Locally, Act Globally

THE PREVIOUS CHAPTERS HAVE addressed specific contributions NGOs make to development, both in traditional project work and policy advocacy. Though the latter has broader impact, it generally focuses on specific reforms such as changes in the marketing of baby formula, changes in specific "problem projects," redesigning adjustment programs and persuading local governments to "listen to the people."

These changes may have dramatic consequences for millions of people, but they do not challenge the mainstream development model itself.

By not challenging it, we affirm the basic framework. We imply, by our silence, that the rules of the game are inviolate, and that the task in hand is to make the best of things for the poor, given the constraints of the system.

An increasing number of NGOs, however, are questioning the framework itself. They do so with difficulty. Their background is mostly practical, grassroots, small-scale and popular. They do not engage easily in academic discussion about macroeconomic theories. However, their experience, properly marshalled, amounts to a damning indictment of prevailing economic values.

The pivotal challenge NGOs face throughout the 1990s is to build the alliances that are necessary to convey that indictment and to search for alternatives. The time is ripe. The "democracy contagion" triggered by recent changes in Eastern Europe and elsewhere, the growing awareness of the interdependence of nations brought about by environmental problems, AIDS, narcotics trade and other factors, and the manifest failure of orthodox economics all combine—along with a mounting "end of millenium fever"—to present unparalleled opportunities to challenge the old order.

NGOs in both North and South comprise a broad spectrum. They adopt widely differing styles, differing approaches, different constituencies. But increasingly they share a common perspective on the failure of the conventional development models to address the problems which need to be tackled. Some may be more vocal than others, and the policy changes they favor may differ, but there is a growing consensus that present world priorities serve neither the interests of the poor nor the environment.

This analysis stems, not so much from research programs and intellectual debate but from pragmatic observation of reality. NGOs who worked with the Brazilian poor through the years of that country's "economic miracle" saw a dramatic change in the situation of the *rich,* as the country climbed from fortieth position to ninth position in the world economic league table, but remarkably little change in the situation of the *poor.*

NGOs working with forest-dwelling tribal people throughout the Third World have seen logging operations contribute to national prosperity but to local misery. And NGOs campaigning for more official aid from Northern governments have seen billions of dollars wasted in Africa with little to show but "cathedrals in the desert."

Such tales are told, increasingly, by television documentaries and NGO campaigns. These help win specific reforms to correct the injustices highlighted but do not amount to a fundamental challenge of the development model itself. NGOs by themselves are usually poorly equipped for the research and analysis tasks, and are not confident in the macroeconomic language of government decision makers. To overcome these obstacles they must build alliances with dissidents in fields of economics, planning, agriculture and theology, and with others who are better equipped to challenge the sacred cows of orthodox economics but who may lack grassroots experience.

This strategic collaboration can provide the foundation for a compelling international movement for real change. The maxim for such a compact is—to reverse a familiar slogan—"think locally, act globally."

Five Fundamental Flaws

1. Dollar-Centered or People-Centered Economics

Conventional economics puts money, not people, at the center. Good economic management and sustainable growth are important, but they are not all that is important. Good management of human and natural resources, equity and social justice are just as crucial.

Progress should not be equated to economic growth. Development economists mostly agree that the objective of development is to improve the human condition, not simply the aggregates. But what they find easiest to measure are the aggregates.

In focusing so exclusively on GNP or GDP, decision makers commit two fundamental errors. First, they dwell on the means to the ends rather than on the ends themselves, and in so doing treat human beings as by-products of the economic machinery. Second, they concentrate on measuring what can readily be measured, rather than on what needs to be known.

The word *Economics* derives from the Greek *oikos* (house) and *nomos* (manage). The American economist, Herman Daly—whose recent book, *For the Common Good*,[150] has influenced many of the ideas in this chapter—describes the important distinction Aristole made between *oikonomia* and *chrematistics*. Oikonomia is "the management of the household so as to increase its use value to all members of the household over the long run," while chrematistics is the "manipulation of property and wealth so as to maximize short-term monetary exchange value to the owner." Oikonomia has three virtues in comparison with chrematistics: it takes a long-run view, it considers costs and benefits to the whole community, not just to the owners of wealth, and it focuses on concrete use value.

Sadly, most modern economics—with its emphasis on short-term profit, its narrow monetary measurements and its domination by a wealthy few—is essentially chrematistics.

NGOs are well placed to promote a new economics which reasserts the old values of collective and sustainable benefit.

2. Value-Added Vandalism

"Value added" is a concept that needs reappraisal. The lucky owner of a Rembrandt portrait—worth $1 million—could cut the one-meter canvas into one centrimeter squares. If he mounted each on a brooch and sold them with a certificate guaranteeing authenticity for $200 he would realize $2 million. By destroying a precious treasure, according to standard economics, the "value added" would be $1 million. In reality, of course, he has "added price" and "destroyed value."

This is a far-fetched illustration of an all-too-familiar phenomenon: the rational application of imperfect market forces leading to irrational actions. This manifests itself in the rapacious logging of virgin forests which have taken millenia to evolve in order to make a fast buck, or the drainage of rare wetlands for commercial exploitation. The value ascribed to such precious habitats is systematically understated, because the exploiter pays the cash-register cost, not the value to society.

As economist Judith Rees said recently, within orthodox economics "all pricing assumptions are based on the notion that *willingness to pay* is the same as *value*."[151] She went on to point out that in the Third World the limitation is usually the *ability* to pay.

By the same token, income levels are not, as some textbooks would have it, an accurate measure of people's effort and of the value of their output, but are determined by people's accumulated wealth and power throughout history.

3. Gross National Profanity

The most important yardstick for economists is the gross national product (GNP). Growth in GNP is seen as a sign of economic health, stagnation or decline as a malaise. The assumptions are that GNP measures something of importance to the economy, and that GNP growth contributes to the total well being of people. This faith is not justified.

In some countries there is a strong correlation between GNP growth and improvements in social indicators but elsewhere there has been little discernable correlation. Similarly, rapid growth rates are often associated with rapid environmental destruction.

The GNP is an indicator which is so partial as to be artificial. It fails to take into account the depreciation of assets. For example, if Britain were to export its entire stock of national art treasures in a single year the GNP would show a sharp growth though, self-evidently, the nation would be poorer. If the natural resource base were stripped to make a quick buck, again the GNP would increase. And if each breadwinner paid a wage to her or his spouse, and charged an exactly equal rent, this would (ignoring taxes) increase the GNP but not make an iota of difference to physical well being.

No business would survive long with economic management as arbitrary as that of national accounting systems. The business equivalent of *GNP per capita* would be *turnover per employee,* which says precisely nothing about the company's viability. If the profit margin is small then a high turnover can still not yield enough to cover overheads and generate a surplus. Hence companies measure their profit after essential expenses have been deducted. For a country, the equivalent measurement might be something like the per capita purchasing power after essentials for survival (food, health care, shelter, education, etc.) have been deducted. The term profit would be rather appropriate. Sadly, it would be extremely difficult to calculate this profit, but the argument points to why social indicators are more important than the GNP. UNDP has taken a step in this direction by expressing GNP in terms of "purchasing power parity" (an estimate of spending power, comparing the cost of the same goods in various countries).[152]

Orthodox economists are recognizing the need to revise their formulas, especially as they try to find ways of accommodating environmental factors in their calculations. Hence the IMF has recently described in its house journal three factors which should be included in the UN System of National Accounts:

1. depletion of resources extracted for sale (e.g. oil, timber);
2. defensive expenditures to prevent or correct for environmental damage (e.g. reforestation, environmental education);

3. degradation of the environment as a result of economic activity (e.g. acid rain, pollution of fishing grounds, soil erosion).[153]

These factors, deducted from the GNP, lead to a more realistic "net national product," or NNP, although the measurements, especially for the last factor, can be very imprecise.

4. Standards of Living or Standards of Spending?

Even if the calculation of Net National Product could be precise, the results would only represent an indicator of *economic* welfare. Other, social, factors need to be considered. For this reason, some economists have made efforts to consider the physical quality of life index, which measures infant mortality, life expectancy and literacy, but they resist efforts to combine this with the GNP to arrive at broader indicators of human welfare. They prefer to keep the economic separate from the human indicators. As a consequence, the latter become marginalized as they are regarded as imprecise measurements, while GDP can be determined to six significant figures. (The GDP of India in 1986 was recorded as US $203,790 million, the comforting precision of which belies immense inaccuracies such as the unknown size of the informal sector, unrealistic official exchange rates and imprecise population data.

Herman Daly suggests going further. He takes into account twenty variables, including environmental factors, income distribution, public services such as health, education and roads, household labor, depreciation of consumer variables (which is much more rapid in the disposable age of today than when it was customary to have household goods repaired rather than replaced when they broke down), costs of commuting and car accidents and expenditure on advertising. He arrives at the per capita index of sustainable economic welfare (ISEW), which he calculates for each year for the United States.

According to Daly's impressive calculations, though per capita GNP in real terms rose from US$3,976 in 1956 to $7,226 in 1986 (an 82 percent rise), the ISEW only rose from US$3,157 to US$3,403 (8 percent). Americans may appear richer now than they did thirty years ago but much of that wealth is illusory since it is swallowed up in ways which do not improve standards of living, or is outweighed by deterioration of the environment.

Such calculations would be virtually impossible for developing countries since the raw data is unreliable or unavailable. The UNDP has recently launched a more rough and ready human development index, combining purchasing power, life expectancy and adult literacy.[154] UNDP intends to broaden the index in the future to include other factors.

5. New International Human Order

The debates about revising systems of national accounts, about estimating environmental damage in economic terms and about calculating more realistic alternatives to GNP are important, but it would be wrong to suggest that, so modified, economics might then be the perfect science. It would still be arbitrary and imprecise. Economic calculations can never be a substitute for making value judgments based on people's needs.

Introducing taxes on energy and fertilizer use, making polluters pay for the damage they do and similar financial penalties are important, but they are not substitutes for further-reaching governmental programs to safeguard the environment.

Welcome as a New International Economic Order would be, even more important is a New International Human Order. Economic factors blind present-day governments to the social and environmental priorities.

A New Economic Framework

NGOs who have been learning macro lessons from their experience and working with sympathetic economists are refining a critique of the present development model. The alternatives they advocate appear more plausible as Earth's ailments become more glaring, and their evangelism is becoming increasingly sophisticated.

The Other Economic Summit (TOES), with participation of NGOs from North and South, has become an annual sideshow to the Group of Seven Summit. Similarly, the Annual Meetings of the IMF and World Bank are occasions in which NGOs confront finance ministers, Bank and Fund officials and the media with their alternative economic view. Networks of Southern NGOs have emerged, such as the Penang-based Third World Network, the Latin American Forum on Debt and Development and the Asian NGO Coalition) which are coordinating efforts to present development alternatives.

NGOs must continue with their more traditional activities, but they have an overwhelming responsibility to help shape a new world view.

The Challenge for NGOs in the 1990s

Least Action

A brave new world order is required and NGOs have an important role to play in forging this. Against such a monumental challenge many of the specific recommendations made in this book may appear too modest. They smack of minor reforms when nothing short of total revolution is required. Readers who believe that such a total and sudden revolution is *possible* in our age, who believe that all political structures, ideologies and cultural frameworks can be torn down and the world constructed anew, may find the recommendations disappointing.

It is relatively easy to agree on the basic shape of the future order we want but not the path for reaching it. Economic decisions and lifestyles should be tempered by environmental sustainability. There should be equity between nations, within nations and within families. All people should enjoy full democratic, human, political and economic rights—the truly enabling environment. Governments must prioritize international cooperation to overcome global problems such as AIDS, narcotics and marine pollution. And governments should be required to hand on to future generations a world unscarred by their term of office.

The question is how do we get from here to there? The "there" may be an attractive goal, but there are countless obstacles to overcome. Short of revolution, the challenge is to pick a path of change which is sufficiently incremental to be plausible, yet sufficiently rapid to save the world. The revolutionary strategy may be more urgent and sweeping, but who knows how long it will take for the necessary awakening of the collective public vision?

There is a law of physics which is apt for democratic politics—the principle of least action. This principle states that the path charted by any natural process is such as to minimize the effort required at each step (somewhat like a schoolchild's approach to homework!).

It explains, for example, the course taken by mountain streams. In its passage downhill, the water may come against a boulder. At this point it has to "choose" a path around the obstacle. This will always be the path of least action—the path in which it experiences least resistance. The numerous obstacles it encounters determines its course. The stream's flow appears to be random, but it is in fact completely logical. The water does not find the quickest way downhill, neither does it necessarily reach the bottom. It may get no further than a pool halfway down.

The ultimate destination is the cumulative result of all the earlier choices of immediate expediency. A small dam upstream, or the gouging out of a brief channel, or even perhaps shifting just one boulder, can completely alter the destination of the water in that particular stream.

Similar principles apply in politics. A given set of circumstances have led to the society we have today—the cumulative result of countless choices, each one of which was determined by the political expediency of the moment. The alternative society we aspire for may be miles off. The art of influence is to spot the opportunities to erect a blockage here, to create a channel there or to shift an obstacle, and by so doing alter the course of history towards the society we desire.

The direct route from the old values to the new may not be realistic. Water cannot flow uphill. It is necessary to consider what are the precursors of the new society in terms of changed perceptions, reformed institutions, novel practices and legal reforms which are feasible within the constraints of today. These will help pave the way to further reforms and so on until the full social change is achieved.

Civil engineers who set out to bring water from a mountain spring to a far-off village cut a channel which closely follows the contours—even though that course may at times move away from the village, because they appreciate the principle of least action.

The political equivalent is to chart a reform path which is guided by the contours of public opinion and expediency, and which is selective as to the values and paradigms it challenges. The path must be carefully strategic as to when, where and how it attempts to make its intervention.

Without losing sight of the longer-term vision, these are the tactics which effective pressure groups must heed. By doing so their initial actions and successes may appear modest, but they could be helping to shift the world toward a different course. It has been the purpose of this book to suggest ways in which NGOs from both North and South can make such a contribution, to describe examples from practical experience and to draw lessons from this experience.

In spite of all the resources at their disposal—perhaps *because* of this resource abundance—development NGOs cannot yet claim collectively to have made a contribution to be proud of. Though uniquely placed to witness the impending global crises and to see what must be done to avoid them, they have typically been more concerned with building their projects or increasing their turnover than with marshalling their influence. In contrast, the women's movement, environmental pressure groups and other citizens' movements have, with a fraction of the resources, done considerably more to change attitudes, reform institutions and change policies.

Progressive development NGOs are beginning to realize the shortsightedness of their approach and are searching for new strategies which could unleash their potentially immense influence. NGOs must be mindful of the principle of least action, and they must strive for maximum effect.

Maximum Effect

To maximize their impact, NGOs must be ever aware of the need for change; change in the way they think and plan, change in the way they work and change in the way they relate to others. Such reformation is not easy. It requires considerable sacrifice, particularly on the part of Northern NGOs. If they resist change and opt for a more comfortable, static existence, they risk becoming insignificant bystanders on the world stage as major battles relating to the survival of the planet unfold.

NGOs must be guided by a new vision of development. The new vision should be directed not just toward the problems and struggles of an array of disconnected communities, but also toward the global issues.

NGOs must see that they cannot act in isolation, otherwise they will become marginalized as world crises deepen. As alternative welfare or planning ministries they will help many people but solve few problems. To do the latter they must position themselves as catalysts for change within the broader arena of decision makers.

They should help push for a redefinition of just development and good governance. Development in the sense of improved infrastructure and state apparatus is needed, and this requires a healthy economic growth. Poverty alleviation, through the universal provision of basic needs, is a prerequisite for a civilized society. So far most governments would agree, but the NGO should argue that the *style* of growth is critically important. It should be driven by the principle of equity, not just for moral reasons, but because experience shows that equity, including gender equity, is the surest path to sustained growth. The development path must also be environmentally sound. Unsustainable use of the natural resource base is an economic sleight of hand—borrowing from the future. Similarly, to achieve short-term success at the expense of oppressed populations is neither durable nor efficient. Good governance demands a strong civil society and this requires democracy in its broadest sense and full respect for social justice.

Good governance, then, calls for *development, economic growth, poverty alleviation, equity, natural resource base preservation, democracy and social justice: the DEPENDS formula for just development.*

Such a redefinition is possible in today's climate. There is a growing realization of the interdependence of nations. This has been kindled by issues such as global warming, the spread of AIDS and narcotics, the growing problem of environmental and economic refugees, the clamor for democracy within centrally planned states and military dictatorships and the evident repercussions for the world of conflict and repressive actions within one state. The old ideas of national sovereignty must be revised in this new climate of interdependence. Moreover, there is a shift in popular political consciousness in much of the world from an old-style adherence to production politics, concerned with the ownership of the means of production, to consumption politics, concerned with what is being produced, for what kind of society, with what kind of values.

Environmentalism is causing a rethinking of economic principles. Rapid growth is not the panacea but the poison if it is ecologically unsustainable. This does not mean—as the "deep Greens" would have it—that we should strive for zero economic growth, but that healthy economic growth should derive from value added by human creativity and labor, not by depleting the natural resource base. The environmental balance sheet is more important than the financial one.

The political events in Eastern Europe, Latin America, Southeast Asia and elsewhere are also causing a rethinking of the importance and meaning of democracy. Democracy is not just about the right to vote for a president. It is about the accountability of the state, freedom of information, citizens' rights to have a say in decisions that affect them, freedom of speech and association and political equity. Democracy, so defined, makes for more efficient, effective and sustainable governance.

Applied to development, these principles amount not to structural adjustment—a fine tuning to make the system work better—but to *structural transformation,* a transition to a new order and new values predicated on the needs of people, both today and in future generations. Such transformation is not the task of Southern governments alone. Indeed it is simply impossible without equally sweeping changes in the North.

NGOs—particularly those who work in both countries of the North and the South—have a unique capacity to argue the case for this structural transformation.

References

1. Fernandes, Walter (ed.). *Voluntary Action and Government Control* (New Delhi: Indian Social Institute, 1986).

2. Robertson, James. *Future Wealth: A New Economics for the 21st Century* (London: Cassell Publishers, 1990).

3. World Bank. *World Development Report* (Washington D.C.: World Bank, 1989).

4. Lehman, David. "Basismo as if Reality Really Mattered," mimeo, chapter from forthcoming book (Cambridge: 1989).

5. McGranahan, Donald, et al. *Measurement and Analysis of Socio-Economic Development* (Geneva: United Nations Research Institute for Social Development, 1985).

6. Cornia, G.A., Stewart, F., and Jolly, R. *Adjustment with a Human Face* (Oxford: Oxford University Press, 1987).

7. Chambers, Robert. *Rural Development: Putting the Last First* (Harlow: Longman, 1983).

8. Bangladesh Rural Advancement Committee (BRAC). *The Net: Power Structures in Ten Villages* (Dhaka: 1980).

9. Uphoff, Norman. "Relations between Government and NGOs and the Promotion of Autonomous Development," paper presented to the Conference on the Promotion of Autonomous Development (Ithaca, N.Y.: Cornell University, 1987).

10. Chambers, Robert. *Rural Development: Putting the Last First* (Harlow: Longman, 1983).

11. Lipton, Michael. *The Poor and the Poorest: Some Interim Findings* (Washington, D.C.: World Bank, mimeo, 1985).

12. Tidrick, Gene. *World Bank Operations and the Alleviation of Extreme Poverty* (Washington, D.C.: World Bank, mimeo, 1986).

13. World Bank. *Poverty and Hunger* (Washington, D.C.: World Bank, 1986).

14. World Bank. *World Debt Tables* (Washington, D.C.: World Bank, 1989).

15. World Bank. *World Development Report* (Washington, D.C.: World Bank, 1990).

16. Korten, David C. *Getting to the 21st Century: Voluntary Development Action and the Global Agenda* (West Hartford, Conn.: Kumarian Press, 1990).

17. Ibid.

18. Landim, Leilah. *NGOs in Latin America,* in World Development (Supplement), vol. 15, *Development Alternatives: the Challenge for NGOs* (Oxford: Pergamon, 1987).

19. Organization for Economic Cooperation and Development (OECD). *Voluntary Aid for Development—the Role of NGOs* (Paris: OECD, 1988).

20. Brodhead, Tim, and Herbert-Copley, Brent. *Bridges of Hope? Canadian Voluntary Agencies and the Third World* (Ottawa: North-South Institute, 1988).

21. Korten, David C. *Micro-policy Reform: the Role of Private Voluntary Agencies,* Working

Paper no. 12 of the National Association of Schools of Public Administration (NASPAA) (Washington, D.C.: NASPAA, 1986).

22. Clark, John. *Milking Whom?* (London: International Coalition for Development Action, 1979).

23. Twose, Nigel. "European NGOs: Growth or Partnership?" in: *World Development* (Supplement), vol. 15, "Development Alternatives: the Challenge for NGOs" (Oxford: Pergamon, 1987).

24. Hellinger, D., Hellinger, S., and O'Regan, F. *Aid for Just Development* (Boulder, Colorado: Lynne Rienner, 1988).

25. Theunis, Sjef. *Development Forum* (Brussels: May/June 1989).

26. Organization for Economic Cooperation and Development (OECD). *Voluntary Aid for Development—the Role of NGOs* (Paris: OECD, 1988); also private correspondence with OECD, 1990.

27. Fox, Thomas H. *NGOs from the United States* in World Development (Supplement), vol. 15, "Development Alternatives: the Challenge for NGOs" (Oxford: Pergamon, 1987).

28. Hellinger, D., Hellinger, S., and O'Regan, F. *Aid for Just Development* (Boulder, Colorado: Lynne Rienner, 1988).

29. Fox, Thomas H. "NGOs from the United States" in: *World Development* (Supplement), vol. 15, "Development Alternatives: the Challenge for NGOs" (Oxford: Pergamon, 1987).

30. Hellinger, D., Hellinger, S., and O'Regan, F. *Aid for Just Development* (Boulder, Colorado: Lynne Rienner, 1988).

31. Brodhead, Tim. "In One Year, Out the Other?" in: *World Development* (Supplement), vol. 15, "Development Alternatives: the Challenge for NGOs" (Oxford: Pergamon, 1987).

32. van der Heijden, quoted in Hellinger, D., Hellinger, S., and O'Regan, F. *Aid for Just Development* (Boulder, Colorado: Lynne Rienner, 1988).

33. Organization for Economic Cooperation and Development (OECD). "25 Years of Development Co-operation," Development Assistance Committee Report, Chapter 5, "Co-operation with NGOs" (Paris: OECD, 1985).

34. Berg, Robert. *NGOs: New Force in Third World Development and Politics* (Washington, D.C.: Center for Advanced Study of International Development, 1987).

35. Tendler, Judith. "Turning Private Voluntary Organizations Into Development Agencies: Questions for Evaluation," Program Evaluation Discussion Paper no. 12, (Washington, D.C.: US Agency for International Development, April 1982).

36. Pinstrup-Anderson, Per. Seminar given at Oxfam UK (Oxford: 1987).

37. World Commission on Environment and Development, chaired by Gro Harlem Brundtland *Our Common Future,* 1987.

38. Tendler, Judith. "Turning Private Voluntary Organizations Into Development Agencies: Questions for Evaluation," Program Evaluation Discussion Paper no. 12, (Washington, D.C.: US Agency for International Development, April 1982).

39. Self Employed Women's Association (SEWA). *We the Self Employed: Voices of Self Employed Workers* (Ahmedabad, India: SEWA, 1984).

40. Fowler, Alan. "NGOs in Africa: Achieving Comparative Advantage in Relief and Micro-development," Discussion Paper 249 (Sussex: Institute of Development Studies, 1988).

41. Brown, L. David. "Organizational Barriers to NGO Strategic Action," *Lok Niti,* vol. 5, no. 4 (Manila: ANGOC, 1988).

42. Annis, Sheldon. "Can Small-scale Development be Large-scale Policy?" in *World Development* (Supplement), vol. 15, "Development Alternatives: the Challenge for NGOs" (Oxford: Pergamon, 1987).

43. Yudelman, Sally. "Integration of Women into Development Project?" in: *World Development* (Supplement), vol. 15, "Development Alternatives: the Challenge for NGOs" (Oxford: Pergamon, 1987).

44. Conroy, Czech. *The Place of NGOs in Bilateral Aid for Sustainable Development; Final Report to the Royal Norwegian Ministry of Development Cooperation* (London: mimeo, International Institute for Environment and Development, 1989).

45. Brown, L. David. "Organizational Barriers to NGO Strategic Action," *Lok Niti,* vol. 5, no. 4 (Manila: ANGOC, 1988).

46. Tendler, Judith. *Whatever Happened to Poverty Alleviation? A Report for the Mid-decade Review of the Ford Foundation's Programs in Livelihood, Employment and Income Generation,* Washington, 1987.

47. Brown, L. David. "Organizational Barriers to NGO Strategic Action," *Lok Niti*, vol. 5, no. 4 (Manila: ANGOC, 1988).

48. See notes 42, 41, 20, 66, 40, 88, 16 and 35.

49. Twose, Nigel. "European NGOs: Growth or Partnership?" in *World Development* (Supplement), vol. 15, "Development Alternatives: the Challenge for NGOs" (Oxford: Pergamon, 1987).

50. Uphoff, Norman. "Relations between Government and NGOs and the Promotion of Autonomous Development," paper presented to the Conference on the Promotion of Autonomous Development (Ithaca, N.Y.: Cornell University, 1987).

51. Sen, Biswajit. "NGO Self-evaluation," in *World Development* (Supplement), vol. 15, "Development Alternatives: the Challenge for NGOs" (Oxford: Pergamon, 1987).

52. Nyoni, Sithembiso. "Indigenous NGOs: Liberation, Self-reliance and Development," in *World Development* (Supplement), vol. 15, "Development Alternatives: the Challenge for NGOs" (Oxford: Pergamon, 1987).

53. Korten, David C. "Micro-policy Reform: the Role of Private Voluntary Agencie?" Working Paper no. 12 of the National Association of Schools of Public Administration (NAS-PAA) (Washington, D.C.: NASPAA, 1986).

54. Tandon, Rajesh. "The Relationship between NGOs and Government," mimeo paper presented to the Conference on the Promotion of Autonomous Development (New Delhi: PRIA, 1987).

55. Fernandes, Aloysius. "NGOs in South Asia," in *World Development* (Supplement), vol. 15, "Development Alternatives: the Challenge for NGOs" (Oxford: Pergamon, 1987).

56. Organization for Economic Cooperation and Development (OECD). *Voluntary Aid for Development—the Role of NGOs* (Paris: OECD, 1988).

57. Cernea, Michael. *NGOs and Local Development,* (Washington, D.C.: World Bank, 1988).

58. Qureshi, Moeen. "The World Bank and NGOs: New Approaches," speech to the Washington chapter of the Society for International Development (Washington, D.C.: World Bank, April 22 1990).

59. Hellinger, D., Hellinger, S., and O'Regan, F. *Aid for Just Development,"* (Boulder, Colorado: Lynne Rienner, 1988).

60. Clark, John. "The World Bank and Poverty Alleviation," paper prepared for the Washington 1988 meeting of the World Bank–NGO Committee (Oxford: 1988).

61. Twose, Nigel. "European NGOs: Growth or Partnership?" in *World Development* (Supplement), vol. 15, "Development Alternatives: the Challenge for NGOs" (Oxford: Pergamon, 1987).

62. Korten, David C. "Third Generation NGO Strategies: a Key to People-Centered Development," in *World Development* (Supplement), vol. 15, "Development Alternatives: the Challenge for NGOs" (Oxford: Pergamon, 1987).

63. Uphoff, Norman. "Relations between Government, and NGOs and the Promotion of Autonomous Development," paper presented to the Conference on the Promotion of Autonomous Development (Ithaca, N.Y.: Cornell University, 1987).

64. Oxfam UK. *The Field Directors' Handbook* (Oxford: OUP, 1985).

65. Organization for Economic Cooperation and Development (OECD). *Voluntary Aid for Development—the Role of NGOs* (Paris: OECD, 1988).

66. Elliott, Charles. "Some Aspects of Relations Between the North and South in the NGO Sector," in *World Development* (Supplement), vol. 15, "Development Alternatives: the Challenge for NGOs" (Oxford: Pergamon, 1987).

67. Brown, L. David. "Organizational Barriers to NGO Strategic Action," *Lok Niti,* vol. 5, no. 4 (Manila: Asian NGO Coalition, 1988).

68. Aga Khan Foundation. "The Enabling Environment," report of Nairobi conference (London: Aga Khan Foundation, 1988).

69. Beckmann, David. Private communication (World Bank, Washington, D.C., May 1990).

70. *Grameen Dialogue,* vol. 1, no. 4 (Bangladesh: Grameen Bank, Sept. 1990).

71. Uphoff, Norman. "Relations between Government, and NGOs and the Promotion of Autonomous Development," paper presented to the Conference on the Promotion of Autonomous Development (Ithaca, N.Y.: Cornell University, 1987).

72. Tendler, Judith. *Turning Private Voluntary Organizations Into Development Agencies: Questions for Evaluation,* Program Evaluation Discussion Paper no. 12, (Washington, D.C.: US Agency for International Development, April 1982).

73. Elliott, Charles. "Some Aspects of Relations Between the North and South in the NGO Sector," in *World Development* (Supplement), vol. 15, "Development Alternatives: the Challenge for NGOs" (Oxford: Pergamon, 1987).

74. Bangladesh Rural Advancement Committee (BRAC). *The Net: Power Strucures in Ten Villages* (Dhaka: BRAC 1980).

75. Self Employed Women's Association (SEWA). *We the Self Employed: Voices of Self Employed Workers* (Ahmedabad, India: SEWA, 1984).

76. Lehman, David. "Basismo as if Reality Really Mattered," mimeo, chapter from forthcoming book (Cambridge: 1989).

77. Landim, Leilah. "NGOs in Latin America," in *World Development* (Supplement), vol. 15, "Development Alternatives: the Challenge for NGOs" (Oxford: Pergamon, 1987).

78. Lehman, David. "Basismo as if Reality Really Mattered," mimeo, chapter from forthcoming book (Cambridge: 1989).

79. Uphoff, Norman. "Relations between Government, and NGOs and the Promotion of Autonomous Development," paper presented to the Conference on the Promotion of Autonomous Development (Ithaca, N.Y.: Cornell University, 1987).

80. Fowler, Alan. "NGOs in Africa: Achieving Comparative Advantage in Relief and Microdevelopment," Discussion Paper 249 (Sussex: Institute of Development Studies, 1988).

81. Twose, Nigel. "European NGOs: Growth or Partnership?" in *World Development* (Supplement), vol. 15, "Development Alternatives: the Challenge for NGOs" (Oxford: Pergamon, 1987).

82. Korten, David C. *Micro-policy Reform: the Role of Private Voluntary Agencies,* Working Paper no. 12 of the National Association of Schools of Public Administration (NASPAA) (Washington, D.C.: (NASPAA),1986).

83. Ibid.

84. Birch, Isobel. *Oxfam UK's Work in Primary Health Care in Zambia* (Oxford: Oxfam UK, mimeo, 1990).

85. d'Monte, Darryl, in de Silva (ed.). *Against All Odds* (London: Panos Institute, 1989).

86. Lok Niti. "NGOs and International Development Cooperation," Journal of the Asian NGO Coalition, vol. 5, no. 4 (Manila: Asian NGO Coalition, 1988)

87. Ibid.

88. Garilao, Ernesto. "Indigenous NGOs as Strategic Institutions," in *World Development* (Supplement), vol. 15, "Development Alternatives: the Challenge for NGOs" (Oxford: Pergamon, 1987).

89. Cernea, Michael. *NGOs and Local Development* (Washington, D.C.: World Bank, 1988).

90. Brodhead, Tim. "In One Year, Out the Other?" in *World Development* (Supplement), vol. 15, "Development Alternatives: the Challenge for NGOs" (Oxford: Pergamon, 1987).

91. International Council for Voluntary Action (ICVA). *Relations between Southern and Northern NGOs: Effective Partnerships for Sustainable Development* (Geneva: ICVA March 1990).

92. Garilao, Ernesto. "Indigenous NGOs as Strategic Institutions," in *World Development* (Supplement), vol. 15, "Development Alternatives: the Challenge for NGOs" (Oxford: Pergamon, 1987).

93. UN Economic Commission for Africa (UNECA). *People's Charter on Popular Participation* (Addis Ababa: UNECA, 1989).

94. Padron, Mario. "NGOs from Development Aid to Development Cooperation," in *World Development* (Supplement), vol. 15, "Development Alternatives: the Challenge for NGOs" (Oxford: Pergamon, 1987).

95. Minear, Larry. "The Other Missions of NGOs; Education and advocacy," in *World Development* (Supplement), vol. 15, "Development Alternatives: the Challenge for NGOs" (Oxford: Pergamon, 1987).

96. Trivedy, Roy. *Report of Malawi Action Research Project* (Oxford: Oxfam UK, 1989).

97. H.M.G. *Charities: A Framework for the Future* (London: HMSO, May 1989).

98. Lemaresquier, Thierry. "Prospects for Development Education," in *World Development*

(Supplement), vol. 15, "Development Alternatives: the Challenge for NGOs" (Oxford: Pergamon, 1987).

99. Sender, John, and Smith, Sheila. *Development of Capitalism in Africa* (London: Methuen, 1986).

100. Mutahi, Wahome. Quoted in *The Guardian* (London: 11th Sept. 1990).

101. Sender, John, and Smith, Sheila. *Development of Capitalism in Africa* (London: Methuen, 1986).

102. Ibid.

103. Ibid.

104. Ibid.

105. Ibid.

106. Adedeji, Adebayo (Chairman of the UN Economic Commission for Africa). Remarks to an NGO meeting at the UNCTAD Conference on the Least Developed Countries (Paris, Sept 1990).

107. World Bank. *Sub Saharan Africa: from Crisis to Sustainable Growth* (Washington, D.C.: World Bank, November 1989).

108. World Bank and UN Development Program. *Africa's Adjustment and Growth in the 1980s* (Washington, D.C.: 1989).

109. Clark, John and Allison, Caroline. *Zambia: Debt and Poverty* (Oxford: Oxfam UK, 1989).

110. Cornia, G.A., Stewart, F. and Jolly, R. *Adjustment with a Human Face* (Oxford: Oxford University Press, 1987).

111. Report of conference on Rapid Rural Appraisal, Khon Kaen University (Thailand: 1987).

112. Chambers, Robert. *Rural Development: Putting the Last First* (Harlow: Longman, 1983), and "Normal Professionalism, New Paradigms and Development," Discussion Paper 227 (Sussex: Institute of Development Studies, 1986).

113. Trivedy, Roy. *Report of Malawi Action Research Project* (Oxford: Oxfam UK, 1989).

114. Moser, Caroline. *The Impact of Recession and Structural Adjustment Policies at the Micro-level; low-income women and their households in Guayaquil, Ecuador* (London: London School of Economics, 1989).

115. Coote, Belinda. *Debt and Poverty in Jamaica* (Oxford: Oxfam UK, 1986).

116. Clark, John and Allison, Caroline. *Zambia: Debt and Poverty* (Oxford: Oxfam UK, 1989).

117. World Bank. *Sub Saharan Africa: from Crisis to Sustainable Growth* (Washington, D.C.: World Bank, November 1989).

118. World Bank. *World Development Report,* (Washington, D.C.: World Bank, 1990).

119. Mosely, Paul. *International Finance* (October 1987).

120. Griffith-Jones, Stephanie. *Cross-conditionality or the Spread of Obligatory Adjustment* (Sussex: mimeo, Institute of Development Studies, 1988).

121. World Bank. *World Development Report* (Washington, D.C.: World Bank, 1988).

122. van der Gaag, Jacques. *Targeted Programs for the Poor During Structural Adjustment* (Washington, D.C.: World Bank, 1988).

123. Gray, Cheryl. *Food Consumption and Expenditure in Mexico and the Income Effects of Removal of Food Subsidies* (Washington, D.C.: World Bank, mimeo, 1986).

124. World Bank. *World Development Report* (Washington, D.C.: World Bank, 1988).

125. Oxfam UK. Annex to evidence submitted "International Debt Strategy," Treasury and Civil Service Committee (London: HMSO, March 1990).

126. Howe, Sir Geoffrey (UK Chancellor). Speech at the Annual Meetings of the IMF and World Bank (Washington, D.C.: 1981).

127. World Bank. *World Debt Tables* (Washington, D.C.: World Bank, 1989).

128. Griffith-Jones, Stephanie. "Cross-conditionality or the spread of obligatory adjustment" (Sussex: mimeo, Institute of Development Studies, 1988).

129. United Nations Conference on Trade and Development (UNCIAD). *Trade and Development Report* (Geneva: UNCTAD, Sept 1989).

130. Griffith-Jones, Stephanie. *Cross-conditionality or the Spread of Obligatory Adjustment* (Sussex: mimeo, Institute of Development Studies, 1988).

131. World Bank. *World Development Report* (Washington, D.C.: World Bank, 1990).

132. United Nations Conference on Trade and Development. "Trade and Development Report," (Geneva: UNCTAD, Sept. 1989).

133. Ibid.

134. Bourgignon, Branson, and de Melo. *Adjustment and Income Distribution* (Washington, D.C.: World Bank, Country Economics Dept., May 1989).

135. World Bank. *Report of the Task Force on Poverty Alleviation* (Washington, D.C.: World Bank, 1988).

136. Clark, John. "The World Bank and Poverty Alleviation," paper prepared for the 1988 Washington meeting of the World Bank-NGO Committee (Oxford: 1988).

137. Griffith-Jones, Stephanie. *Cross-conditionality or the Spread of Obligatory Adjustment* (Sussex: mimeo, Institute of Development Studies, 1988).

138. World Bank, IMF et al. "Joint Statement on Africa: long term development," statement from meeting chaired by World Bank President (Washington, D.C.: May 10, 1989).

139. George, Susan. *A Fate Worse Than Debt* (London: Penguin Books, 1988).

140. Oxfam UK, Queen Elizabeth House, UN Non-Governmental Liaison Service (UN NGLS). *Debt, Adjustment and the Needs of the Poor,* Final Report of the Oxford UN-NGO Workshop (Geneva: UN NGLS, 1987).

141. Asian NGO Coalition/Environment Liaison Center International. *The Manila Declaration on People's Participation and Sustainable Development* (Manila: June 1989).

142. Major, John (UK Chancellor). Speech to the Development Committee of the IMF/World Bank (Washington, D.C.: April 1990).

143. Hurd, Douglas (UK Foreign Secretary). "The Future of Africa," speech to the Overseas Development Institute, (London: June 6, 1990).

144. George, Susan. *A Fate Worse Than Debt* (London: Penguin Books, 1988).

145. Asian NGO Coalition/Environment Liaison Center International. *The Manila Declaration on People's Participation and Sustainable Development* (Manila: June 1989).

146. Clark, John, and Allison, Caroline. *Zambia: Debt and Poverty* (Oxford: Oxfam UK, 1989).

147. Cornia, G.A., Stewart, F. and Jolly, R. *Adjustment with a Human Face* (Oxford: Oxford University Press, 1987).

148. de Silva, Leelananda. *Weighted Scales* (Geneva: UN Non-Governmental Liaison Service, 1986).

149. Camdessus, Michel. Briefing of IMF Northern Executive Directors (Washington, D.C.: December 18, 1989).

150. Daly, Herman, and Cobb, John. *For the Common Good: Redirecting the Economy Toward Community, the Environment and a Sustainable Future* (Boston: Beacon Press, 1989).

151. Rees, Judith. New Economics lecture (Whitechapel Art Gallery, London: June 28, 1990).

152. United Nations Development Program (UNDP). "Human Development Report," (New York: UN Development Program, May 1990).

153. IMF Survey. (Washington, D.C.: International Monetary Fund June 4, 1990).

154. United Nations Development Program (UNDP). *Human Development Report* (New York: UN Development Program, May 1990).

Index

Abed, Fazle, 83
Academic authors, 143
Accountability of NGOs, 62–63
Adedeji, Adebayo, 164
Adivasis, 52–53
Adjustment with a Human Face, 172
Adjustment, structural *see* Structural adjustment
ADMARC, 128–29
Advocacy activities (*see also* Lobbying), 31–32, 76–77, 127
Advocacy NGOs, 35
Africa, 156–61; agriculture in, 158, 182; bureaucracies in, 163–64; democracy in, 25; export volume of, 184; famine in, 21; indebtedness of, 141; land reform in, 161; reform in, 13–14, 168; state intervention in, 13–14; wealth distribution in, 48

Aga Khan Foundation, 85
Agricultural Development and Marketing Corporation, 128–29
Agricultural input subsidies, 181
Agricultural prices (*see also* Commodity prices), 106, 181, 195
Agricultural reforms, 197
Agriculture (*see also* Farmers), 54–55, 106–8, 158, 161, 182
Ahmedabad (India), 95
Aid *see* Financial aid; Foreign aid
"Alternative conditionality", 193
Alternative marketing organizations, 135
Amul (brand name), 34
Anand Niketan, 105
Andhra Pradesh (India), 98–99
Anecdotal evidence, 127–29
Annis, Sheldon, 54

Asian Development Bank, 117
Audits, 197
Austerity measures, 102, 162, 163
AWARE (organization), 98–99

Baby food, 66, 131, 135–37
"Baby Killers, The", 135
Baby Milk Action Coalition, 131
Backlash *see* Reprisals
Band Aid (organization), 21
Bangladesh: dams in, 117–118; exploitation in, 153; grassroots movements in, 90–95; NGOs in, 5, 7–8, 56, 98; peasant leaders in, 49; pharmaceutical legislation in, 67; politics in, 16
Bangladesh Rural Advancement Committee, 83, 92

Banks (*see also* Debt;
Interest rates; World
Bank), 140, 168, 184,
191
Bargaining power (*see
also* Compromise),
146–47
Basismo, 16
Bataan nuclear power
station, 190–91
Boards of trustees, 57
Bombay, 114–15
Boycotts, 139–40
BRAC, 83, 92
Brazil: electricity
generation in, 182;
grassroots organiza-
tions in, 5, 98; NGOs
in, 30–31; politics in,
16; poverty in, 204;
trade unions in, 96
Britain, 32–33, 42, 130,
137–38, 141–42
British Overseas
Development
Administration, 85
Brown, David, 53, 56,
84–85
Brundtland, Gro Harlem,
6
Brundtland Commission,
48
Budget reform, 179, 194
Bureaucrats, 80, 162–64
Burkina Faso, 104–5
Burma, 155

Camdessus, Michel, 196
Campaign Cooperative,
135
Campaign for Real Aid,
138
Campaigning, public,
144–45
"Capital flight", 191
Carter, Jimmy, 6–7
Cash crops, 153–54, 159,
182
Cernea, Michael, 77, 121
Chambers, Robert, 18
Charities, 38
Child mortality (*see also*

Infant mortality), 17
Chile, 66, 97
China, 12–13, 97, 155
Chowdhury, Zafrullah, 67
Chrematistics, 205
Churchill, Winston, 24
Cinci wa Babili (Zambia),
48
Citibank, 190
Citizen participation,
48–51
Citizen pressure (*see also*
Grassroots move-
ments; Lobbying), 10
Civil servants, 80, 162–64
Code of conduct, NGO,
39
Coffee industry, 135, 176,
198
Colonialism, 157–58
Comilla District
(Bangladesh), 117–18
Commercial banks *see*
Banks
Commodity prices (*see
also* Agricultural
prices), 154–55
Communication skills
(*see also* Literacy
programs), 93
Community leaders *see*
Leadership
Compensatory
programs, 175
Compromise, 120
Conditionality, 188, 192,
193, 199
Confidence among the
poor, 89–90
Conscientization, 31, 75,
90
Consumption politics, 15
Contributions, financial
see Financial aid
Conventional
development policies,
4, 20–21, 27–28,
150–51, 186, 204–8
Copper mining, 155
Corporations,
multinational, 139–40,
156

Corruption (*see also*
Smuggling), 42–43,
164, 190
Credit (*see also* Grameen
Bank of Bangladesh),
91–92, 95, 100, 115,
184–85
Crops *see* Agriculture;
Cash crops
Cross-conditionality, 150
Currency devaluation,
177, 194

Daly, Herman, 205, 207
Dams, 78, 102–3, 115–16,
118, 130, 182
De-linking, 155
Debt (*see also* Lending):
corruption and, 190;
IMF on, 180; lobbying
about, 138–39, 141–42;
of Peru, 165; World
Bank on, 22, 184
Debt relief, 193, 196–97
Decision makers (*see
also* Leadership),
146–47
Decision making (*see
also* Citizen
participation), 53–54
Declaration of NGOs on
the African Economic
and Social Crisis, 126
Democracy, 14–15, 25,
198, 211–12
Democratic govern-
ments, 10, 68
DEPENDS principles,
25–28, 186, 188, 211
Depreciation, 206
Devaluation, currency,
177, 194
Development: defined,
20–22; just, 23–28;
theory of, 100–103
Development agencies,
official *see* Official aid
agencies
Development education,
125, 131
Development NGOs, 210
Development policies,

conventional, 4,
20–21, 27–28, 150–51,
186, 204–8
Dhaka (Bangladesh), 56
Diamond, Larry, 26
Dictatorships, 67–68
Disarmament, 191–92
DISHA, 5
Displaced persons, 78,
115–16, 130
Dominican Republic, 176,
198
Donors *see* Fundraising

Economic austerity mea-
sures, 102, 162, 163
Economic crises, 21–22,
165–85
Economic exploitation,
52–53, 152–53
Economic growth, 23,
158–61, 174, 185, 211
Economic reform, 106,
187
Economic stabilization,
165, 166
Education, development,
125
Elections, 97, 98, 99
Electricity, 182
Elite, 93, 162–64
Elliott, Charles, 90
Employment policies (*see
also* Unemployment),
140
End Loans to South
Africa Campaign, 140
Energy, 181–82, 195
Environment, 24–25, 102,
191, 205, 211
Environmental audits,
197
Equity, 24, 198, 211
Ershad, H. M., 67
Ethiopia, 13, 152
Eucalpytus, 113
European Commission,
21, 156–57
European Economic
Community, 34
Evangelical charities *see*
Charities

Evidence: anecdotal,
127–29; legislative,
137
Exchange rates *see*
Currency devaluation
Exploitation, 52–53,
152–53
Exportation and
importation, 153–54,
159, 177, 179, 182,
184, 195–96

Famine, 13, 21
FAO, 104–5
Farmers, 19, 152
Federation of Voluntary
Organizations in
Development of
Karnataka, 113–14
FEVORD-K, 113–14
Fight World Poverty
(lobby), 138
Finance, international
(*see also* Debt; Inter-
national Monetary
Fund; Lending; World
Bank), 138–39, 141–42
Financial aid (*see also*
Foreign aid;
Fundraising), 39–44
Fishing rights, 92–93
"Five Ls", 76
Food and Agriculture
Organization, 104–5
Food consumption (*see
also* Baby food), 20,
175
Food distribution,
targeted, 176, 180
Food exportation and
importation, 153–54
Food security, 128–29,
197
Food subsidies, 170,
179–80
For the Common Good
(H. Daly), 205
Ford Foundation, 116
Foreign aid (*see also*
Financial aid), 32–33,
42, 138
Foreign exchange, 196

Foreign policy, 139
Forest gatherers, 52–53
Forestry, 112–14, 116
Forum for African
Voluntary Develop-
ment Organizations, 6
FOVIDA, 116–17
Free-market economies,
37, 103, 151
Freedom from Debt
Coalition, 5–6
Freire, Paolo, 31
Functional literacy
programs *see* Literacy
programs
Fundraising (*see also*
Financial aid), 32–33,
36

Garcia, Alan, 165
Garilao, Eduardo, 120,
121
Gender equity *see*
Women
Geopolitical issues *see*
Foreign policy;
Politics
George, Susan, 193
Ghana, 55, 162, 168
GINGOs, 80
GONGOs, 80
Government employees,
80, 162–64
Government services,
195
Government-inspired
NGOs, 80
Governments: demo-
cratic, 10, 68; local, 93,
98–99; NGOs and, 7,
64– 69, 99–100;
Northern, 189–93;
Southern, 55–56, 105,
106, 183, 187, 193–94
Grameen Bank of
Bangladesh, 86
Grassroots development
NGOs, 35, 79–80, 122
Grassroots movements,
15–17, 74, 75, 89–103,
121
Great Britain, 32–33, 42,

130, 137–38, 141–42
Greenpeace (organiza-
    tion), 15
Gross national product,
    20, 206–7
Group of Seven, 141, 208
GSS, 91
Guatemala, 80
Gujarat (India), 5, 33–34,
    52–53

Haiti, 98
Harambe, 50
Havelaar, Max, 135
Health Action Inter-
    national (organi-
    zation), 6
Health care services, 66,
    87, 110–12
Heijden, Hendrick van
    der, 43–44
Housing, low-cost, 36
Housing for pavement
    dwellers, 114–15
Howe, Geoffrey, 184
Human interest appeal,
    147–48
Human rights, 25, 68, 198
Hunger, 20–21

IBFAN, 6, 32, 136–37
Ideology, 152–56, 174
Illiteracy programs see
    Literacy programs
IMF see International
    Monetary Fund
Importation and
    exportation, 153–54,
    159, 177, 179, 182,
    184, 195–96
Income distribution see
    Wealth distribution
Income terms of trade,
    159
Indebtedness see Debt
Index of sustainable
    economic welfare, 207
India: economic
    exploitation in, 52–53;
    legal reforms in,
    51–52; literacy
    programs in, 31;

NGOs in, 5, 68;
    resettlement in, 78,
    130; rural health care
    in, 87; social forestry
    in, 112–114; trade
    unions in, 95–96;
    wealth distribution in,
    48
Indonesia, 133
INFACT, 136
Infant food, 66, 131,
    135–37
Infant Formula Action
    Group, 136
Infant mortality (see also
    Child mortality), 161
Inflation, 13, 168, 194
Information, public, 102
Information resources
    (see also Research),
    121, 172
Infrastructure, 23
Innovations of NGOs,
    51–52
Institutional reform, 182
Intellectuals, 99
Interdependence,
    international, 27, 211
Interest rates, 180, 183
Interfaith Center for
    Corporate
    Responsibility, 136
International Baby Foods
    Action Network, 6, 32,
    136–37
International Chamber of
    Commerce, 190
International Code of
    Marketing of
    Breastmilk
    Substitutes, 136
International Council of
    Voluntary Agencies,
    131–32
International Court of
    Justice, 190
International debt see
    Debt
International finance see
    Finance, international
International Food Policy
    Research Institute, 48

International inter-
    dependence, 27, 211
International lobbying
    (see also Advocacy
    activities), 125–49
International Monetary
    Fund: Extended Fund
    Facility, 184; ideology
    of, 174; on inter-
    national debt, 180;
    lending policy of, 178;
    national development
    strategies and, 106;
    structural adjustment
    and, 167, 168, 170–71,
    178
International publicity,
    94–95, 156–57
Investment, 140, 180–181
Irrigation programs, 116
ISEW, 207
ITT, 159

Jamkhed, 87

Kaira District Dairy
    Cooperative, 33–34
Kampuchea, 5
Karnataka (India),
    112–14
Khulna District
    (Bangladesh), 92–93
Kissinger, Henry, 21
Korten, David C., 26–27,
    33, 66, 108

Labour Party (Britain),
    15
Land reform (see also
    Wasteland manage-
    ment), 161–62; in
    Andhra Pradesh,
    98–99; BRAC and, 92;
    debt relief and, 193;
    grassroots move-
    ments and, 101;
    Samata and, 95; World
    Bank and, 101
Landim, Leilah, 99
Latin America, 16, 98, 99
Leadership (see also
    Decision makers;

Management), 49–50, 56–58, 84, 91
Left (politics) (*see also* Radical NGOs), 161
Legal reforms, 51–52
Legislative evidence, 137
Lehman, David, 16, 99
Lending (*see also* Debt), 178, 187, 188, 190–91
Liberal democracies, 10, 68
Lima (Peru), 116–17
Lipton, Michael, 20
Literacy programs (*see also* Communication skills), 31, 91
Living standards (*see also* Quality of life index), 17
Lobbying (*see also* Advocacy activities), 125–49
Local government, 93, 98–99
Low-cost housing schemes (*see also* Housing for pavement dwellers), 36
Low-income countries *see* Southern governments
"Ls, Five", 76

Macro-policy reform *see* Policy reform
Maharashtra State (India), 87
Mainstream development policies, 4, 20–21, 27–28, 150–51, 186, 204–8
"Making Common Cause Internationally", 131–32
Malawi, 110–11, 128
Maldevelopment, 27–28
Mali, 80
Man and Superman (G.B. Shaw), 104
Management (*see also* Leadership), 84–85
"Manila Declaration"

(1989), 193
Marasmus, 135
Marcos, Ferdinand E., 190
Market economies, 37, 103, 151
Market protectionism, 183, 191
Marketed crops, 153–54, 159, 182
Marketing organizations: alternative, 135, 176; parastatal *see* Parastatals
Marketing practices, multinational, 136–37
Marxist states *see* Single-party states
Matabeleland, 68
Mendes, Chico, 96
Mexico, 180
Micro-policy reform, 33, 109, 110–22
Military budgets, 191–92
Military dictatorships, 67–68
Milk distribution, 116
Minear, Larry, 126
Mission statements, 36–37, 84
Mobutu Sese Seko, 164
Monetary devaluation, 177, 194
Moral compulsion, 147
Morocco, 180
Mortality *see* Child mortality; Infant mortality
Mozambique, 5
Mulanje (Malawi), 128
Multinational corporations, 136–37, 139–40, 156
Mutahi, Wahome, 157
Myanmar, 155

Narmada Dam, 78, 130
National Movement for Free Elections (Philippines), 98
Natural resources *see* Environment

NBTT, 154, 159
Negotiation (*see also* Compromise), 147
Nestlé SA, 135–36
Net barter terms of trade, 154, 159
Net national product, 207
Networking, 6, 86–87, 129, 130–31, 134, 148–49
New International Human Order, 207–8
New Internationalist (magazine), 135
NGOs *see* Non-governmental organizations
NNP, 207
Non-governmental organizations (*see also* Grassroots development NGOs; Northern NGOs; Southern NGOs): accountability of, 62–63; advocacy role of, 76–77; corruption of, 42–43; decentralization of, 85–86; effectiveness of, 46–47; establishment of, 7, 55–56; funding by, 90; funding of, 38–44, 55, 101–2; future of, 208–212; history of, 29–34; ideology of, 152–55; innovations of, 51–52; leadership in, 56–58; management in, 84–85; micro-policy reform and, 33, 109, 110–22; mission statements of, 36–37; networking among, 6, 86–87, 129, 130–31, 134, 148–49; official funding of, 38–39; personnel of *see* Personnel, NGO; policy analysis and, 161–64; policy reform and, 104–22, 161–62;

public image of, 45–46, 81; reprisals against, 7, 84, 92, 94; research by, 60–62; scaling up by, 8–9, 69, 73–81; size of, 52–53; strengths of, 47–54, 81; structural adjustment and, 165–85; supporters of, 145–46; types of, 34–35; weaknesses of, 54–63; women's movement and, 101

Northern governments, 189–93

Northern NGOs, 29–30, 127, 134

Novib, 115

Nuclear power stations, 190–91

Official aid agencies: failures of, 21; grassroots NGOs and, 79–80; NGO funding and, 38–39, 43; NGO innovations and, 51–52; NGO partnerships with, 8, 120–21, 151; research by, 61; structural adjustment and, 105, 106

One-party states, 67–68

Operation Flood, 34

Organization for Economic Cooperation and Development, 39, 41–42

Orthodox development policies, 4, 20–21, 27–28, 150–51, 186, 204–8

The Other Economic Summit, 208

Oxen, 48

Oxfam UK: adjustment research and, 172; African debt and, 141; in baby formula controversy, 131; British overseas aid

budget and, 32–33; debt relief and, 193; funding by, 30; Gujarati forest gatherers and, 52–53; Malawi parastatals and, 128; Zambian primary health care system and, 111–12

Padron, Mario, 126

Pakistan, 85

Palawan, 5

Panchayats, 113

Panos Institute, 117–18

Parastatals, 14, 103, 128, 194–95, 197

Participation, citizen, 48–51

Pavement dwellers, 114–15

Perestroika, 14

Personnel, NGO, 53–54, 58–59, 83–84, 119, 120

Peru, 115, 116–17, 165

Phalombe (Malawi), 128

PHAM, 110–11

Pharmaceutical legislation, 67

Philippines, 5, 97–98, 190–91

Physical quality of life indices, 17

Policy analysis, 161–64

Policy reform (*see also* Micro-policy reform), 74, 76, 104–22, 161–62

Political parties, 93–94

Political reform, 192–93

Political reprisals, 130–31, 148

Politics (*see also* Consumption politics; Elections; Negotiation), 16

Popular development NGOs *see* Grassroots development NGOs

Popular movements *see* Grassroots movements

"Positive conditionality", 192, 193

Poverty: causes of, 18, 152–53; confidence and, 89–90; defined, 17–20, extreme (*see also* Pavement dwellers), 19–20, 47–48; growth of, 169; just development and, 23; World Bank and, 174–75, 185

Powerlessness, 18, 164

Prices *see* Agricultural prices; Commodity prices

Primary health care services, 66, 110–12

Private enterprise see Market economies

Private Hospitals Association of Malawi, 110–11

Profits out of Poverty campaign, 139

Programme of Action to Mitigate the Social Costs of Adjustment (Ghana), 55

Project replication, 74, 75, 82–88, 119–20

Pronk, Jan, 42–43, 193

Proshika, 84, 91

Protectionism, market, 183, 191

Public campaigning, 144–45

Public health care, 66, 87, 110–12

Public image of NGOs, 45–46, 81

Public information (*see also* Research), 102

Public investment *see* Investment

Public opinion, 129

Public service contractors, 35

Publicity, 94–95, 156–57

Quality of life index (*see also* Living standards), 207

Qureshi, Moeen, 77

Radical NGOs (*see also* Left (politics)), 37–38
Recessions *see* Economic crises
Recruitment of personnel *see* Personnel, NGO
Redundancy *see* Project replication; Unemployment
Rees, Judith, 205
Reform (*see also* Economic reform; Land reform; Policy reform, *etc.*), 179–82; in Africa, 13–14, 168; in Ghana, 168; gradual, 174; in Latin America, 16; Northern, 191–92
Replication, project, 74, 75, 82–88, 119–20
Reprisals, 7, 84, 92, 94, 130–31, 148
Research (*see also* Information), 92, 143, 171–72
Research institutes, 35, 61–62
Resettlement, 78, 115–16, 130
Results (organization), 145–46
Rubber tapper trade unions, 96
Rural health care *see* Health care services
Russia *see* Soviet Union
Ruzizi dam electricity project, 115–16

Salaries, 59, 62, 163
Samata, 49, 95
Savings schemes, 91–92
Scaling up, 8–9, 69, 73–81
Scholars, 143
Self Employed Women's Association, 95–96
Self-sufficiency, 155
Self-sustaining projects, 87
"Shared responsibility", 193
Shaw, George Bernard, 104
Sierra Leone, 19
Silviculture, 112–14, 116
Single-party states, 67–68
Smuggling, 180, 181
Social audits, 197
Social cost/benefit analysis, 176–182, 185, 197
Social Dimensions of Adjustment in Africa project, 108
Social forestry, 112–14, 116
Social justice, 25
Society for Promotion of Area Resource Centers, 114–15
Southern governments, 55–56, 105, 106, 183, 187, 193–94
Southern NGOs, 6, 56–57, 132
Sovereignty, 26–28, 55–56
Soviet Union, 12, 25
SPARC, 114–15
Sport Aid (organization), 21
Sri Lanka National Environment Council, 117
Sri Lankan Environmental Congress, 117
Stabilization, economic, 165, 166
Staff, NGO, 53–54, 58–59, 83–84, 119, 120
Standards of living, 207
Starvation *see* Famine; Hunger
State employees, 80, 162–64
State marketing boards, 14, 103, 128, 194–95, 197
Stop the Aid from South to North (campaign), 139
Structural adjustment, 165–85; agricultural reforms and, 108; conditionality and, 187–88; economic austerity measures and, 102; maldevelopment and, 27–28; in Mali, 80; Southern governments and, 105
Structural transformation, 186–99
Subsidies, 170, 179–80, 181, 195
Supporters, NGO, 145–46
Survival International (organization), 133
Survival strategies, 175–76

Tandon, Rajesh, 67
Targeted food distribution, 176, 180
Tariffs, 195
Taxation reform, 179, 195
Tea industry, 135
Technical innovation NGOs, 34–35
Tendler, Judith, 47, 50, 56–57, 88
Third World Network, 6
Tiananmen Square rebellion, 97
TOES (summit conference), 208
Toronto plan, 141
Trade, 138, 177, 183–84, 196
Training of personnel *see* Personnel, NGO
Trincomalee power station, 117
Trustees, 57
Turkey, 185

UN Special Session on Africa (1986), 126
UN System of National Accounts, 206–7
UNCTAD, 184
Under-5 mortality rate, 17
UNDP, 206, 207

Unemployment, 175
UNICEF, 136, 172, 195
United Kingdom, 32–33, 42, 130, 137–38, 141–42
United Nations (*see also headings beginning* UN), 134
United States, 42, 43, 47, 50, 137
Upper Volta, 104–5
USAID, 42, 104

Value addition, 205
Voluntary organizations *see* Non-governmental organizations

Wages, 59, 62, 163
War on Want (organization), 131, 135
Wasteland management, 113–14
Wealth distribution, 13, 48, 198
Wealth indices, 17
Westinghouse (firm), 190
Women (*see also* Self Employed Women's Association): in agriculture, 54–55, 106–8, 161; financial schemes of, 91–92;

just development and, 24; in Lima, 116–17; NGOs and, 54–55
Women's movement, 101
Women's Savings Club, 92
Wood production, 112–14, 116
World Bank: on African democracy, 25; AKSP evaluations of, 85; Brazilian power sector and, 182; Cernea on, 121; development theory of, 100–101; equity and, 26; extreme poverty and, 19; ideology of, 174; Indonesian transmigration and, 133; on international debt ratios, 22; lending policy of, 178; Malawi parastatals and, 128–29; Narmada River dam and, 130; national development strategies and, 106; net contributions of, 39; NGO advocacy role and, 77; poverty and, 174–75, 185; Ruzizi dam project

and, 115, 116; Social Dimensions of Adjustment in Africa project, 108; structural adjustment and, 167, 168, 170–71, 174–75, 178, 184
World Development Movement, 135, 138
World Development Report, 17–18, 26, 175
World Food Conference, 20–21
World Health Assembly, 136
World Health Organization, 136

Yatenga project, 87
Yudelman, Sally W., 54–55

Zaire, 115–16, 164, 180
Zambia: development priorities in, 49–50; economic vulnerability of, 155; inflation in, 13; oxen in, 48; poor in, 152–53; public health in, 66, 111–12; subsidies in, 170, 180
Zimbabwe, 68

Other important books from KUMARIAN PRESS:

Beyond the Clinic Walls
Case Studies in Community-Based Distribution
JAMES A. WOLFF, ROBERT CUSHMAN, JR., FLORIDA A. KWEEKEH,
C. ELIZABETH MCGRORY, SUSANNA C. BINZEN
MANAGEMENT SCIENCES FOR HEALTH

Change in an African Village
Kefa Speaks
ELSE SKJØNSBERG

Community Management
Asian Experience and Perspectives
EDITOR: DAVID C. KORTEN

A Dragon's Progress
Development Administration in Korea
EDITORS: GERALD E. CAIDEN AND BUN WOONG KIM

The Family Planning Manager's Handbook
Basic Skills and Tools for Managing Family Planning Programs
EDITORS: JAMES A. WOLFF, LINDA J. SUTTENFIELD,
SUSANNA C. BINZEN
MANAGEMENT SCIENCES FOR HEALTH

Getting to the 21st Century
Voluntary Action and the Global Agenda
DAVID C. KORTEN

Keepers of the Forest
Land Management Alternatives in Southeast Asia
EDITOR: MARK POFFENBERGER

Managing Organizations in Developing Countries
A Strategic and Operational Perspective
MOSES N. KIGGUNDU

Opening the Marketplace to Small Enterprise
Where Magic Ends and Development Begins
TON DE WILDE, STIJNTJE SCHREURS, WITH ARLEEN RICHMAN

Reports that get Results
Guidelines for Executives
IAN MAYO-SMITH

Seeking Solutions
*Framework and Cases for
Small Enterprise Development Programs*
CHARLES K. MANN, MERILEE S. GRINDLE, PARKER SHIPTON
HARVARD INSTITUTE FOR INTERNATIONAL DEVELOPMENT

Transforming a Bureaucracy
*The Experience of the Philippine
National Irrigation Administration*
EDITORS: FRANCES F. KORTEN AND ROBERT Y. SIY, JR.

Training for Development
Second Edition
ROLF P. LYNTON AND UDAI PAREEK

The Water Sellers
A Cooperative Venture by the Rural Poor
GEOFFREY D. WOOD AND RICHARD PALMER-JONES
WITH M. A. S. MANDAL, Q. F. AHMED,
S. C. DUTTA

Working Together
Gender Analysis in Agriculture, Vols. 1 & 2
EDITORS: HILARY SIMS FELDSTEIN AND SUSAN V. POATS

❖   ❖   ❖

For a complete catalog of
KUMARIAN PRESS titles, please call or write:

KUMARIAN PRESS, INC.
630 Oakwood Ave., Suite 119
West Hartford, CT 06110-1529 USA

tel: (203) 953-0214 • fax: (203) 953-8579